See-Saw

Published in 2021 by Ballpoint Press
4 Wyndham Park, Bray,
Co Wicklow, Republic of Ireland.

Telephone: + 353 86 821 7631
Email: ballpointpress1@gmail.com
Web: www.ballpointpress.ie

ISBN 978-1-9160863-8-8

While every effort has been made to ensure the accuracy
of all information contained in this book, neither the author nor
the publisher accept liability for any errors or omissions made.

Book design and production by Joe Coyle Media&Design,
joecoyledesign@gmail.com

Front cover sketch by CRD

Printed and bound by GraphyCems

This book is made of materials from well-managed forests and
controlled sources, which guarantees a reduced carbon footprint.
Forest management helps to maintain biodiversity and protects ecosystems.
This book is printed with vegetable oil-based inks.

See-Saw

A Perspective On Success,
Leadership And
Corporate Culture

Fintan Drury

Ballpoint Press

Dedication

To,

Brenda, Aoife, Cillian, Conor and Cliodhna who were the constants on much of the journey and whose support, even during the roughest times, never wavered. Thank you.

• • •

Mike Burns, Kevin Healy and Gerry Barry the gifted and generous men who mentored me as I set out on my professional life. Mike, prior to his death, constantly encouraged me to write this book and Kevin guided me through it all with great care.

Contents

'See...

Dr. Austin Darragh of the Institute of Clinical Pharmacology exploded with anger at me during a break for commercials on RTÉ Radio's *Morning Ireland* in 1986. I was co-presenter of the programme then with the legendary David Hanly and while there were occasional skirmishes with interviewees, we shared a belief that most could be persuaded to part with relevant information without beating them up live on air. Dr. Darragh was brought into the studio while the advertisements were running and I quickly referenced that I'd be asking him about one contentious issue when the programme restarted. The interview would be the next item on the show.

Austin Darragh was founder and Chief Executive of the Institute of Clinical Pharmacology which was listed on the New York Stock Exchange, a company that did clinical trials for many of the world's leading drugs companies. It was considered to be both successful and innovative and the interview was timed to coincide with the release of its annual report. The year before, a 31-year old man, Niall Rush, had died when undertaking trials at the Institute, so as soon as Dr. Darragh was seated I told him the interview would include questions about Mr. Rush.

In the minute or so remaining of the ad break he became aggressive, threatening me that he would walk out, pointing out that he was the 'resident' doctor on the Gay Byrne show, was friendly with the station's most popular broadcaster, but also with the Director General and that if I asked him about it there'd be serious consequences for me. The outrage was so intense that, even if I had wanted to respond, there was no time so a couple of minutes into the interview, I asked him to explain what had happened to Mr. Rush.

Austin Darragh was caught in a moment of time. The flashlights of success had been dimmed replaced by the red light of a live radio news programme that was fixed steady and must have seemed unrelenting in its intensity. Still he was bright and articulate so, in spite of his visible anxiety, he handled it well knowing however, that as he trudged his way through the unfortunate circumstances of Mr. Rush's death, his bloated status had taken an unwelcome hit. It was good radio, though maybe not for Austin Darragh.

• • •

With the exception of my time as a news reporter and presenter with RTÉ, most of my professional life has been spent, in the background advising others in business, sport and politics. In the 2000s, however, I was in demand as a non-executive director of Irish corporates, expected to guard shareholder interests across some very substantial businesses in technology, gambling, energy and financial services. It represented an endorsement of sorts of my capacity as an adviser and, over that decade, I was paid very well to support the necessary governance of a number of plcs and large privately-owned companies.

I was a non-executive director of Anglo Irish Bank between 2002 and 2008. I retired on completion of a second three-year term in May 2008 when, in spite of gathering storm clouds on the global financial markets and a concern over the level of shares owned by Cavan businessman, Seán Quinn, the bank appeared in good shape. In 2007 independent researchers had named Anglo the best-performing small bank in the world over the previous five years but it took less than five more for the bank to collapse, be nationalised, and in March 2011 to post losses of €17.7 billion. This was easily the largest loss ever posted by any Irish business; its collapse and the dire state of the whole Irish banking industry was to have disastrous consequences for the Irish taxpayer.

I was chairman of Paddy Power plc (now Flutter plc) for the same six years as I was on the bank's board, a period of exceptional growth for the Irish gambling company with a massive increase in shareholder value. That role as chairman and how I fulfilled it remains, in business, a notch on my corporate belt, the antidote to the Anglo Irish virus. Under the leadership of the board that I chaired, Paddy Power was to the vanguard of the global development of online gambling, the phenomenon that has completely transformed the industry with the company's market capitalisation at c. €25 billion today. This quite extraordinary growth has enriched an already highly profitable industry but with the transformation to 24/7 gambling have come grave societal consequences.

In 1990, I established Ireland's first-ever, full-service sports management business, one that was to help steward the careers of many leading Irish footballers and rugby players, project-manage the 2006 Ryder Cup, and stage pre-season tours for top football clubs including FC Barcelona and Real Madrid. While Platinum One (UK) continues to trade, I and friends who'd supported me had lost money by the time we chose to wind-up the Irish company in 2021.

Throughout the 1990s I worked in a strategic advisory role to a number of government departments and ministers on national programmes and on crises, most notably the Hepatitis C crisis sparked by a failure of governance in the Blood Transfusion Board. I did some professional work with Brian Cowen, early in his ministerial career before we became friends and I morphed into an unpaid political counsel to him for much of the remainder of his time in public office. In this way I've had some involvement in politics most of my professional life.

• • •

My career started with doing exactly what I had always wanted, even from my early teens. I was a newsman. There are few jobs where you are more visible or central to what's going on than news journalism, and perhaps even more so if that is in broadcasting. My 15 minutes of relative fame came in my 20s when I did some reasonably high-profile work as a broadcaster in RTÉ, particularly the two and a half years co-presenting *Morning Ireland*.

My younger self was enthusiastic and idealistic about journalism but, time would tell, without the conviction that would have seen me stay the course. In my mid-twenties I engaged in emotional and mental pinball around whether I would go into politics or stay in journalism? Would I stick or twist? Then, within a few years, I'd moved into business, a decision that lacked real or deliberate intent. I had never aspired to being a businessman, yet that's what I chose to do, not consciously, but I did it, nonetheless.

My personal life was unaltered. I socialised with the same people, my close friends were and are principally people from my youth, along with others who were clients of my sports agency and a few from politics and business. I changed nonetheless; never to the point of an outward or obvious arrogance, but I did become too self-assured, not just in myself, but also about the integrity of nearly all of those with whom I worked.

Maybe my ascent to senior roles on the boards of some of Ireland's largest companies influenced whatever change occurred in my corporate persona. This could be a post-rationalisation but I did become excessively confident about myself and the businesses where I worked. Perhaps this was a natural consequence of operating at a particular level corporately, but certainly I became less discerning and less sceptical. I trusted stories that I would have previously doubted and I donned the gown of *faux* respectability that comes with success in business or at least the sense of it.

I experienced many incidents of poor corporate behaviour, fuelled normally by arrogance, often with a shake of greed, most of which I was able to manage or I chose to walk away from, wiser but largely unscathed. There are two exceptions: Anglo Irish Bank and Paddy Power which are legacy items that, in different ways, have concerned me greatly for more than a decade. In one case, it's obvious why but the other which, from a purely business perspective was a huge success, troubles me – the journalist and the socially-aware me – even more. I was part of the leadership of both institutions at critical points in their evolution.

Leadership is something I've witnessed across the gamut of my professional life. At its core it's about knowing your position, understanding it and behaving accordingly. I've been in leadership positions where I have performed but there were other occasions when I allowed events carry me along, where I wasn't at all reflective enough or I failed to fully trust myself.

In other situations where I have been in close attendance to leadership, I have seen it both brilliantly expressed and woefully betrayed. I've seen its status and power used for personal gain; watching from the margins I've sensed its greatness as much as I've observed its abuse. Remarkably, I have sometimes failed to see those different manifestations when I've been in the room, seeing the phoney leader from a distance but not the one within my own circle.

Success can blind us and not just our own. Arguably we're even more prone to error when we imbibe the success of others or, as I've experienced more than once, when the leadership in an organisation gets stoned on its success. It doesn't matter how bright or savvy we are, how principled we believe ourselves to be, success softens our senses. It did mine in a number of situations over my years in leadership roles across business.

Anglo Irish Bank's success, in the context of an Ireland that wasn't only economically vibrant but wanted to believe in the robustness of its economic miracle, meant some in senior positions were too trusting. I know that I was. I believed, assumed even, that governance standards were being met. In most cases they were but, when you're a board member of a financial institution, it being compliant most of the time is not enough. What happened represented a totemic failure of leadership, starting with the CEO, who was later chairman and many in positions of responsibility, including this non-executive director.

Leaders are those whom we choose to follow. I followed Seán FitzPatrick because I believed in him. I was wrong; he was not the person I thought him to be. I and others failed to see the characteristics that made him but also meant that, in the end, his leadership was deeply flawed. I can see those characteristics now but that's not a great deal of comfort because I'm left asking how I failed to see them at the time?

My failures were conditioned by the circumstances in which I worked, exacerbated by failures in regulation but they were failures, nonetheless. It is important to highlight them but also how deep cultural and behavioural considerations were the dominant features of the bank's collapse. The learnings need to be amplified because without deeper debate on the fundamentals they'll continue to be repeated, as they have been through the ages.

As though to prove the point, in spite of the hardship, drama and humiliation that accompanied the deep fracturing of Ireland's banking system in 2011, it didn't take long for another financial services business to display the identical features of cultural arrogance and greed that had marked the Anglo failure. That those very fundamentals that undid Anglo a decade earlier were manifest in 2021 in the damage done to Ireland's largest stockbroking company, Davy Stockbrokers, is remarkable.

The Central Bank assessment of what happened there read like something from a corporate echo chamber; a group of senior Davy executives conducted a transaction on their own behalf, breaking compliance regulations in a manner that the regulator described as 'reckless'. Davy, established in 1926, was just five years from its centenary when its culture of overbearing omnipotence, on display for decades, finally weakened the foundations to threaten its proud history.

That the survival of an independent business, approaching its 100th centenary, was undermined by the malpractice of some senior executives is nothing new. In 1494, *Banco dei Medici*, then Europe's largest bank, collapsed just three years short of its 100th anniversary, the cause, historians say, being the 'venality' of its leadership. So Davy's failure is as much a reflection of the failure of this big 15th century financial institution and many more over the centuries, as it is representative of the same corporate arrogance at the heart of Ireland's banking crisis of the early 21st century.

• • •

While the scale of Anglo's collapse understandably damaged my career, my failure to see the fault lines in its leadership and governance is as nothing compared to how I'd missed the destructiveness of Paddy Power's growth into a global powerhouse in the gambling industry. I led a board that conducted its business ethically, delivering strong shareholder value in the process but here again the blinkers were on, blocking from me the growing societal consequences of that success.

The founders of Paddy Power established it because they saw commercial potential in taking on the UK bookmaker brands in Ireland. Success came quickly but it was easily managed until it changed from private to public ownership when it floated on the London Stock Exchange in 2000. From that moment the dynamic changed. Making profits, achieving growth, was now the expectation of a much larger community of investors – both private and institutional – and success meant that was the absolute imperative.

I followed the Paddy Power dream because I believed in it. I was wrong because its flawless business model shows a disregard for the public good. Any assessment of my business career would most likely feature my leadership of Paddy Power as the high watermark but, for me, it represents something less edifying. I did a good job. I was well paid to do it. The shareholders were happy with my tenure but, for all the commercial positives, it's the role that troubles me most. It highlights the scale of my transition from an actively curious journalist to, at least, a passive subscriber to the unique importance of corporate Ireland.

• • •

There is nowhere that leadership comes under greater scrutiny than in national political life; there is no professional calling more important than politics. There is no career choice that carries the same responsibility, so no other leadership role can have the same white-knuckle feel as that of being responsible for leading a nation. There can be no level of responsibility that leaves an individual so exposed to the criticism of peers than being a politician who assumes leadership or who finds themselves in that position. There is no area of life where integrity matters more than politics.

I followed Brian Cowen because I believed in him. I was wrong because, for all his special talents, he displayed characteristics, especially a marked lack of ruthlessness, that meant sustained political leadership would be beyond him. When he became Taoiseach I was expectant. I shouldn't have been. The conditions of his premiership were the most challenging that any Taoiseach has ever experienced but it wasn't just the circumstances of the time that sundered his political career so prematurely.

• • •

I'm not sure that over my 30 years working the turf of Irish corporate, political and sporting life, that I changed to any real extent but in the halcyon days of the mid 2000s I was, however unconsciously, riding the wave of my own success, of how I was seen. With that, I succumbed to a form of corporate inertia that dulled my capacity to challenge, and not just others but, much more importantly, myself. I've come to understand how, even if it's only a light weave, a fabric of invincibility is potentially lethal and is most likely donned wherever success is in evidence.

Failure prompts introspection (or should) and when that failure is on a grand scale, vastly greater than the years of success and is accompanied by institutional investigation and public attention, the need to better understand what happened and why is compelling.

In recent years, while continuing to work in business, I returned to some journalistic work, largely opinion-writing in Ireland and the UK on migration, gambling and football. Since my testimony to the Oireachtas (Parliamentary) Banking Inquiry in 2015 the journalist in me has been intrigued by my own professional journey. It has been so markedly different to everything I had anticipated and expected of myself when I started my career, as part of the first-ever group of graduates recruited as trainee journalists by the national broadcaster, RTÉ.

SHOVELHEAD

The reviews had been relatively positive. Then, Alpho O'Reilly, Head of Design and a respected choreographer, spoke: he was hesitant, the initial words of encouragement weren't easily offered, as though to signal that ultimately his judgment might be less forgiving than those who'd provided assessments of my voice, diction and script writing. It was 1981. I and a few others had just completed a screen-test which consisted of writing and then presenting a mock TV newscast which was the final part of an evaluation to determine whether Ireland's national broadcaster, RTÉ, would offer any of us employment as journalists.

As though for dramatic effect, in his markedly camp way, Alpho excitedly asked the technician to freeze-frame my image on screen and then said that I must always pay attention to the way my hair was combed whenever I'd be on television. "Mr Drury, you must sweep your hair off your forehead to the left or the right. It cannot be just brushed down the middle because as you can see, it accentuates the fact that your head is shaped like a shovel." Welcome to broadcasting!

Sadly, the same Alpho O'Reilly, who was a respected figure in television and theatre in Dublin from the sixties, disappeared in January 1996. He was never found. On the few occasions when we talked after the first occasion when he had so clinically determined that I had a face for radio, I found him somewhat eccentric but interesting and pleasant. The advice he'd offered was correct though it mattered little because most of my broadcasting was on radio. In any case I was losing it at such a rate that what little hair I had wouldn't have taken a comb.

When I'd joined RTÉ, the young boy who had been reared to be curious, who had followed world events through radio and newspapers in a home with no television but where, even from a young age, curiosity and opinion were encouraged, was beside himself. Even at university I'd a little routine with a few close friends where, at the end of an anecdote, I'd sometimes sign myself off, as though *reporting on some big news story. So, for me being drafted by RTÉ was a dream come true, one which knew no boundaries at the anticipated excitement of being a news reporter. It was, I felt sure, the start of a life in journalism where the only boundaries to what I could do would be the stories that I could find. In fact I spent only about seven years there but they were formative for much of what followed.*

I

The Dream Job

In RTÉ my first permanent post was with the Radio News Features Unit that produced two daily news magazine programmes at 1.30 p.m. and 6.30 p.m.; *World Report* on Saturday mornings; and the respected *This Week* at 1pm on Sundays. News Features had a reputation for excellence and independence. That independence was hard-earned in an organisation managed with a stifling civil service culture where careers were advanced largely based on length of service not talent and where salaries were directly attributable to how long you'd been on the payroll rather than the quality of your work or importance of your brief.

In contrast, News Features was an oasis of enlightenment under the stewardship of Mike Burns, Kevin Healy, and Gerald Barry. Though exceptional broadcasters themselves, they made sure that neophytes like me were given the latitude to develop. I thrived, loved it and advanced quickly to a position where, when I chose to leave RTÉ and journalism, I'd already had seven years reporting and presenting at the highest level. I was 29.

I had reported from Northern Ireland for a period; been a frontline radio news presenter; covered a US Presidential election; done other overseas reporting; interviewed some famous people from the Libyan leader Colonel Gaddafi to tennis player and boyhood hero Ilie Nastase; covered general elections; and made both television and radio documentaries. More importantly, given how I would spend the next 30 years of my professional life, I'd learned about teamwork, leadership, management, graft, timing and the need to make do with whatever resources you have. Most importantly, in a profession where ego is powerfully present, I'd seen its power and its destructiveness at close quarters.

The great benefit of working in the small News Features unit was how its leadership made teamwork paramount. It was the key to exceptional programming. So as to deliver quality output twice a day, everyone's contribution was respected. This was learned by the speed with which you could be handed a starring role as the programme presenter, then the following week be working largely off-air. While I'd first learned it playing university football, here I learned the primacy of teamwork ahead of personal ambition in any workplace.

In April 1983 I was presenting the lunchtime news. When I arrived in the office that morning there was a note from a colleague, Joe O'Brien. Quiet and unassuming, Joe lived the idea of teamwork ahead of personal ambition. In his note he said that an Irish Columban priest in the Philippines, Niall O'Brien, had been arrested with two others on suspicion of a multiple murder and it was likely he would face charges. The Columban Fathers were concerned and Joe's note finished with a phone number for the prison in the village where the priest was being held.

It was a blank canvas; no other media seemed aware of the story. I contacted the Columbans in Dublin to check a few things and then, mid-morning, wandered down to the studio, more curious than expectant. Today, we communicate with the rest of the world as though it's the place next door. Then, the idea of phoning a prison on a tiny Philippine island and being able to talk to an inmate was absurd. I asked the technician to record from the point at which I'd start to dial the number, just on the off-chance we'd get anywhere.

It was well that I did. Remarkably, the jailer spoke English and readily agreed when I asked him if Fr O'Brien could be brought to the phone. It's rare to know instantly that you've landed on a big story but, when we'd finished, I had – by simply asking the most obvious questions – uncovered a story that would come to dominate the news in Ireland for months. It was a time when the church in Ireland was revered almost without question. Once broadcast, the priests' plight received extensive media and political attention. It was carried in Australia, triggering a similar interest in the fate of Fr. Brian Gore who was also detained.

When Joe O'Brien arrived to do that evening's news programme, what he'd been on the cusp of breaking 24 hours earlier was an international news item. It was Joe's scoop, but I was the one congratulated for my work. In a newspaper we would have shared the by-line, but radio offers no such opportunity. It was now my story. Joe O'Brien had been airbrushed out.

This reflected the idea of teamwork within our News Features unit but even still I'm unsure that had the roles been reversed, I'd have been as constructive and resisted the temptation to sit on it for a day. I would probably have convinced myself that I would do a better job on chasing it down and conducting any interview that might follow. Within hours, as the story triggered a major political reaction, a colleague, Charlie Bird, who had no involvement in it was sent to the Philippines with a film crew to cover the fallout.

In that moment I learned how management decisions that fail either the test of logic or reasonableness are rarely good ones. Joe O'Brien or I should have been sent but some other obscure agenda was playing out, representative of much of what passed for management in RTÉ then. Charlie Bird, rightly, took the opportunity and used the story as the base on which he built his career as one of the more curious and persistent news journalists in Ireland. It was poor management though; effective management starts with the mindset of those in charge and with their attitude and their capacity to see events through the lens of those who work with them, a feature that's frequently ignored. I know that, where I've been an effective leader, it's been where I have been fearless in promoting ability and talent. Just so, among the reasons I have failed is allowing myself to be compromised on that essential.

• • •

In my teens it had been the excitement of overseas reporting that had most attracted me to journalism, drawn to the idea of reporting on world events. In the 1980s RTÉ newsroom such opportunities were very rare. I relished these assignments partly because when you were sent overseas, being an RTÉ journalist meant that you worked at the same level and pace as your international colleagues, but with a fraction of their resources. You wanted to be as good as them though always that meant being more resourceful.

In 1984, I was sent to Libya to cover a serious diplomatic crisis between Britain and Libya after a policewoman, Yvonne Fletcher, was shot dead outside the Libyan Embassy in London. It was alleged the shots had been fired from inside the embassy and there was understandable outrage across politics, the media and the public in Britain. The situation was so serious that I was dispatched to Tripoli within 24 hours to report for TV and Radio News and all radio current affairs programming. That's just how it was: a major event happened and you had to react to it.

The previous year I had spent a challenging fortnight in Paris, where the Loughney brothers, who owned pubs in Dublin and Paris, bankrolled me because I had been sent at such short notice to cover the bombing campaign of the notorious Jackal. I had no idea how the financial arrangements worked but they booked my accommodation and I went to them for French francs so presumably they had some system with RTE management to recoup their funding of a news reporter.

More seriously, at 1.20 p.m. on Saturday December 17th of that same year, the IRA detonated a car bomb near a side entrance of Harrods department store on Brompton Road in central London. The bomb exploded as four police officers in a car, and another on foot, neared the suspect vehicle. Six people were killed, three police officers and three civilians. I had finished editing a lengthy pre-recorded interview with Cardinal Tomás Ó Fiaich, for the next day's *This Week* programme but by early afternoon I was in a cab on my way to the airport and that evening I was at the scene, doing interviews and preparing a detailed report for the *This Week* which I co-presented from London. The interview with the Cardinal was never broadcast.

When you're a young journalist you crave these kind of stories, want to report on them and be as close to the action as possible. One of the three civilians killed by the Harrods bomb was a journalist, Philip Geddes, who got a tip-off and was so close by that he rushed to the scene, only to be caught by the explosion. We were the same age. Another colleague of a similar age was ITN's Terry Lloyd who was killed by US military when covering the 2003 invasion of Iraq. I knew him quite well because we'd worked in Libya together in 1984 and he was a correspondent in Belfast for much of my time there with RTÉ.

• • •

I was good at my work. I loved being a newshound, researching and building stories. I was fortunate to have a good voice and while, as my close women friends were always at pains to point out, I was no oil painting, nor did I have any physical features that would distract the viewer, so a move to television was possible and had, for some time, interested me.

The outlet of choice for anyone with my experience was *Today Tonight* (a forerunner to the current *Prime Time*) which was then edited by Joe Mulholland, a legendary editorial figure with whom I wanted to work. Joe seemed similar in approach to the men who'd led and supported me in radio, perhaps more demanding but he was both story and talent oriented. I knew *Today Tonight* was recruiting and I'd met him to discuss a role and been given a sense that a job there was pretty much mine to lose.

I was called for an interview. I presented myself on the day, expectant, arrogantly so, only to face a completely formal and rigorous interview. In the cocktail of panic and shame that I can still recall, I did a terrible interview. It quite rightly ended *Today Tonight*'s interest in me. The technical side of television broadcasting is different, but by then I'd extensive experience of live television so my failure was due to something more basic, more personal. I had lost the opportunity to progress through a failure to prepare. It was a good lesson. I learned from the humiliation I felt when I left that interview, knowing that my arrogance and carelessness had cost me a job I had coveted.

I moved to Northern Ireland as a correspondent in 1982. RTÉ's editorial commitment there was immense, unsurprisingly given it was, throughout that period, a story of major international importance. There was a team of eight journalists and two camera crews, a large studio and never any shortage of material to cover. My mother's family came from the North and I'd always followed political developments there with interest. When I was 16, I had won a national essay competition run by the *Irish Independent* on the subject of Northern Ireland so there may have been an element of destiny about my being posted to Belfast.

It was in the immediate aftermath of the 1981 Hunger Strikes, a place where the hard-line direct rule of Margaret Thatcher's Conservative government couldn't address the lawlessness that was fomented by the very bigotry successive British governments had supported. That hardness wasn't the exclusive preserve of the Tories, as Northern Secretary for three years in the late 1970s Labour's Roy Mason facilitated a sharp increase in covert operations by the SAS. Northern Ireland, constantly on edge, was a society with a nervous twitch of lawlessness which the Republican movement leveraged to build its community base that would later shift to constitutional politics, through Sinn Fein.

For a young journalist with a still somewhat romantic sense of the job, Northern Ireland was the compelling issue of the time, so to be in a position to cover it was exciting. I had experienced colleagues who'd worked the same Northern 'turf' during the 1970s when the levels of violence were staggering. In 1969, the year the 'Troubles' started, 16 people were killed. Over the next decade the death toll was 2,084 and over the five years between 1972 and 1976, 1,500 people were killed.

That part of our island could fairly have been described as being at war, not in the conventional sense perhaps but colleagues who covered Northern Ireland at that time described something that had many of the hallmarks of ongoing armed conflict. It is remarkable how little this reality impacted life in Dublin 140 kilometres from that theatre of bloodshed.

I was 14 when Bloody Sunday occurred and I started university in 1976 a year when just fewer than three hundred people were killed. Three hundred! I was studying politics, had an above average interest in current affairs and I was of northern stock – the grandson of Joseph Connolly, who stood for Sinn Fein in the 1918 Westminster election in Mid Antrim. Somehow the remorseless regularity of the killing inured many of us to its reality. It may seem perverse, it certainly does now, but apart from those in border communities, life in the Republic was unaffected. Most in Britain were largely ignorant of Ireland, indeed as I was to learn most of its leading politicians neither understood it nor showed any great interest in its welfare.

What was more remarkable was the attitude of my peers. It has long mystified me how little interest people in the Republic have in the wellbeing of those with whom they share the same tiny island. The peace that was hard-won is still young and tender. The more time that passes without a serious threat of any return to violence is welcome but history teaches that the experience of those who recall its horror helps toughen the resolve of a community to prevent its return. The serious rioting that occurred in the spring of 2021 should have served to remind us of how precarious peace often is for generations after it has been reclaimed. It might alert younger people to the ease with which a return to violence could occur.

• • •

That sense of it being a war of sorts meant that not infrequently in the 1970s and the '80s the institutions of the state were prepared to break their own laws in pursuit of a required outcome, while republican paramilitaries took the fight to England intermittently, as though to remind the British public of their continuing presence. We suspected then, but we now know that it was considered acceptable for the British state to pervert the course of justice if it meant that the 'men of violence' could be curtailed.

In that time, on the small part of this small island where it had sovereignty, the United Kingdom believed the republican threat warranted interventions that included, on occasion, breaking the very laws it was supposed to uphold. This happens across the globe. It's the 'the end justifies the means' argument and I reported on a number of state-sponsored killings during my time as a correspondent in Belfast.

Even in their immediate aftermath you could sense their source. It seemed that, for a period in the early 1980s, the Tory government believed the republican threat was so serious, it was appropriate to sanction 'special forces' to engage in state-sponsored, extra-judicial killings. The British government's focus was the preservation of its interests and those of the population in Northern Ireland who were loyal to the Crown. While it claimed to govern with an even hand, it viewed the welfare of the unionist community as preeminent, reflecting its title of, Her Majesty's government of the United Kingdom and Northern Ireland.

The circle of violence was perpetually vicious and it was spinning faster and faster. The nationalist community was becoming more confident, more assertive and within its ranks were those who believed almost any level of violence against the Crown, was justified. Westminster then allowed itself the latitude to behave inappropriately in its attempt to assert control. It, or agents acting on its behalf, stepped outside the law in the pursuit of putting an end to the violence and, when those occasions arose where scrutiny of their actions was required, it generally found ways of muting an effective analysis of events.

Those actions of the Thatcher government were wrong. The SDLP's Seamus Mallon used to quote the 17th century Dutch philosopher, Baruch Spinoza, *if you sacrifice justice in the pursuit of security you will lose both.* Government must have moral authority and nothing can place that at greater risk than for it to depart from due process to facilitate the killing of its own citizens. Those who choose to operate outside the law should be held accountable but, in a democracy, it can hardly include the government sanctioning that suspected paramilitary activists be shot dead on sight.

With such an approach real authority is lost. With such tactics lecturing people on the evils of paramilitarism or violence sounds hollow and erodes credibility. What are citizens to make of such hypocrisy? What should we expect in a society where people see convicted paramilitaries facing appropriately serious sentences for violence towards police officers but see no accountability where the police or army chose to mete out justice on the side of the street or down a country lane?

More than any other single consideration, the lack of an impartial, professional, accountable police service in Northern Ireland bedevilled progress towards peace. In the early 1920s, at the very point when my grandparents needed to migrate from Belfast, 21% of the RUC was Catholic. This had halved when the 'Troubles' started in 1969 and by 1998, displaying the utter distrust of the nationalist community in its police service, the figure had dropped to 7.5%. While the percentage of Catholics in the police service today is considerably higher it remains below desired levels.

Covering Northern Ireland was made more challenging by Section 31 of the Irish Broadcasting Act which prohibited journalists from broadcasting interviews with members of banned organisations. It was reactionary and flawed legislation brought in by elements in government as right-wing on law and order as Ireland has known. The British government followed suit, though not until 1988, so throughout my time reporting on events in Northern Ireland, colleagues working for BBC, ITV and local media in the North could access and use that side of the 'argument' whereas those of us working for the Irish state broadcaster faced the prospect of jail were we to do the same.

We went on strike in August 1985 for a couple of days. That one pathetic blink of defiance apart, I have often wondered at how, with a very few honourable exceptions, we could have been so accepting of such blatant and counter-productive State censorship. There were some of our number who agreed with it but most thought that Section 31 wasn't a force for good. It was about the containment of a voice that might have been unpleasant and even threatening but that our democracy, however immature and unsophisticated, was robust enough to deal with. Journalists went on strike once, held the odd protest demonstration, but otherwise we just muttered into our pints about the sheer stupidity of it all. Section 31 of the Broadcasting Act neutered broadcasters. It made it very difficult to bring a lens of objectivity to how the Northern Ireland story was told and how developments could be explained.

• • •

I left Belfast in summer 1984 to return to Dublin after I was chosen to co-present a new morning radio news and current affairs programme *Morning Ireland*, scheduled to start that November. It had been a difficult decision. I loved reporting from Belfast, had done some of my best work covering notable events including the Darkley massacre and two of the three so called 'shoot to kill' incidents that were later investigated by John Stalker. I was enjoying it but the opportunity was too great, especially as the new programme was under the control of the News Features department. It would be a return home in more ways than one. It was to be ground-breaking because, a few pirate stations apart, Irish listeners then had a choice between RTÉ and the BBC. I was pleased to have been recruited for the role.

Morning Ireland was going to be a milestone event in the history of Irish broadcasting so the choice of presenters didn't sit well with some more experienced colleagues. I returned to a News Features thick with testosterone-laden intrigue. There were all sorts of pressures on management; not only was the programme going to break new ground but, statistically, it would represent a doubling in the daily output of the News Features unit.

A relatively new recruit to broadcasting, David Hanly, and I had been selected as the best partnership to present the programme. I was ushered from Belfast on that account. David was to become the programme's star through his calm, distinctive, quizzical style and husky voice but the choice to have me partner him, was now being challenged by some, much more experienced, colleagues. In early autumn, as preparations continued, the pressure for a senior presenter to be given the role grew and eventually management agreed so I was jettisoned.

I was annoyed especially as I had been happy in Belfast but there wasn't a great deal I could do about it. In some form of compensation I was sent to Washington to cover the US presidential election between Ronald Reagan and Walter Mondale. So, when *Morning Ireland* first broadcast on November 4th, 1984, I was not co-hosting the programme but was instead in the studios of National Public Radio in Washington, reporting on the dullest Presidential election in modern US history.

It turned out those who had lobbied against me did me a favour. The programme had a very difficult start. Within weeks, RTÉ's chairman, Fred O'Donovan, showing a complete disregard for his employees and internal morale, pandered to newspaper and early audience opinion by acknowledging publicly that the Authority was considering taking the programme off air. That was just months after the programme had launched. The atmosphere around the News Features unit was awful for that period and my treatment by newsroom management was part of the intrigue.

I chose to just get on with my work on other programmes and to avoid the gossip and manoeuvring. I was avaricious for 'airtime'. I did some strong work in the months after my return from Washington, including on stories in Northern Ireland. Then, in early 1985, about four months after the programme had been launched, New Features management asserted itself and insisted on returning to its original plan to pair me with David Hanly who, despite the programme's difficulties, had already made his mark.

• • •

When I took over as his co-anchor, *Morning Ireland* was already beginning to turn a corner. The timing couldn't have been better for me as the audience was starting to build and, with the different dynamic of my relationship with David Hanly, listenership figures climbed. David was emerging as a star and my status was enhanced, partly on the coattails of his popularity and certainly on the public's growing enthusiasm for the programme. It turned out I had been fortunate in not being the co-host when the programme had launched to a disgruntled public and a cynical media.

David Hanly and I were very different broadcasters and interviewers, in voice and in tone but we shared one important journalistic ingredient – curiosity. We were curious about nearly everything; we also enjoyed each other's company, something an audience will sense because it makes co-hosted programmes easier to listen to, particularly in the early morning.

In 1985 the programme quickly moved from one the chairman of RTÉ wanted to disown to a big success. While David was its star, a great deal of the transformation was down to our exceptional producer, Tom Savage. Tom knew how to balance items and to work us as a partnership; he moulded David and me into a pair that brought morning news and current affairs to a growing audience over those first years. We worked hard. The very early hours were punishing but the whole team had a great pride in being part of something that was new, and which gradually moved to a position where it often set the news agenda for the day.

Decades on, some of the excellent programmes remain with me. The great individual interviews were just that and most of them were David's but the best journalistic endeavours – certainly the most satisfying – are when there's a team involved. The programme on May 30th, 1985, was my standout experience in live programme-making throughout my whole time in RTÉ. The previous evening I sat down at home to watch Liverpool and Juventus play the European Final at Heysel in Belgium.

Within moments it was obvious a human catastrophe was unfolding, one that would end up claiming the lives of 39 football fans and see about 600 others injured. The early TV pictures didn't leave much doubt but that the biggest night in European football was the backdrop for an emerging tragedy of scale. I left the house immediately, jumped on my bicycle and pedalled furiously the couple of miles to the studios to work on the following morning's programme.

When, 12 hours later, *Morning Ireland* ended, we'd brought the Irish public the most comprehensive coverage of the horrific loss of life at what should have been a memorable sporting event. I remember our boss Mike Burns, the Head of Radio News, working all night as if he was a trainee. Gary Agnew was dispatched to Dublin port to get accounts of returning Irish Liverpool fans and did it brilliantly but, most of all, I remember an Eamon Dunphy polemic on how the behaviour of many English fans was a reflection of deep social ills in Thatcher's Britain.

I was interviewing him and, in the moment, I was somewhat bemused by how he segued from football to a general commentary on the ills of British society. It may have suited his political disposition but it proved to be a telling and prophetic perspective, delivered as always, with that swagger of utter belief in the profundity of his opinion. I think it was one of Eamon Dunphy's finest journalistic moments. It was extraordinary and distressing, 35 years later, to see the violence of thousands of English fans around Wembley Stadium on the night of the European Championship final in July 2021. In so many ways, football serves as a bellwether of sorts for how England is with itself.

The two years plus I spent presenting *Morning Ireland* was the most fulfilling time of my career as a journalist. Everything about the programme represented the essentials I had learned from my time in News Features and indeed working with the team in Belfast. The work ethic, teamwork and focus on excellence were what made it so rewarding as well as the recognition that went with being involved in a programme that was gaining huge listenership and credibility. Public figures either wanted to come on the programme or knew that, in certain circumstances, whether or not they wanted to, it was the right thing for them to do. Still, two and a bit years on I was getting restless, quite why I don't really know.

II
Change of Plan

When I chose to leave the world of journalism and broadcasting, the only professional life I had known, I had no career plan and certainly no personal drive or motivation to move towards the world of business but, strangely, that's what I did. There was no family history or connections in business. I had never displayed any interest or aptitude for it but I left what I loved doing, did well and what was certainly a natural habitat, for something that was completely unknown. Money may have been part of it, we had one small child and planned more, but I didn't lack confidence in how far I could go in broadcasting, my wife was a successful professional, so no financial imperative was at the heart of the decision.

I was too young to appreciate the enormity of the change. A move from journalism to public relations might not appear substantive but, particularly when you're a news journalist, it is and it's why the trite profile of 'poacher turned gamekeeper' attaches so easily. I simply didn't think of it at all deeply enough. Nor, however, did I feel any great excitement about embarking on a career in public relations and business. It just seemed like something I could do and make a success of without changing who I was. I was wrong. I did have some initial success but with that came an elevation within business circles and while little in my personal life changed, professionally I allowed this to compromise the essence of who I was in my earlier years.

The decision wasn't feckless but nor was it deeply considered. I was 29, had no business training nor obvious skills that could allow me to succeed in business as I did in the world I was leaving. We all change over time, we're constantly learning as we advance through our careers but in that moment I don't believe I knew what I was doing. In my early years in business, the journalistic instincts and training occasionally benefited me but, predictably perhaps, they became dulled over time which meant that years later, when a journalistic nose – that somewhat jaundiced view of things as they might appear – could have benefited me, its sensory powers had been lost. I drifted into a world that was alien but to which I adapted in order to survive.

I was no more ambitious in business than I had been in broadcasting but the corporate environment demands certain behaviours. Sustained achievement is bound up with corporate belief that consumes everything including, normally, your capacity to probe and to evaluate purpose. My peers will dispute this, pointing to senior management or board meetings where debate is encouraged, stimulated by those in charge but it's not that level of corporate belief that's at issue. It's not operational curiosity that's often missing, it's much more substantive questions like 'what we are doing?'; 'why we are doing it?'; and 'how do we choose to do what we do?' These issues are critical to ensuring shareholder returns don't come at the expense of more fundamental considerations; these are important to the establishment of a positive organisational culture.

In time, with more apparent success, a certain momentum built behind my status, first as a strategist beyond just communications, then as a senior adviser before I became a professional non-executive board director. The feeling was almost uniformly positive, I was in demand, valued and respected as much as I had been in RTÉ. There was however one great difference. In business there wasn't the regular evaluation based on your last programme or your last interview. Not only that, the small community of business leaders was protective of the tribe; membership was hard won but once ordained, it was difficult to fall out of favour.

Unwittingly, I started to adopt a sense of impregnability. I had gained enormous self-confidence through my career in RTÉ, particularly presenting live news programming over a number of years. I had carried that through to the establishment of my PR and sports management businesses, the former a new entrant into a highly competitive market, the latter the first of its type in Ireland. Over the first decade of my business career the success of these companies fuelled my sense of self-worth. It also brought me to the attention of others.

When I was appointed to the boards of Paddy Power plc and Anglo Irish Bank plc in early summer 2002, my ego was further inflated. When you are on a number of boards, growing your own business and consulting at an elite level, you're working so hard, earning such great money that you forget to pause, to consider things holistically and ensure that you 'reboot', centred on your core values. Others may do this but during those extraordinary times, I didn't, or certainly not often enough or with the requisite depth.

My basic principles were never threatened; no amount of perceived success or real financial rewards would have tempted me into actions that I knew to be wrong and most of those with whom I worked closely had a similar outlook. Not everyone had though, and as I grew into the corporate environment my comfort with the surroundings made me less discerning on issues of character. The curiosity quotient, the pursuit of facts so essential to news journalism are not encouraged as widely in corporate life. Over time I allowed my curiosity to be dulled as, unconsciously, I embraced the primacy of profit orientation towards realising shareholder returns.

It was to be in the aftermath of the biggest corporate collapse in Irish history and one of the biggest ever in the world, that I began to re-centre. To that point in business, I was seen as a leadership asset, someone who would bring strong experience and alertness to a board or to senior strategic consulting roles. I believe I was seen in some quarters as a bit 'straight', inflexible around how certain situations would be managed, but that meant I rarely found myself in uncomfortable positions. I was able to choose the roles I wanted which, for me, normally started with the character of the person asking and the culture of the organisation.

Organisational culture can change, sometimes subtly and with little risk to the fundamentals of the business but, more often than is appreciated, the change can be driven by a leader or a leadership cohort that wants to fulfil very particular ambitions. Those targets might appear consistent with those of the organisation but they cannot be if they are given more weight by those in charge; the pursuit of personal ambitions leads to an almost inevitable erosion of the pre-existing, purer corporate culture with a potentially ruinous outcome.

Leaders come in all shapes and sizes. While it's changing, however slowly, most leaders are male. The power and self-centredness of the male ego adds to the threat that organisational success is driven by personal leadership ambition. This can be a precursor to organisational culture change which, if it's not monitored, can undermine the original corporate purpose and style. I have seen this at close quarters in a number of instances but I failed to appreciate what was happening in real time.

It is the leader or leadership group who set the culture in any organisation. They constantly influence how it is shaped, but without the close attention of senior colleagues, especially non-executive directors, their personal ambitions may assume precedence so their actions start to undermine certain fundamentals of the culture they should be protecting. The erosion of corporate culture can long go unnoticed until a point is reached where the edifice gives way with often dire consequences.

My drift – and that is what it was – from journalism into business meant that I lacked certain basic attributes as well as any formal training. In contrast, when I'd joined RTÉ in my early twenties I had many of the attributes and underwent a period of intensive training that had allowed me progress quickly in news and current affairs broadcasting.

What did follow me on the transition was my curiosity, interpersonal skills and my ability as a communicator. However, when I most needed to be sceptical, probing, doubting and disinterested in the accepted narrative I was, instead, too vested in things being just as they appeared to be.

MELTDOWN

Seán FitzPatrick was a remarkably likeable person. Over the years I knew and worked with him I met only one senior business figure who knew him, thought otherwise and consistently warned me that he was not trustworthy. I know scores of spoofers who would tell you now that they never trusted him or didn't like him, including some business journalists, but they are just that, spoofers. In some ways his status was represented by how widely, well beyond business circles, he became known as 'Seanie' in that talismanic way some people attract monikers of their names like 'Gaybo' (the broadcaster, Gay Byrne); 'Charlie' (former Taoiseach Charles Haughey) or even his government press secretary 'PJ' (P. J. Mara) who was so beloved of the satirists of that time.

I first met Seán FitzPatrick on the Sports Development Board of University College Dublin in the early 1990s. I remember the first meeting; his warmth, speed of thought, charm, all wrapped in a physical presence that, in spite of his short stature, allowed him to dominate the room, any room. I'm expressive. I'm drawn to others who are too but this was different to anything I'd known, certainly in business. He had eyes that engaged you, hands that worked the air as if conducting the rhythm of his dialogue and he was very tactile, an unusual feature for Irish men of that vintage.

In my years as a journalist I'd interviewed powerful and famous men but few had an aura like his; being in his company that first evening was intoxicating as it was over the following decade and a half when we worked together and became friends. It was only when I met him for the last time, in the first days of January 2011, that I saw him as he had become, self-absorbed and manically driven to promote the image he'd spent his lifetime to create. In that meeting, throughout what was a last ever discussion between us, he offered no acceptance of responsibility for what had transpired.

Seán FitzPatrick faced a number of criminal charges but, apart from public opprobrium, the loss of certain professional accreditations and considerable sums of money, he escaped penalty for the collapse of Anglo Irish Bank at a cost to the Irish taxpayer of multiple billions.

David Drumm was as low-key as Seán FitzPatrick was business box office. From north county Dublin, he was more like your cliched accountant than his predecessor, quiet but with a steely resolve that allowed him progress quickly in the upper levels of the bank. I didn't know David well but his personality was reserved to the point of appearing distant on occasion. My impression of him was of someone who was solid and dependable.

I don't remember when I first met him but I assume it was after I became a director of the board. That was in 2002. I was a member of the board's Nominations Committee that appointed him as Chief Executive of the bank in 2005. David Drumm was head of operations in the United States and one of the senior executives I knew least well but, from those under consideration, he was the best candidate to replace Seán FitzPatrick as CEO. I believed that then and I still do.

The committee was unanimous and the international consultants the board had retained to advise also considered him the best candidate. The real problem was that so too did Seán FitzPatrick whom we'd agreed should be appointed board chairman, fatally contributing to extending his control over a publicly quoted financial institution that he'd come to see as his own.

David Drumm made some bad decisions but, most seriously, the courts found him guilty of false accounting and conspiracy to defraud, reflecting grave errors of judgement by someone who was vested with leadership of a financial institution. These actions compromised the very idea of ethical behaviour and contributed significantly to the demise of the bank.

The criminal charges David Drumm faced necessitated his extradition from the United States, something he resisted for a period before being brought home to Ireland in March 2016. He was convicted in 2018 and served two years and six months of a six year sentence before being released in early 2021.

In the 2000s, Seán Quinn was as widely admired for his business acumen as Seán FitzPatrick but not as liked. That wouldn't have bothered him, both men enjoyed money and power but Seán Quinn had little interest in and never sought popularity, certainly not for *its own sake. What he did cultivate was a legend around his business brilliance and his concern for and munificence toward the people of Cavan and Fermanagh. Like much legend it might have had some truth but most of it was the stuff of Aesop, Rowling and the like.*

I met Seán Quinn around that time. It was the kind of meeting you wouldn't easily forget, one that made any idea of further meetings not at all attractive. I'd been asked by a friend to accompany him to the meeting which was at Seán Quinn's Slieve Russell hotel on the border. It lasted a couple of hours where my friend got little by way of advice but a great deal on the Quinn family's private business interests across the world and how fabulously wealthy he was. It was part-Flintstones, part-Trump but it was alarming because the certainty and the naked ambition to continue a pursuit for more and more billions of earnings included investments in two companies where I was a director.

Seán Quinn's behaviour around Anglo Irish Bank was a significant contributor to its ultimate fate. In 2012 he was sentenced to a short period in jail relating to court orders to reverse asset stripping and, in sentencing him, Justice Elizabeth Dunne of the High Court said that he had 'only himself to blame'.

Anglo was my professional nemesis. I was a non-executive director for two terms, the second of which ended six months before the bank started to teeter towards its ignominious end. I thought that I'd performed my duties well but I had not. I had acted honourably and professionally but those are characteristics, not measures of how well a job is done so it was inevitable that the public angst and controversy surrounding the bank's collapse and that of much of the banking system disfigured what had, to that point, been a reasonably positive CV.

My insider's view is of an institution that became weighed down by the sheer force of one man's personality and his need for its success to always be tied to him, and by another man who, from outside, deployed a considerable amount of his family's capital investing in the bank through the use of Contracts for Difference (CFDs), a form of derivatives which the globally renowned investor, Warren Buffett, has described as financial weapons of mass destruction. The Quinn family used them to build a considerable position in the bank with enormous consequences personally and ultimately for the bank.

My interest in this economic catastrophe and other experiences over the course of my professional life is heightened by my training as a news journalist and my first love, being a news reporter.

III
Accountability

One Sunday morning in July 2009, I was on the panel of RTE Radio's *Marian Finucane Show* discussing the week's events and weekend newspapers. I had done it from time to time and there was nothing remarkable until, after an ad break, I was asked to address the collapse of Anglo Irish Bank as the show had received calls from listeners on the issue. I'd been a non-executive director of the bank for six years so, while I wasn't expecting to be asked about it, the public reaction to my being on morning radio was hardly unreasonable. The scale of Anglo Irish Bank's failure within a generally battered financial services sector meant the Irish economy was collapsing. My experience of live broadcasting allowed me to deal with the unexpected question adequately. I said all that I could say at that point, that as a former director I would address my fiduciary responsibilities in any criminal cases and, as a citizen, I'd cooperate fully with any state investigations.

Six years later, on July 30th, 2015; as I drove into the city for my session with the Oireachtas Committee on the Banking Crisis, I thought back to a talk that I'd given some 20 years previously at an Anglo Irish Bank senior management meeting. I was a young professional consultant and Seán FitzPatrick, whom I was only getting to know, had asked me to address my view of the bank. I provocatively painted an exaggerated profile of its executives and how they did their business; a bank that was customer friendly, flexible but perhaps too sure of its emerging status. It was amateur satire and the muted applause told me it hadn't gone down well. Most present liked the idea that Anglo was 'different' and 'edgy' but railed at my characterisation of its executives as somewhat 'wide-boyish'.

When I finished as a consultant to the bank in 1999, I'd have counted the start of a process of 'gentrification' of Anglo Irish Bank as one of the better achievements of our role as consultants. The work we'd done with senior management was considerable. Some of it was against the Anglo grain but progress had been made on moving to an appreciation of the need for the bank to present itself differently, to reflect more the essence of what it meant to be a bank. The work was about fundamental change and senior management seemed to embrace it. The culture was to change still more over the next decade and yet, as someone who'd joined its board in 2002, I later came to see how some of the problems that manifested themselves in its demise were still deep-rooted.

At the end of my evidence to the inquiry I got up from where I'd sat for about four hours and went to shake hands with each of my interlocutors. Some were friendly; others looked hesitant as if it wasn't the 'done thing' but, no matter how fractious it may have been at times, slinking out stage-left is not really me. I might have imagined it but I sensed a correlation between those who looked me in the eye and those who'd been the more impressive in their interrogation of my account.

Fianna Fáil's Michael McGrath and Fine Gael's Eoghan Murphy were thorough but Donegal Sinn Féin TD, Pearse Doherty, was the best prepared and the most difficult combatant; most others were adequate and a couple were not – though they may well have thought the same of me. While I was pleased that the hearing was over, I was upset too. My testimony had been controlled before it even began, meaning that I'd been forced to ignore part of the narrative I considered critical to a full understanding of what had gone wrong at Anglo.

Six years after my Sunday morning comments on RTÉ Radio One, when I had committed to giving as full account as possible of what had happened in Anglo, I left the Dáil after my day of evidence to the Oireachtas Inquiry, frustrated. The process that I had long anticipated – court cases and political inquiries – was at an end but I'd been obstructed in addressing the most important learning of all from the collapse of the once revered bank – a massive failure of corporate culture. It would be another few years before the seminal importance of organisational culture was bootstrapped, formally, by the Central Bank to the oversight of financial institutions.

• • •

In 2019, a decade after the collapse of Anglo Irish and other banks in Ireland and overseas, the Irish Banking Culture Board was established with the stated aim of *rebuilding trust in the sector through demonstrating a change in behaviour and overall culture.* Other changes driven by the European Central Bank had already been introduced with more robust regulatory considerations but, for the first time, explicit references were made to issues like *behavioural risk* or the need to focus management resources on the wider *corporate environment or culture.*

The financial crisis Ireland experienced wasn't unique but the scale of it burned what occurred into the soul of the nation. The global damage is reflected in more robust regulation including an apposite focus on organisational culture. The Irish Central Bank is uncompromising that, under the new regimen, it would *monitor and challenge the banks on the delivery of Behaviour and Culture plans* because, from a prudential and conduct perspective, it appreciates that cultural behaviours affect outcomes. The Davy Stockbroker issue of 2021 only served to reinforce the necessity for a much more culture and leadership focused approach to regulation.

This is a marked step change for the Central Bank; the focus is no longer on simply making sure the banks comply with the regulations and codes but that *the people who lead those firms set about building a culture that serves their customers, their shareholders and the wider economy in which we license them to operate.* It is a change that has a profound impact on how non-executive directors and senior management in financial institutions must perform.

My first experience of organisational culture was the positivity of the cocoon of RTÉ's News Features department. I had carried important learnings into my own business when I founded Drury Communications in 1989. Billy Murphy, a close friend who was working in Murray Consultants, then the premier PR firm in Dublin, agreed to join. It was a leap of blind faith but, however unsteadily at first, we found our way to quickly gain a foothold in the market and within a few years had become an emerging threat to the bigger firms.

We did a number of things well from the outset. We used different language, actively promoting 'communications consulting' rather than 'public relations' or 'PR' and constantly pushing the importance of a 'corporate reputation' to any company's pursuit of sustainable success and respect. While we were innocents, we set about running Drury Communications like it was IBM, with a proper board, management structures and reporting.

I knew David Kennedy, the former CEO of Aer Lingus. David was a neighbour who was a respected and sought-after non-executive director. Somehow I persuaded him to become chairman of my fledgling operation. Billy and I grafted but all the time we focused on the centrality of the mission around teamwork which was the ultimate arbiter as to whom we recruited to meet our growth expectations.

Our egos were never allowed get in the way of business development. When we recruited we looked for people who could be better than us, just as my mentors in RTÉ had done. We hired well – Rosheen McGuckian, Tim Collins, Padraig McKeon, Paddy Hughes, Trish Morrissey and others – always looking for those who could add to, not just complement what we did. Critically, they had to be team players and be mature enough to respond to a light-touch leadership culture. Once the team was deepened, whatever formal leadership there had been, became flatter still but, as senior colleagues passed me out as advisers of choice, I turned to broadening the corporate ambition.

With the business performing exceptionally, I prompted the board about opening an office in Northern Ireland. There was a great deal of talk about an emerging all-island economy so my family connections and my journalism in the North pulled me towards Drury Communications leading the way. I wanted to show that an Irish professional services firm needed to have an office in Belfast if it was to lay claim to provide a coherent all-island service.

The political situation was still very tense and while it was absent the excesses of violence that marred the 1970s and 1980s, it remained unstable, with a very real risk of a descent back into the violence-studded instability of that period. In 1995 Drury Communications in Belfast was formed with Tom Kelly as its CEO. Tom was a writer and former political adviser to Dr. Joe Hendron, SDLP MP. We appointed a Belfast businessman and the then chairman of the

Unionist party, Lord Dennis Rogan, as chairman and he joined the board of the Dublin company. To illustrate how toxic the atmosphere remained, on the evening when David Kennedy, Tom and I met Dennis to formalise his appointment to the board, there were rioters on the streets and cars were being set alight nearby the restaurant in central Belfast where we were having dinner.

Drury Communications was the first business in the public relations sector and one of the first across all professional services, to have offices in both cities to provide a seamless, all-island service. Once it was firmly established, I recommended we consider the central European block of Hungary, Poland and Czech Republic for further expansion. After a year's research, in 1997, we opened Drury Kft (Limited) in Budapest, with two staff in a tiny office just beside the magnificent State Opera House. We won a sizable contract within a month and did reasonable business for a number of years.

Throughout, Drury Communications was run by an independent board which sought to support management's ambition but never without question and never without protecting the core principles of the business. I learned the importance of trust but also that it's best for all if it is qualified, never unquestioning. I learned the primacy of teamwork in a business environment but the experience, set by David Kennedy as chairman, was so devoid of individual egos that I got no schooling in how destructive of corporate wellbeing, personal ambition can be. I learned the value of debate where it is real, and where asking or challenging is encouraged and not looked on askance as almost an act of disloyalty. Some of these learnings were absorbed, others taught but, as with anything, what certain experiences subsequently showed me is that good practices need constant reaffirmation, positive lessons need regular revision.

I sold Drury Communications to the management in 1999, on the 10th anniversary of its establishment. I knew that while I was enjoying aspects of the work and I was good at parts of it, the world of public relations wasn't where I wanted to be. I had set up a sports management business where I wanted to work more directly with the small team. It was another junction on the road for me.

It's a source of pride that Drury Communications remains a leader in its market. In the more than two decades since I retired as its first

CEO, I've had no involvement in its growth and development, so the success has been achieved by the brilliance of others. Ultimately, it is testimony to Billy Murphy's quiet but effective stewardship. While he remained focused on that task, my career meandered for a number of years before in the early part of the 21st century I was to reconnect in a very profound way with two of the bigger clients I had managed in Drury Communications.

• • •

Some argue that managing small organisations is considerably easier than those of scale but the same issues arise and, in many respects, the challenges are greater. What determines excellence in leadership and management are attitude and behaviour. When organisations succeed it reflects well on the standards of those in charge so, when they fail, it's normally a consequence of poor behaviour, often manifest in a flawed corporate culture. That has been my experience. The risks to business come from various areas but with major corporate difficulties, financial or operational, irrespective of sector or size, the cause is normally people-related. It's been that way forever.

One of the more notable cases of the last 50 years was the bankruptcy of the US energy giant, Enron. Shareholders filed a $40 billion lawsuit after the company's share price fell from $90 per share to less than $1 in 18 months. It was the largest corporate bankruptcy in U.S. history. In the 1990s Enron developed a sophisticated system of accounting loopholes that allowed it to hide billions of dollars. Its CFO and other senior executives not only misled the board but also pressurised its auditor Arthur Andersen to ignore the issues. Andersen had its license voided and the partnership collapsed with the loss of 85,000 jobs across its global practice. It might be called the law of eighty five thousand unintended consequences!

The 2015 Volkswagen scandal where it was found to have fitted at least 11 million cars worldwide with a device that dramatically lowered emissions in testing, is well known. VW's share price fell by 35% in 48 hours. It had been a deliberate act of deceit signed off at the highest levels. The company paid a fine of in excess of €4 billion in the US and in 2018 its CEO was charged with fraud and conspiracy.

In recent years Boeing has staggered from crisis to crisis to the point where presuming on its survival became questionable. What's not is that its defective 737 Max aircraft lead directly to the deaths of 346 people who, if they hadn't flown on it would be alive today. The crashes led to the dismissal of Boeing's CEO and the commencement of a criminal investigation amid growing evidence that the company's problems had stemmed from a corporate culture that put the focus on saving time and lowering costs rather than on quality production.

There may only be few sectors where the perversion of a corporate culture by arrogance or greed can lead to a direct threat to life but there are many where, indirectly, the consequences of board and or management failures can be far-reaching. The unintended consequences of a lax corporate culture can be extremely serious.

In early 1994 the Irish Blood Transfusion Service Board (BTSB) announced it may have administered a contaminated blood product to women in childbirth, potentially affecting as many as 100,000. The scandal was that the service had been alerted three years earlier by a British hospital that a batch of donated blood may have been contaminated but no action was taken. 1,200 women were found to have been exposed to blood with the Hepatitis C virus almost 300 of whom died as a direct result.

I saw this sad episode at close quarters. Then Minister for Health, Brendan Howlin TD, acted swiftly and decisively to address the problem and vested responsibility in Drury Communications to direct the national communications response. The cultural flaw in the BTSB – to a degree brought to light by the intervention of Dr. Joan Power – was evident from the very first moment we started our work. The Irish state paid out circa €2 billion in compensation. A cavalier culture had directly led to the organisation missing a clinical warning years earlier that could have reduced those numbers. The consequence of the lax culture and organisational failure was catastrophic. Like with Boeing, 300 lives were lost which puts the €2 billion cost to the exchequer in some perspective.

• • •

Following the global financial crash in the early part of the 21st century, central banks and regulatory authorities everywhere started to review corporate governance and regulatory systems. The evidence that human behaviour will always find a means to undermine and corrupt systems cannot be challenged.

Medici Bank of Florence was the most important financial institution in 15th-century Europe. It collapsed after 100 years of success, the cause was the greed and indiscipline of key personnel. Barings Bank was founded in 1762 so when it failed in 1995 it was heading towards 250 years trading but a lack of internal controls, illustrative of corporate arrogance, allowed a 25 year old employee bet on his judgment of the markets. Imagine an institution of that scale and importance being destroyed by one young employee?

Lehman Brothers had lasted even longer. It was one of the world's largest investment banks and was almost 160 years old when it collapsed in 2008 giving the lie to the idea of "too big to fail". The causes were a mixture of overstretching and malfeasance and again, just as with Enron, questionable audit practices. The culture of the firm had been perverted.

These examples of jobs lost, families ruined, even significant social upheaval, are all consequent on corporate arrogance. Whether it was 500 or five years ago, or even within the last year, the root cause is normally human frailty. The fuel we bring to any endeavour, the oxygen only human creativity, imagination and drive can give to an enterprise can be corrupted by our less palatable characteristics, often with long-term damage to the business, to a whole sector and even society as a whole. Wherever humans are involved, others need to be smart and imagine the unimaginable because that's the best hope of not being surprised or caught off guard.

While it's accepted that an organisation with an ethical core, built on a set of proper values, is less likely to do bad things, even by accident, this is hardly enough. The motivation of any business, whatever it does, must be more than to simply operate within the law or to just obey the rules. The ultimate test and certainly the best way to avoid a corporate calamity is to be ethical and actively so. The behaviours of those in the most senior positions matter most to the culture of the organisation.

Then, around fundamentals, a good board must apply its standards actively not passively. This is more difficult than it might appear. It needs leadership by the chairman but all senior experienced people must insist on standards that they are comfortable with, must live them and ensure the board and the company is meeting them. Achieving this as an active, almost living, process is the challenge.

To have any prospect of the achievement of excellence at board level, it's essential that there's a collective commitment of all its members to more than simply a shared set of values. That is a fundamental, a basic prerequisite if any organisation is to function and thrive. What's paramount, however, is that the board provides an active, perhaps even hyperactive, stewardship of management and its commitment to the pursuit of economic success based on agreed standards. This is all critical to corporate culture.

• • •

It's hardly surprising that the governance and regulatory standards of the financial services sector have been considerably strengthened since the period leading up to the global financial crisis. They are the black and white rules that all those in positions of leadership must adhere to; they have the force of the law behind them but while they are stronger now than before the financial crash, they were sufficiently robust even then to have led to a much better outcome.

Viewed through todays lens, the Anglo Irish Bank board was relatively passive and certainly not doubting or interrogative enough. I thought Seán FitzPatrick shared a belief system about basic behaviours that, for example, would have considered it inappropriate to move personal loans off balance sheet to avoid them being discovered by the annual audit. Everyone on the board would have thought likewise; it's hardly an unreasonable presumption to make of an institution's leader.

Were Seán FitzPatrick operating to the values all board members and most senior executives expected then, quite simply, he couldn't have thought it acceptable to boomerang a large part of his loans annually as we know he did for years. There was a great deal more about the bank that contributed to its demise but this practice alone would have been so alien to the standards of his board colleagues, it's little wonder that he never shared it. The responsibility for that is his and his alone.

There was a wider problem however, where across board members and senior management there was too much mutual regard, an excess of belief in the bank's impregnability and the 'genius' of its leadership. The internal mood reflected only how the bank was seen externally. The uniform view of Anglo, in Ireland and internationally, was so positive, it made us less likely to question, made it more difficult to imagine the unimaginable. It should, in fact, have made us more attentive. This goes to the heart of the matter.

The critical thing that really good non-executives do is to ignore what's in front of them, to doubt the accepted narrative and relentlessly pursue the 'what if?' It may be that in most cases such an approach proves to be unnecessary, even an apparent waste of board time. That inconvenience, that notional waste of resources is as nothing compared to how money, jobs, even lives, can be saved in the small percentage of cases where things go disastrously wrong.

I know that I had never thought of Seán FitzPatrick acting in a manner that was not, exclusively, in the best interests of the bank. The fault for having had that level of trust is mine. The contract between senior management of any business and their non-executive colleagues should be one of expectation that nothing they say will be taken at face value, that would represent the best means of a board protecting both the shareholders and, indeed, management itself.

There were technical weaknesses at board level too. While I applied myself diligently to my task as a director I didn't appreciate fully the levels of borrowing on the international markets that allowed Anglo continue lending beyond a point where that was sensible. Money was too easily available from the overseas capital markets, and as a board member I'd failed to anticipate just how quickly this funding could dry up in a crisis.

What happened is a source of great regret. Anglo's failure is not down to me, nor is the bank's collapse the sole cause of Ireland's going through the great economic hardship it did at the turn of the first decade of this century. There were many different and related factors at play but the fact is that some in senior positions – including this non-executive director – have to recognise and acknowledge their shortcomings.

Seán FitzPatrick always said he wanted board members who would never be afraid, irrespective of the circumstances, of expressing their point of view. I now realise that was not true; it was a recruitment message aimed at men, predominantly men, who wanted to believe that of themselves. It was certainly a recruitment message that I heard and believed. I appreciate now that it had to be pitched in a way that made it credible to me because if I had doubted it, I wouldn't have accepted the position.

This was perhaps the first moment when my metamorphosis from journalist to businessman was manifest in my own behaviour, in my decision-making. The curious, cynical me was subdued. Otherwise I would have doubted why I was being recruited. I chose not to interrogate the point. I suspect I wanted to believe and did at the time, that it represented acknowledgement, a recognition of what I had to offer. It's almost impossible to be completely objective about opportunities for your own personal advancement and being recruited to the board of Anglo Irish Bank certainly represented then a big step on the ladder of corporate respect.

Even in 2002, Anglo was quite 'big ticket' and being recruited to its board did make a statement. The bank was in the ascendent. My years of consulting had contributed to its burgeoning reputation but my business experience was limited, so I should have given more oxygen to the small doubts I had about my selection. I didn't, not beyond the smallest reflection because, to have done so would have damaged my self-esteem, made me worry about my motivations, perhaps even question those of the bank's leader in choosing me. I wanted to believe what he told me, so I did.

Seán FitzPatrick may have convinced himself that he wanted independent, strong people around him but the evidence suggests differently, that in fact he largely wanted those whom he knew to admire him and thought he could influence. With the bank continuing to grow, the approach remained centred on what he alone considered best. In real time I never suspected how dominant was his sense of his own omnipotence, something that's reflected in how he'd built Anglo Irish Bank in his own likeness.

Ironically, the Anglo board did oversee a strengthening in corporate governance but with the bank's spectacular growth, it was done in a way that didn't threaten the fundamentals that had got Anglo to where it was. The board didn't appreciate how carefully the momentum around the bank's growth and success was being choreographed. Seán FitzPatrick was supportive of, on some points even an advocate for, greater governance but change was being managed by him in a way that allowed him to turn up or down the governance dial within an increasingly centralised control model. This approach, within a fealty culture, was central to the bank's undoing.

It is true that this controlling behaviour under the nose of a largely admiring board wouldn't have mattered as much were it not for externalities. The global and domestic economic environments turning so sour, the heightened risk profile of some lending, the behaviour of Seán Quinn and the failures of the industry regulator created what's termed, 'the perfect storm'. This is not unusual, it's what happens: deep organisational flaws are normally exposed when wider, external, circumstances bring them to the fore. In Anglo's case this meant that where others experienced violent business disturbance, its position right on the economic fault line of Irish lending – property – could have only one outcome, an earthquake of once-in-a-lifetime proportions.

Before all that, the Anglo board would have passed muster, indeed it did under most criteria that determined board effectiveness so, as the bank's success increased, the institutions, the rating agencies, market analysts and the media competed with each other to 'out-eulogise' on the bank's performance. Like in any relationship, flaws that prove fatal to business tend to be deeply embedded and can remain obscured for a long time.

As Anglo Irish Bank experienced sustained strong growth, questions around it were about its dependence on property lending and, within that, the focus on development, as well as on a perceived lack of a geographic spread, in earlier years. Some of these factors contributed to its undoing but they were not the core issue which was, the cultural fissure at the heart of a centralised leadership model dressed up as something else.

• • •

I was on the board of Anglo for six years to May 2008, retiring just six months before the bank failed in early December. For all my time on the board, it had been a badge of honour. Anglo was the darling of the rating agencies, the institutions and the media. I remember in 2004, at a social event in England, meeting the CEO of a large UK plc who, without any prompting, went into a monologue about what he could offer as a non-executive director. It took some time before I realised that we were at cross purposes. I thought he was promoting his credentials for the Paddy Power board which I chaired but it was Anglo Irish Bank. When I explained this to him he made his apologies and disappeared. I've wondered about him occasionally since, as Paddy Power/Betfair now Flutter plc has had spectacular success while the Anglo embers are long since grey and cold. It's just how it was then, Anglo was a corporate mecca of sorts.

In spite of all the accolades, there was no apparent smugness around the Anglo board table nor was there any conscious undue risk-taking in the management of the bank's affairs. There's no non-executive who saw it as other than a professional and robust financial institution. In my time the investment in internal audit was significant, the work of the external auditors seemed of a high standard, so to have anticipated a collapse in profits would have been hard, never mind imagining anything approaching what ultimately came to pass.

We shouldn't spend our professional lives catastrophising but, equally, we shouldn't fail to imagine that bad things happen. They do. Often it happens easily, with little notice, that corporate success can become corporate calamity. I could never have imagined that I'd be a board member of a bank that would collapse creating havoc in the Irish economy; be a witness in criminal trials brought against its former CEO and chairman; spend almost four hours giving evidence to a parliamentary enquiry or that, understandably, I'd find myself largely ostracised professionally as a result.

I should at least have imagined that those things were possible, but I never did because the idea would have been so alien. I should have because being alert to danger is a positive. I should have because when you are a non-executive director you are paid, above everything else, to be a doubting presence, to insist on looking under the carpet, to refuse to take at face value the excellence of the results or commitments of management and you should never, ever, accept what you are told as the truth.

The non-executive director's job is to step back and take the widest possible lens to look for risks and opportunities on the horizon. When a business environment is overwhelmingly positive, as it was for the majority of my time on Anglo's board, it makes that more difficult. It certainly dulled my capacity to be assertive. I've little doubt now that with the truly spectacular success of the early years of the 21st century a degree of corporate *hubris* set in that reflected a change in its sense of itself as an institution. Seán FitzPatrick had changed too; the personal and corporate brands were always in step.

• • •

I was one of the last witnesses to be called by the Oireachtas Banking Inquiry. I had been a member of the Risk and Compliance Committee over my term on the board so even though my retirement after serving the standard two terms, came six months prior to the bank's collapse I was a person of interest. Any parliamentary inquiry, in any jurisdiction, has a dual purpose and often the public interest is secondary to the political capital to be gained from poring over whatever events are at issue. That's just as it is but my friendship with the former Taoiseach, Brian Cowen, was as much why I was called to give evidence as my performance as a director.

There was some basis for the political curiosity in my appearance at the inquiry. Events, contemporaneous with but not connected to the bank's travails involving me and Brian Cowen, had received considerable public attention. None of that concerned me as, no matter how things might have appeared in some reporting, nothing untoward had occurred. I am an experienced communicator but there's no greater ally to ward off intense interrogation than the truth. I had it and I was so sure of its strength that I had neither spoken with Brian Cowen nor looked at the testimony he had given the inquiry a few weeks previously. I was as certain of his truthfulness as of my own and, furthermore, I knew most of the inquiry members, including his political opponents, would not doubt his integrity.

So, on the morning that I was preparing to enter the parliamentary bear pit of Leinster House with TDs and Senators looking for some new, preferably dramatic, testimony, I could afford to dwell on my primary thesis that one key learning had to be around organisational culture. In that context, I thought back to that meeting in my earliest days advising the bank. In some respects, its organisational culture had changed markedly from that point to when I'd finished as a director but in other crucial areas around leadership, it hadn't changed at all. Organisational leadership, both substantively and in tone, is set by the person at the top. In the case of Anglo that meant no amount of professional advice or intervention would amend its culture to any fundamental degree. This was where I wanted to focus attention. However, it was, it appeared, of no great interest to my political inquisitors.

My testimony was delayed for three hours as I battled with counsel for the inquiry over two issues, the need for me to be free to address the bank's leadership and to establish the facts around an event in the bank attended by Brian Cowen.

The ruling against my being able to discuss the seminal importance of the leader's role in organisational culture seemed wrong; part of my treatise had been culled before I'd even left the ante room. While some of the specifics like the chairman's outrageous annual 'bed and breakfasting' arrangement of his personal loans; the deposit agreement with Irish Life and Permanent and the Maple 10 issue all warranted attention and critical analysis, the culture of an organisation that could have allowed such things to happen was what needed most study. However there was to be no opportunity for me to give my perspectives on what I considered a really fundamental consideration.

There was another complication. That week the Director of Public Prosecutions ruled the committee couldn't take testimony by video link from the bank's former CEO, David Drumm who was in the US awaiting extradition proceedings. Instead, he had provided a written statement that included an important reference to a dinner at the bank attended by Finance Minister Brian Cowen in the weeks between his appointment as Taoiseach and taking up that office. The statement had been leaked to the newspapers.

Strangely, even though David Drumm's statement which had referenced the dinner, had already been published in the media, the DPP still ruled that it could not be used by the committee in its deliberations. That represented quite a problem. I was being told by counsel to the inquiry that I could not advert to his statement in my testimony. The ruling meant I was supposed to give evidence as though I didn't know the testimony of another individual, even though it was covered extensively in that morning's newspapers. The DPP's ruling may have undermined the committee's endeavours, but I was the person most discommoded by it. I was the person 'in the dock' so to speak.

I had spent a considerable part of my professional life either being the person asking tough questions of leading figures live on radio or preparing businesspeople and politicians for all forms of public debate but this time I'd to face scrutiny of my period as a non-executive director of Anglo Irish Bank between 2002 and 2008. While I'd retired five months before the bank's full 'implosion', my term meant that my testimony would be relevant especially as my friendship with Brian Cowen had allowed numerous conspiracy theories to take hold.

Without referring to David Drumm's evidence, I chose to establish that no discussion about the bank had happened at the dinner. The following day David Drumm acknowledged, publicly, that what I said was correct, claiming however that, over the course of the evening, he'd spoken privately with the incoming Taoiseach about the strains on the bank, something Brian Cowen has always denied. Brian and I had arrived together that evening and were the first to leave, again together.

IV

Ego Games

My appointment to the boards of Anglo Irish Bank and Paddy Power went against a corporate bias that would have decried the small and medium business (SME) sector. Certainly, journalism and public relations were two roles that many in business didn't value. I wasn't of the standard board gene pool but I'd have been seen as quite pugilistic, not someone who would endorse wrong-doing or corner-cutting.

For the six years I was on the Anglo board, not one shareholder, analyst, or commentator questioned the suitability of any non-executive but once the bank collapsed a disorderly queue formed in double quick time. That's not to suggest that the post-apocalyptic determination by some commentators that the board of the bank had not performed was surprising or unreasonable. It wasn't. However, the scale of the financial collapse revealed such a systemic governance malfunction that it wasn't exactly difficult to conclude that the boards of all the Irish banks hadn't performed but, in real time, no commentators had registered any flaws in their makeup.

One of the more consistently referenced observations about board performance is the closeness or even inter-relationship of non-executives. Some business academics and journalists are fixated on it as though it is the root of much, if not all, evil. In an ideal world it might be best if there were very limited inter-connections or none at all, but that is challenging in smaller markets like Ireland. Still, there are those who argue it's the primary cause of poor governance. I'm unconvinced. It happens that one of the most dysfunctional experiences I've had was on the board of a large business where I knew no one before I joined.

This is not to dismiss the point, rather not to overweight it as more than one of a number of issues to be factored into the work of an effective nominations committee in its board recruitment and certainly to include restrictions on new cross-business relationships emerging. Flogging the point, as some are prone to do, risks the issue assuming an importance out of proportion to the reality.

There are or there should be obvious points of control. Seán FitzPatrick was, for a time, a small shareholder in a business I owned. It was declared and not relevant to anything that occurred, but it would have been wiser for him not to have been. Separately, he and I explored a potential project in central Europe. We were acting in our private capacities and, despite the noise pedalled by one source, the conduct of the project which ultimately led nowhere, was at all times appropriate. Still, it would have been better had we not considered that project together.

There needs to be a balance on concerns about interrelationships in the composition of board and leadership teams. Otherwise, excellent people who could add considerably to the endeavour can be lost because an overly formulaic approach determines they cannot even be considered. It is the behaviours that matter.

When I was chairman of Paddy Power plc. I recommended to the board that a non-executive vacancy should be filled by Patrick Kennedy, who was then Finance Director of food business, Greencore plc. I declared that I knew Patrick, that his father had been a valued non-executive chairman of Drury Communications. I made it clear that it was Patrick's standing as an emerging talent that gave me confidence he would be a great addition to the board. I was proven correct.

A number of years later John O'Reilly was retiring after a successful period as Paddy Power CEO, so the board appointed independent consultants to lead the process of recruiting his successor. All the non-executives thought Patrick who was still with Greencore should be considered and I asked him to allow his name to go forward. The consultants included him in their deliberations and their independent process identified him as the best candidate. Patrick Kennedy turned out to be one of the best CEOs in Irish business and drove exceptional shareholder value over his tenure. I was chairman for its first phase.

In our time working together our personal relationship never once prevented Patrick from asking tough questions of me as chairman when he was a non-executive nor did it make me any less robust in chairing the board when he became chief executive. Recruitment is never an exact science and, while nepotism and favouritism are not to be recommended, nor should existing relationships be an obstacle to the selection of someone with the right skills and experience.

To have appointees with no other connections may well be preferable but it's not crucial; within months close relationships can be formed where there were none previously. Ultimately performance has to be rooted in the integrity of each individual, especially those in key leadership positions. Advances in technology suggest that it's possible to 'engineer' almost anything but the one great exception is human behaviour. Wherever we place the judgment of humans at the heart of an endeavour we need to realise that underperformance will be a reasonably regular occurrence.

The economic damage done by the financial crash means many central banks have placed emphasis on more sophisticated and rigorous standards of recruitment to boards of financial institutions; regulatory disciplines have been strengthened along with a move towards much higher levels of individual accountability. These positives are among the measures necessary to reduce the risk of future financial shocks of scale. The board dynamic will have profound influence on the outcome, positive or negative. It is rarely neutral.

A fundamental is to find ways of proactively and regularly cross-checking that everyone understands the values of the business, shares them and lives them. Another is about having a means of establishing and regularly confirming each board member's commitment to this principle as the bedrock of the business. This is not easily done; it will take time and resources, but it may be critical to delivering sustained success and it's certainly crucial to a reduction in the number of business collapses.

This is where attention should be directed. The principle of a regular, robust programme of board assessment to ensure that each board member is completely focused on meeting the needs of the business in an ethical, disciplined and transparent manner, is critical. That is what puts a spine, a backbone, into any business. It is perfectly possible that a board would appoint someone as a non-executive who was not known to the other directors but who would find the CEO and the chairman intimidating and not be able to muster any form of worthwhile contribution. The converse is equally plausible.

The board has a leadership role; its importance, its responsibility, cannot be overstated. It follows that its composition influences both how an organisation is perceived as well as how it performs. That is why the issue engenders so much debate. The primary source of the complexity around it is that human behaviour means complete security around board performance, even conduct, isn't possible. It is why I believe that no matter how robust the systems, the most essential consideration is still to always imagine the unimaginable.

• • •

My appointment as a non-executive to boards represented the start of a new phase of my career. It was an initially successful period but was to lead to some notable failures and a decade of stress that was degenerative of body and soul. Much of this was my own fault but there was an amount of bad luck and ill circumstance involved too. Most, though not all of it, was down to my tenure as a director of Anglo Irish Bank.

The fees I earned of about €400,000 over six years as a non-executive director were considerable, as was the status attached to being a member of its board. In different ways, in my mid-40s, each represented a validation of sorts of the move I'd made from journalism to business, 15 years previously. While I can reflect on that now, at no point then did I see it that way or even feel the need to justify my career decision.

Over this period when I was generally sought after for business counsel any doubts I might have had about what I had to offer, fell away and I became more assured, arguably excessively so. The trust I had always placed in my gut instinct about people and the direction of organisations was replaced by something softer, something less defined or rigorous. My instincts had been corporatized. I still evaluated what I saw but I did so from a position of belief not doubt. I still questioned certain things but not with the same precision; I had found a means of assessment that calmed any natural instinct of concern or worry. I never stopped doing my best professionally but I was unaware that I had reconditioned myself, that I'd donned a less demanding approach, one shaped by organisational success and the pursuit of profit.

In Anglo Irish Bank, I was the board member best equipped to monitor corporate culture and, arguably, to have seen what was happening. Strangely I just didn't have my eyes open to the betrayal of trust that was woven into the fabric of the bank, profiled not unreasonably, by the *Financial Times* as the *buccaneering culture created by its founder*.

In my journalistic career in RTÉ I'd learned the importance of trust. It is fundamental to being a broadcaster. Without it how could you, with any confidence, broadcast live every morning? The frontline programme presenters could not do their job unless they had absolute trust in the wider team, be certain that they were all focused on their responsibilities to the full. That's how programmes get made. Those with the profile roles are highly dependent on those who aren't known at all, being just as competent and motivated as if they were the household name.

In my own businesses – both Drury Communications and Platinum One Sports Management – leadership was rooted in the idea of a team ethic where people knew their roles and fulfilled them to the best of their ability without being supervised and managed at every turn. Although small, these businesses had active boards which included experienced non-executive directors. The relationship between the chairman and the CEO was pivotal to this because there might be occasions when a CEO would want to share something with just the chairman without elevating it to the whole board but a decision on that would, properly, rest with the Chair.

Over my six years as chairman of Paddy Power that's exactly how I'd managed things with first John O'Reilly and then Patrick Kennedy as CEOs. The reality is that no matter if it's an SME or large plc, a board's standing and reputation is wholly dependent on the judgment and integrity of the fulltime executives, especially the CEO. 'C' stands for 'Chief', after all.

When I was chairman of Paddy Power there was no occasion when non-executive directors were not informed of any and all information germane to the exercise of their role. In the case of John O'Reilly and Patrick Kennedy I was dealing with exceptional executives who would never have countenanced keeping critical information from me as chairman. We would, on occasion, have consulted on how and when to bring sensitive matters to the full board but never in a manner that could leave board colleagues or the business exposed.

What I and my Anglo board colleagues came to know from the level of scrutiny brought to bear by the report of Professor Peter Nyberg in 2011, by the various legal investigations and by the Oireachtas Banking Inquiry, was that the same could not be said of a few of the bank's most senior executives, especially Seán FitzPatrick. Personal failings duly acknowledged, and in particular that of not being more challenging, it is also the case that some important information wasn't shared with non-executive directors. This was reflected in the testimony of others and was evident from various inquiries as a contributing factor, but only that, to the board's failings.

• • •

At the same time as the different criminal cases and various inquiries were advancing and oddly, given the incalculable damage that Cavan businessman Seán Quinn had done, the Quinn family chose to rattle the sabre of a civil action against the non-executive directors. Quinn's insatiable desire to maximise his personal wealth contributed significantly to Anglo's drift towards acute instability and then speedily to its collapse.

When I had met him on that one occasion in 2007 and listened to his treatise on how to make billions, he spoke of the family's share portfolio which included both Paddy Power and Anglo Irish Bank. During his assessment he gave no hint that he knew that I was on the board of the bank and chairman of Paddy Power which meant he either didn't know or, less likely, he wanted to see how I might react. I didn't but I did leave there somewhat concerned at how he'd spoken of their importance to him.

I raised the matter informally with Seán FitzPatrick, not, at first, out of anything other than curiosity, but later, as the board became aware there could be a problem with Quinn, I spoke with him and David Drumm. David was already on the case and as things progressed the board became aware that Quinn represented a risk that was difficult to manage.

My lunch meeting with Quinn had made me aware of how obsessive he was about his family's money and that his extraordinary arrogance meant he could be a dangerous shareholder. So, as chairman of Paddy Power, I raised questions formally at board about the Quinn family holding and whether we could determine if there was a risk it held more through CFDs? The base position wasn't threatening but it was something that we kept a close watch on because the Quinn family wasn't a shareholder the board would have wanted to see building a large stake in the business.

• • •

The crisis in my business life that first hit in 2009 wasn't due only to my involvement with Anglo Irish Bank because, just as its contamination was seeping into my corporate bones, my own sports business hit heavy turbulence. I was heading the executive team. I was also the majority shareholder so if I was disposed to buck-pass, there wasn't much relief out there.

The future looked bright in the wake of our management role in the 2006 Ryder Cup, the successful staging of FC Barcelona's pre-season in 2007 and 2008, but an acquisition we had made, against the judgment of my chairman Johnny Fortune, started to cause difficulties. It's interesting to reflect on how that certainty in my own judgement overrode the concerns of my trusted chairman; some of the behaviours I failed to see elsewhere occasionally manifested themselves closer to home. The two most material errors I made in the almost quarter century over which I'd founded and managed both the communications and sports agency businesses coincided with the turmoil of years dealing with the Anglo fallout. They were of relatively small consequence though some friends and family lost money.

So, all in all, for a number of years there was a weariness with the endless pursuit from a range of interests. It was a difficult time for most of the Anglo Irish non-executives but my relationship with Brian Cowen meant I had also a political target on my back.

This added another layer of difficulty to my management of the vortex of intrigue in which I found myself. Even though Brian had retired, anything that could deepen the political damage to Fianna Fáil would have enduring value. Its political opponents pursued every facile angle, worked and reworked any material, no matter how tenuous, even though no politician of substance doubted Brian Cowen's integrity. I was at a social event where a Fine Gael minister whom I know asked after him then bemoaned the tawdry nature of the pursuit of *a man we all know to be decent and honest.*

This is just the standard rules of political engagement and, were the roles reversed, Fianna Fáil would have gone after Fine Gael people with equal vigour. Post-Anglo, the longer the whiff of a problem prevailed the more likely electoral benefit could be achieved. That wasn't helpful to the former Taoiseach but nor was it great for me.

• • •

Anglo Irish Bank's collapse traumatised me in ways I still struggle to understand. Within a few years my professional career was in a full-blown crisis. My standard working day had gone from one where I dealt with positive, constructive things to labouring through seemingly endless threats to my integrity and the family's financial well-being. The onslaught was like a tsunami at times, media queries and quarter-baked conspiracy theories circulated which, once dealt with, would be replaced by new ones or by old ones dressed as new. My confidence drained away.

There were not uncommon private rows with acquaintances who showed little sensitivity to the nature and scale of the personal challenge. I wondered if people whom I knew were suppressing anger because of failed investments that I was in part deemed responsible for. One friend moaned at every turn about the banks, Fianna Fáil, Brian Cowen. There was hardly an occasion where he didn't vent on how all parties had conspired to hurt (though I knew not excessively) his wallet. Everyone excepting himself was responsible and, more often than not, he wasn't that subtle about where he directed his ire.

A number of years after the news interest peaked I received a by then very rare invitation to speak at a conference. The session went well. Later I found myself in the bar with a quite well-known entertainer discussing a whole range of subjects. At some point he brought up the issue of the banks so, well-versed in just this scenario and how it could go wrong, I interrupted to say that I'd been on the board of Anglo Irish. In such circumstances I always chose to declare it in case someone found out later and was embarrassed by whatever they might have said. On this occasion I needn't have worried.

It was like I'd flicked some behavioural switch as he went into Doberman mode. In seconds he was red-faced, aggressively challenging me about things that couldn't have been anything to do with me. The final moment of vitriol was delivered with the line that he hoped he'd never again have to spend another minute in my company and, with a theatrical flourish, he put down his drink and left.

These unfortunate situations, some with friends, even family, but more regularly with strangers, were just that and they paled in comparison to the real angst that a great many people were experiencing at the time. The occasional abuse I suffered had to be seen in the context of the scale of economic damage, the numbers of families that were dealing with serious financial difficulties, with little sign of a resolution on the horizon.

I had serious worries but they were nothing to the wider, deeper hardship felt by those for whom the Celtic Tiger had been probably the first time anyone in their family had the opportunity to spread their financial wings. That's not to forget those for whom it had never called, those who have flat-lined economically for generations. Among the real victims of the confluence of failures were families that had sensed they could improve their long-term welfare by taking risk, people who would never have borrowed except for special, normally 'one-off' events or needs now chose, courtesy of the Celtic Tiger, to leverage for a different lifestyle or a more attractive future.

Few of this cohort would have been customers of Anglo Irish; its customer base was narrow but its performance, with all the inherent flaws, had been mimicked across the financial services sector and both directly and indirectly the damage done was widespread and deep. Many citizens who chose to take some unprecedented financial risk over-extended themselves but the conditions then prevailing were so benign that the temptation to do so was hard to resist. The problems were certainly not exclusive to Anglo.

• • •

The other banks liked to lay all the blame at its door. They argued the problem wasn't just the scale of its own losses but also that Anglo's aggressive lending practices during the boom had forced them to follow. The truth is that for a long time, the much larger Allied Irish Banks and Bank of Ireland had been running a very different course to Anglo but later had both tacked to run alongside.

Their timing was less than propitious: some distance ahead on the horizon was a squall that would quickly turn into the violent storm that destroyed so much caught up in it. When it finally abated, many senior crew members of the larger banks chose to present what had happened as though Anglo had been responsible for their decisions to run into the storm rather than to navigate a safe course around it. It wasn't. The responsibility was theirs alone.

The more the media, analysts and the markets had raved about Anglo the more the two big powerhouses of Irish retail banking had allowed it to get under their corporate skins. Their sense of superiority was so deep that, as senior executives and board members began to shift their ground to compete with Anglo, few acknowledged the new strategy was related to the success of their smaller, niche, rival. It was, in fact, classic peer market pressure at work.

Those boards, like Anglo's, were male-dominated and by men of a particular cohort where few doubted their own worth. The result was that as Anglo achieved stratospheric growth and global adulation, this began to grate on individual board members elsewhere and they started to pressurise their senior management teams to follow the once mocked little bank on Dublin's St. Stephen's Green. In time that's precisely what the management of the other banks did so that, when the implosion happened, no board of any Irish financial institution could ignore the charge of having 'followed' rather than 'led', as boards are supposed to do.

In changing tack to compete with Anglo, they displayed a lack of confidence in their own strategic direction, allowing themselves to be distracted and to drift off course. It was a markedly different failure of leadership to Anglo's but nonetheless that's what it was. The two largest Irish banks failed to stick to their business model and to ignore what Anglo was doing as not essential to their growth or to meeting the needs of their shareholders. The financial crisis exposed serious cultural flaws in how both AIB and Bank of Ireland conducted their business.

When the tsunami hit, they attempted to perform a complete *volte-face*, suggesting the problems were uniquely Anglo-related. I saw one piece of correspondence from the chairman of a large financial institution, admittedly written during the worst of the crisis, where he irately chose to lay all the problems of his bank at Anglo's door. Pontius Pilate would have blushed.

• • •

While there were many factors that contributed to Ireland's economic plight there was no escaping that Anglo Irish Bank's 'implosion' was the most significant of them. I had been a board member for six years. I believed that I had served the interests of the shareholders but, as we entered the second decade of the 21st century, it became clear that, as a bank director, monitoring your responsibility through such a narrow prism is not remotely sufficient. The police and different state agencies wanted to meet and interview me about what I knew with the emerging likelihood that I'd be required as a witness in criminal trials.

When I refer to the importance of board members, of senior people in business, regularly taking time to imagine the unimaginable, this is exactly what I mean. Never in all my years of work had I ever thought that the behaviour of senior colleagues, men whom I trusted completely and my own professional failings, could have led to such circumstances. What I do know is that, however challenging my board membership of Anglo proved to be, it could have been worse.

Gillian Bowler and I had never met until, as chair of Fáilte Ireland, she took a personal interest in some of the plans for the 2006 Ryder Cup, an event that, through my sports management business, I was the lead consultant on. I had been working on the project for many years before she chose to engage. The reason she did was that government had allocated an additional budget towards the Opening and Closing Ceremonies which had been added to the more golf-related programme of work we had to undertake. The government spend was many millions and it was being managed through Fáilte Ireland so, about a year out from the event and not unreasonably, she sought direct contact with me to ensure the taxpayers' interests were protected.

We met regularly in advance of the event. Gillian was methodical but not risk-averse, direct and pointed in establishing what she expected and unconcerned by anything other than delivery against reasonable expectations. There was no grandstanding or need to consider her profile, her only concern was that I would match the sizeable budget she was guardian of with an undertaking to ensure the 2006 Ryder Cup was the best-ever staged.

We established a relationship which ultimately led to her placing trust in me to ensure the public spend was managed appropriately. When, despite the most appalling weather imaginable over its first days, the event was a great success and recognised as such internationally, she was quick to both publicly and privately acknowledge our work.

I respected how she went about her business. I liked her and it seemed mutual as she wanted to keep in touch, meeting occasionally to share ideas and talk about general business issues. In mid-2007 she asked to meet to discuss something 'important and private'. To my surprise she asked if I would consider joining the board of Irish Life and Permanent (ILP) plc. once my term as a director with Anglo ended. She was ILP chairman and said she was working with its CEO, Denis Casey, on identifying candidates whom they thought suitable as non-executive directors.

I was flattered but I told her that, while I wouldn't be extending my term with Anglo, nor would I be open to joining the board of another financial institution. We had a number of further meetings at which she tried to convince me and when I continued to resist she said that she'd like to talk with Seán FitzPatrick about it. I chose to do so myself to bring the matter to a close. Fate's hand is never far away. If I had joined the board of ILP, given the massive interbank loan arrangement it agreed with Anglo in September 2008, few would have believed that I wasn't somehow instrumental in it or that there hadn't been collusion between the two boards.

While in corporate Ireland I was damaged irreparably, I had also had some fortune on the timing of my retirement from the Anglo board. The Nominations Committee chose the retiring managing partner of PWC, Donal O'Connor, to replace me. The rules of the practice prohibited him from taking any directorships until 2009 so a few months before I retired in May 2008, Seán FitzPatrick asked if I would extend my term for six months. I declined and, to his great misfortune, Donal O'Connor got a derogation from the general partnership rules of PWC and took up the position in June 2008.

V

Fast and Loose

It's impossible to try to understand what went wrong with Anglo Irish Bank without focusing on Seán FitzPatrick. A large part of the bank's story is simply a corporate reflection of his story. We are all products of our time, our upbringing, and for many organisations the personal DNA of a leader becomes transposed into that of the business. Just as Seán FitzPatrick's personality, his make-up and style as much as his undoubted intellect were pivotal to Anglo's growth, that personal capacity to overstretch and to continually push the boundaries of the possible were integral to its demise. That is a large part of the Anglo story.

Seán FitzPatrick was grounded; he came from a modest background and his career was not noteworthy until, with the acquisition of Irish Bank of Commerce in 1986, Anglo Irish began to emerge in Irish banking. Initially it remained a relative minnow, but under his stewardship and a small executive team it was to emerge as a niche force domestically, then a bank of global significance within its sector. The first phase involved shaking up the non-retail banking sector in Ireland where AIB and Bank of Ireland were consumed by a corporate arrogance reflected in generations of privilege.

This was at the heart of Anglo's emergence, it was key to what spawned Seán FitzPatrick's odyssey. The career of a young accountant leading a tiny financial institution to a man credited with building what in 2005 was rated the most admired small bank in the world. There were legions of fans but, in time, perhaps no one believed more in the legend of Seán FitzPatrick than the man himself which is, I believe, a consideration in understanding what was to unfold.

In its early years Anglo set about providing an offer that was radically different in terms of decision-making and relationship management. It was needed. By the mid-1990s, at the point where its model was more refined, the new Ireland of aggressive property development, commercial risk-taking and exceptionally high levels of personal wealth, was taking root. The new breed of younger corporate players represented a different Ireland. They frowned upon the formality and pomposity of the two big banks and were a good customer match for the emerging Anglo.

There was another consideration – the major one – that the bank's lending model worked. Its process seemed every bit as secure as its competitors but more efficient. The labyrinthine approach of the 'big two' had been there for so long that no one had thought to offer something different. Anglo's executives also worked harder. The model was simpler but, as the results over those first 15 years show, it was robust and Anglo's growth as a business began to translate into its being favoured by investors, first in Ireland, then across Europe and finally, globally.

In the mid-1990s I was its strategic communications consultant. Drury Communications saw right into the heart of this evolving narrative, working at close quarters because a critical part of our work related to Anglo's interactions with the investment community of stockbroking analysts and funds. The period between the mid-1990s and 2007 was one of sustained and, by any standard, spectacular success. Seán FitzPatrick morphed from being a bright, energetic and radical force to a serious and increasingly respected business figure but someone, whom I believe came to see, fundamentally, that this successful bank was 'his' bank.

It's not unreasonable now, in the fullness of time, to conclude, however uncomfortable it may be, that he also saw the board I was sitting on as 'his' board. Seán FitzPatrick managed it so Anglo could exude the impression of having become more corporate whereas, in critical areas, the bank's cultural DNA was unchanged.

I failed in my responsibility as an Anglo board member because I failed to see how it was being led by someone who, both as chief executive and chairman, was orchestrating its behaviours. The board wasn't alert to the absence of standards at the very top. We were 'blindsided' by some behavioural patterns that betrayed a casual arrogance but, allowing for how some of the interaction with the board was controlled, I know now that I should have been more searching. I and others had come to believe so strongly in Seán FitzPatrick that, however unwittingly, we helped to fuel his belief system, failing him also, in the process.

Following the bank's collapse, the non-executive directors were interviewed by detectives from the Office of Corporate Enforcement and it became clear to the authorities that there had been some gaps in our knowledge, that when it came to being informed, we weren't always playing with a full deck. That is not to excuse the failings. Personally, I know there were enough signs to have made me more vigilant and less trusting, to have been more demanding and more insistent that the standards I might have presumed existed, were in place and being monitored.

It is also the case that in certain areas, some of us may not have been sufficiently conversant in aspects of the technical side of Anglo's business. This wasn't hidden; there was never a pretence that it was otherwise and it was similarly true of non-executives of other financial institutions. There has to be a balance; boards should not be filled with those who are technically adept but bring no other skills, including the often derided 'soft' ones that are essential to effective governance.

The new dispensation of financial regulators means 'not knowing' will no longer be a defence for senior management or board members. Not thinking deeply enough about the behaviour of colleagues; being passively rather than actively observant may amount only to 'sins of omission' but sins they are, nonetheless. My greatest regret for my failings over this time is the hurt done to those whose lives were damaged to any extent by the lack of alertness on my part to what was unfolding.

Somehow the best board, no matter how bright or experienced its members, needs to create an environment where everyone feels empowered to raise any issue, no matter how small. The board member who is fearless about asking questions, the one who is completely unfazed by any possibility of appearing stupid or overly zealous is the most valuable board member. This should be a positive, something that is valued and not frowned upon but in actuality it's more difficult to achieve. It is more difficult still when the business is performing well.

Whenever I led a board – Paddy Power (Flutter plc); Web Reservations (Hostelworld plc); Mainstream Renewable Power; RTÉ – it was always understood that anything at all relevant to the business could be brought up and discussed, no matter how obscure or challenging. The only condition I insisted upon was that questioning of management was always conducted respectfully. The chair and the CEO must create the environment where board members are encouraged to question and probe and should appreciate that such a culture offers them greater protection as much as it does their non-executive colleagues.

There's more about the Anglo debacle that's worthy of reflection. Even a decade on much of the commentary has been about the monoline nature of its lending, some of which is accurate and reasonable, some of which is not. Others have reflected on a perceived lack of controls around lending to a relatively small cohort of Irish developers, even though Anglo was the first bank to press the brakes and make no new loans into the Irish market. It should have done so sooner and not have continued, as it did, to lend to some trusted long established clients.

It's easy now to see the bank's growth trajectory as too steep over that period but it's about more than hindsight. It should not have been beyond a board to have worked out that it was problematic. Personally, that I didn't do more to interrogate the bank's growth trajectory, is hard now to understand.

• • •

The appointment of David Drumm was not the reason Anglo Irish Bank became a corporate calamity and however questionable some of his decision-making, he was hopelessly compromised as CEO from the outset. The process of his appointment was impacted by the outgoing CEO who, while he did everything to appear to distance himself from it, in fact, did nothing of the sort.

Years later I could recall one conversation where Seán FitzPatrick emphasised how important it was that the selection committee acted independently of him. The point was so laboured it should have been clear to me then that there could, for him, be only one acceptable outcome. It was a consummate performance; the nominations committee's work was subtly controlled and it was only with the passage of time those of us involved could come to understand its genius.

David Drumm was the best candidate from those shortlisted but neither the board nor the consultants had cast the net widely enough. While that was an error it wasn't the main problem. What we had failed to realise was that Seán FitzPatrick was quietly managing the process toward only one outcome.

The board's decision to elevate Seán FitzPatrick to the position of chairman contaminated David Drumm's appointment as CEO as it would have any appointee. It left him hopelessly compromised as, effectively, the management of the bank remained centred on the man who had come to believe its success was exclusively down to him. The damage was greater because the appointee was internal and so it was that David Drumm came to be to Seán FitzPatrick as Dmitry Medvedev was to Vladimir Putin. The change of role mattered little as, with his own man as Chief Executive, it allowed Seán FitzPatrick remain in control.

The board's decision to appoint him as chairman was contrary to the general advice of the Association of Investment Managers (IAIM) the body that represents large institutional shareholders in plcs. However Seán FitzPatrick was then considered to be an exceptional business leader and someone whose standards were beyond reproach. There was no commentator, no meaningful voice inside or out of the bank who thought otherwise, so the board had reason to consider the value of retaining his influence and intellectual capital.

Still the market wisdom was that departing CEOs should leave the organisation completely on their retirement. It was a firm view, one that was seen as immutable but the board sought to see if an exception would be made in Anglo's case. The argument was that, whoever the new CEO was, they would benefit if the board retained the unique skills and experience of Seán FitzPatrick in the role of chairman.

To my surprise IAIM recommended making an exception to its

own guidelines. There's no doubt that, had it decided otherwise, making the appointment would have been problematic because you don't normally consult with the institutions and then ignore their counsel. Still, IAIM did not tell us to appoint Seán FitzPatrick as chairman, that was our collective decision as a board.

It would seem that it wasn't just Seán FitzPatrick's ego that needed him to stay in control. The movement of a large number of his loans to another institution at audit time each year would have been hard to continue if he wasn't the chairman. There was a risk to him that certain behaviours could be exposed were he no longer a presence through his appointment to the position of chairman. It's a decision that we made as a board but that we were guided towards by the very man who needed to ensure that his own hand remained firmly on the tiller.

The board missed how Seán FitzPatrick hadn't really absented himself from the deliberations over his departure as CEO as he'd promised he would and, on the surface, as he had appeared to do. The control bug never left him and it may be that, given the intensity of his Anglo journey, it was unrealistic to ever imagine that he'd really release it. It was, though, fundamentally unfair to whomever would be chosen; it damaged the integrity of the process and it inhibited the future of the bank.

The best way to profile the depth of this 'control' problem is to personalise it. I have a naturally cynical disposition, I dislike hero-worship and I've a background in journalism which teaches you to doubt or to question. Somehow, in that time I suspended my capacity to interrogate the accepted wisdom which was, in fact, no wisdom at all. I wasn't alone but I'm surprised I didn't navigate through the hyperbole and see the truth. In real time I had failed to see the need.

Seán FitzPatrick was a brilliantly effective corporate tactician, every move was planned and executed in a manner that delivered the outcome he thought best. Debate was encouraged but it was just that: debate. Any analysis of corporate behaviour would be shaped by questions he wanted answered and, fatefully, whereas in his earlier years he'd have pushed back against idolatry, he began to thrive on it. With that transition in his own sense of himself and of the bank, its welfare was put at risk.

Many factors contributed to the destruction of Anglo Irish Bank but the most important considerations were flawed culture and leadership. Seán FitzPatrick was no ordinary man; he towered over most of his peers through an energy and self-belief that's rare in any walk of life. He was a nonconformist which was part of what made him so well liked. It is hard to profile just how different he was to the leaders of the other banks; that difference was part of what many in business, including most media, really liked about him.

His character was as critical to Anglo's success as it was a contributor to its and his own business demise. It was also pivotal to the bank's great strengths, its energy and 'can do' attitude that allowed many good businesses to grow, that facilitated some remarkable development across the country, in the UK and in parts of the United States. The entrepreneurial bank had an entrepreneur at its helm but one who, tragically, failed to appreciate the fundamental value of appropriate levels of disinterestedness, truly independent board control and the strictest of strict compliance.

• • •

Seán FitzPatrick is one of the most persuasive people I've ever known and while he didn't lack self-belief, he'd also a tremendous capacity to make those whom he valued see their own potential. Over the time I'd known him well I would have counted him among the more honest, direct, generous and courageous people I knew; the truth is that's how most saw him. What I'd missed was how in my time on the board he came to manipulate me, how his brand of persuasiveness was, not infrequently, about achieving an outcome that he wanted at a cost to the independence of my thinking.

I had some small sense of foreboding as my second term was coming to an end. It wasn't concerns about the bank's financial welfare but I had started to doubt Seán FitzPatrick, to become uncomfortable at some of his ways. This wasn't marked, it was no more than a gentle sense of unease but it was in my gut and I chose to ignore it. I chose to ignore an emerging personal discomfort even though it should have been telling.

A year before my second term finished, Seán FitzPatrick asked me to be chairman of the board's Risk and Compliance Committee. I wasn't comfortable with the idea even though I had served well as a member of the committee for five years. It did important work and it was very demanding especially as the Basel Guidelines – a series of accords that set global regulatory guidelines around reserves and risk in banks – were being reviewed and implemented. The executive team was excellent as was its chair, Michael Jacob. I had contributed well to the committee but did not feel that I was the right person to be its chair especially when Michael, the most risk-knowledgeable non-executive on the board, was being moved off the committee.

I resisted, strongly at first, but in the end I allowed Seán FitzPatrick to persuade me. I should have held my ground and refused but equally, as I had expressed strong reservations, my reluctance should have been respected. It's revealing that a chairman would pressurise a non-executive director to take on a role, even for a short period against their clear wishes. I wouldn't push someone into a role they were reluctant to do; it's the antithesis of positive leadership. This only added to the small discomfort I had when it should have triggered a considerably more serious reaction.

I told the Nyberg and Oireachtas inquiries that, in the months prior to finishing as a board member, I had insisted on the Nominations Committee minuting that any future chairman of the board's Risk and Compliance Committee be either an accountant, corporate lawyer or an experienced banker. The volume of material was vast as the committee wasn't just responsible for risk across the whole bank but also compliance which, with the advent of the proposed new Basel regulations, meant the complexity of its function was extended regularly. I believed the scale of its work meant, as with the Audit Committee, that the chair should be a specialist.

The general rule when you're appointed to the board of a plc. is that you commit to serve one term but in the expectation that you would be asked to serve another. It's rare for people not to be re-appointed after their first term, rare and not generally a good sign. In some cases people do more than two terms but I had always believed no one should serve more than two 3-year terms. It's why, when I was doing my first chairman's statement for Paddy Power, I wrote that I would serve only two terms as chairman, even though some colleagues wanted me to leave open the possibility of a third.

So, towards the end of 2007, six months out from the end of my second term on the board I met Seán FitzPatrick to establish that, in the event that any consideration was being given to asking me to stay on, there were no circumstances in which I would accept. It's a delicate matter; you're ruling out something that others may not even be considering but, perhaps reflecting a just emerging strain in our relationship, he offered little resistance. Still, I had no sense of foreboding about what lay ahead for Anglo.

Within a year of that meeting and just six months after I retired as a board member, in December 2008, Seán FitzPatrick was forced to resign as chairman. The immediate cause was the elaborate management of loans that he'd choreographed during the annual audit period since well before I had even joined the board in 2002.

The rules on this were clear. Annually, the company secretary would remind us of the regulations around the confirmation of any loan arrangements directors had with the bank. All board members had to sign a reconciliation of indebtedness for the period. Dated, it simply noted the extent of any loans you had, they were then aggregated, were filed and appeared in the bank's Annual Report to shareholders. Seán FitzPatrick got around the system by moving a considerable portion of his loans to another institution during the audit, markedly reducing the levels of his loans as reported.

We were to learn years later that this practice was neither illegal nor contrary to accounting rules but it was a breach of trust. It meant every year we signed off on accounts which, as CEO and later chairman, he knew did not accurately report the directors' loans. That realisation was stark; the very person we and every shareholder regarded as the bank's leader was involved in an accounting sleight of hand that would have done credit to the wiliest card shark at the table. It showed too, the limitation of financial accounting as no more than a report on observable past performance where its reliability is dependent on those responsible being able to observe everything.

Seán FitzPatrick led Anglo Irish Bank but we now know that he misled colleagues which meant that the board, unknowingly, carried that misrepresentation to the shareholders and the public in its annual reporting on the bank's affairs. He talked about trust and integrity but, to use one of his own favourite phrases, he *played fast and loose with it*. In his world there was a hierarchy of interests and, too late, I was coming to see that his generally came first.

• • •

In spite of my annoyance and the anxiety I experienced in the immediate aftermath of the bank's collapse, following his humiliating resignation, I tried to remain in touch with Seán FitzPatrick. My lawyers advised against this but I felt compelled not to completely desert him. My anger was tempered by a sense that he had been completely abandoned by others and, initially, a naive belief that most of what had happened had been outside of his control.

Seán FitzPatrick's fall from grace was precipitous and dramatic. It was total, at a level that meant ignominy wasn't an overstatement so I felt some sympathy for him but I was particularly sorry for his family whom I knew and liked. In those early months I endeavoured to keep in touch and offer some level of succour. It was no more than that; there was nothing practical that I could do to assist him but while I felt let down by some of his behaviours and concerned by the scale of the problem, I was disinclined to abandon him.

While the immediate focus was elsewhere, even for me the Anglo climate wasn't exactly temperate. Long periods of relative calm would be broken by some new storm of intrigue often fuelled by political opportunism. Most of the time I was blindsided by whatever issue was getting media attention. I remember being in hospital and receiving a call from a reporter, someone I have known for decades, who somewhat embarrassedly said his editor wanted to know if I was *one of the Maple 10*? When I had to explain that I didn't know what the Maple 10 was, he apologised, muttering that he'd suspected as much.

Over a period of about a year there were a number such enquiries, most of them from the same political source, a TD of limited ability who seemed determined to promote all sorts of mischievous stories about me. I got some odd calls over that period and while most journalists knew the various suggestions were groundless they had a job to do and I understood that better than most. For all that many politicians and journalists distrust each other, they have a mutual need which means they flirt on occasion.

My relationship with Brian Cowen, the Taoiseach, was something that offered up both news and, for opposition parties, political capital around the collapse of Anglo Irish Bank. My deep knowledge of both the media and politics meant I'd an acute sense of how the pursuit of me would go. As long as Brian had political opponents there would, among them, be people looking to expose some imagined wrong-doing and I would most likely be drawn into it. From the media perspective, the pursuit of the story was completely legitimate; in fact, not to have chased every angle would have been negligent.

It's entirely correct to pursue links between those in business and in politics to see if there's evidence of any breach of the standards in public office expected of an elected representative. The media had a responsibility to pursue every line, no matter how uncomfortable that might have been for me and, in time, Brian Cowen. There were certain immutable facts that neither he nor I ever disputed so it was the media's job to parse the narrative and probe for any weaknesses that might appear. When you're in the media's sights about something so serious, it's a comfort to know you've done nothing wrong. I have often thought since how unbearable the pressure must be when you have the media hounding you about actions that did involve wrong-doing.

• • •

The pressure on me was immense for those early years but it's nothing to what Brian Cowen faced. I was simply a means to an end, even more so with those in politics who stood to gain from exerting more pressure on an already embattled Taoiseach. Over an 18-month period it was relentless and the tales about me grew ever taller, the most serious being that I had been within the inner cabinet sanctum on the night of the Bank Guarantee. This was made up. I told the journalist who contacted me that I'd made two phone calls over that period, one for Anglo and one for Royal Bank of Scotland, the former to an adviser to Finance Minister, Brian Lenihan, and the latter to an adviser to the Taoiseach.

These were wild days as new rumours emerged to replace those that had been debunked. One Saturday a news editor phoned to say a reporter and a photographer had been despatched to my home and as they were going to be there for the day, I might like to get any young family members out of the house within the hour. I thanked him but asked about the story they were pursuing. Within minutes I was able to establish that it was utterly groundless but added there was little point in going to my home as I was working overseas and not flying back till later that evening. I then gave him the flight details for my return to Dublin and said that while I wouldn't be making any comment, if he still thought the story was worth the effort, his journalists could meet me off the flight.

I remember how on the flight home I chatted to the guy sitting with me but all the time I was paralleling what could await me at the airport, rehearsing my look of disdain and refusal to even say 'no comment' as I walked past any waiting journalists. There was no one there but it's what my life was like for a few years. It was hard on my family too. All the time, while I appeared to be functioning as normal, I was dealing with a different private reality, constantly anticipating problems, reviewing events and re-evaluating behaviours. It was an almost 24/7 phenomenon; something I'd never experienced before where, as I lead my daily life, there was another one being played out in my head, at least a great deal of the time.

While it was destructive and I knew it to be, I couldn't seem to loosen its grip but I was also conscious of those who carried a real exposure and I wondered how they could function at all. I wondered in the midst of all this about my friend Brian Cowen who was dealing with a crisis of almost incalculable scale.

One part of my strategic management experience meant that I'd earned a reputation for working with organisations and individuals through major crises. I believed I was particularly skilled at seeing the challenge through the widest lens possible to establish perspective and a sensible way forward. Now, in the midst of my own drama, for the first time, I appreciated how debilitating such an experience is for those directly involved and, when you're in the storm, just how narrow the lens becomes.

I wasn't even a central character but the pressure was relentless, suffocating, to the point that sometimes it was as though the simple act of breathing, staying calm or measured, as the scale of what might be involved became clearer, was difficult. That may appear overly dramatic, especially as I knew I had always acted properly but I understood the lens of perception, how easily it can frame truth. I had spent years advising others on crisis management so I could foresee the range and scale of complications that arise in these type of circumstances. I was working my way through it, evaluating how even tangential issues could spark media and political interest, bringing other parts of my life under scrutiny. I wasn't wrong!

• • •

In spring 2010 I heard from Seán FitzPatrick for the first time in many months. I was surprised and on my guard when he phoned, even more so when he explained why; that he was thinking of writing a book and wanted my opinion about the wisdom of doing so. I was blunt. I told him it would be reckless, that it would draw only more attention on him and his family: a book could and should wait.

Seán FitzPatrick said close friends had advised him to make public his version of events. It was poor counsel. He was facing criminal trials; by then he was so damaged the public wouldn't have believed anything he said but he seemed determined. The friends had advised him against speaking with me, preferring that he would consult with the experienced PR professional, Jim Milton. Jim had advised Tony O'Reilly for most of his career so I encouraged him to do so, knowing that he would get a clinical assessment of what course he should take. A week later he rang me back to say Jim Milton's advice was the same as mine and that he would not be proceeding with the book.

The next time I heard from him was the following Christmas, when he asked if I'd meet him to discuss something "very important". I went to his home where he explained he'd gone ahead with the book with Brian Carey business editor of the *Sunday Times* and Tom Lyons a reporter with that same paper, two respected journalists. He told me they had agreed it was time he told his story.

I remember a well-known public figure, about whom some very unpleasant rumours were circulating, asking my advice about the wisdom of doing an interview with Pat Kenny on 'The Late Late Show'. The show had courted him, saying it would be the best way to 'slay' the rumours. This was the programme feeding him a line to serve its interests for an item the producers knew would deliver a strong audience. I pointed out that, in his anxiety, he was missing the fact that if he chose to go on the show considerably more people would know about the rumours than if he chose not to. Journalists often go on safari with a licence not just to look at all the wildlife but to try to capture those creatures who might be weak and make the best prey.

What was to emerge over that brief and my last-ever discussion with him was that, in spite of what Jim Milton and I had advised, he had gone ahead with the book. In not advising me of this until days ahead of publication he was, again, controlling the agenda. Many months previously he had been definitive that he wouldn't be proceeding and over all that time he'd never sought me out to advise me otherwise. There was, as I had now come to understand that there always had been, a reason for his reticence.

One of the things that he had done was to share information on a range of non-Anglo matters including that he had attended a confidential meeting that I had set up with Brian Cowen, then Taoiseach, in July 2008. The meeting was completely unconnected with the bank, indeed banking hadn't been discussed. I had both the agenda and the meeting notes to prove it. When I reminded him of this he said he had pointed this out to the journalists but that they had still wanted to include it.

Seán FitzPatrick knew the timing of that meeting would, of itself, trigger further controversy and offer capital to the political forces that already wanted to undermine the Taoiseach. It was obvious that, given how the meeting had been months before the bank's implosion, it could only suggest an agenda that was completely at odds with its actual purpose and indeed the origins of the group. I reminded him that while the others present were known to Brian, he had been included on my recommendation.

It was in that moment that I really saw him for the person he was, someone who was so focused on self-preservation that it allowed him to do anything necessary to protect his own self-interest even if that was at the cost of someone else's welfare. I remember how it was that, in the midst of my protests, he said *I know it was wrong but I suppose I was just a bit fast and loose with the stories*. I had my full final awakening to his utter selfishness. Just as his management of the bank had been focused on his personal interests, as he faced the emerging criminal and possible civil trials his need for self-protection meant he was prepared to manage the truth, knowing that while it would unfairly damage the Taoiseach, it might just serve to distract public attention from his own failings.

In the conversation he continued to profess his sadness over what he had done but it was so studied, the whole performance so choreographed, that I got up and left. I was sickened by it but horrified by the scale of the betrayal. As I left his home, I remembered the meeting with Brian Cowen in the spring of 2008 when I'd pushed him to gather some private sector minds to brainstorm on the macro-economic issues facing the government. Brian's constant refrain was that it had to be private and, as usual, that there could never be discussion about peoples' sectoral interests but I was so used to how he worked and thought on these matters I confidently reassured him on this account. Fatefully, I had been just as confident in recommending to him that Seán FitzPatrick be included in that group.

Most of all, it was the moment I realised that a drowning man is prone to do anything to save himself. In whatever fight he thought he could wage to refurbish his profile, it seemed Seán FitzPatrick would scatter every and any piece of information about others that might distract or divert attention from where most of it should have been focused.

The infamous meeting and the nine holes of golf that followed it with Brian Cowen had no relevance to Anglo which at no point, not once, had been discussed. Indeed, the banking sector wasn't discussed at all. Seán FitzPatrick knew that and acknowledged it to me that winter morning when he told me about his book. There was no consideration of the damage it would do to a good person, the Taoiseach who, through me, had trusted him as someone of integrity. I saw this as just part of Seán FitzPatrick's playbook then; the more distractions he could create the better it would serve his interests, with no thought to the impact on others.

There was another consideration and it was part of the reason Seán FitzPatrick had wanted to talk with me. I now knew about the book and some of the likely damage so I would have to give advance notice to others – including the Taoiseach – of its imminent publication and some headlines of what it would contain.

That day I knew for certain that Seán FitzPatrick's only concern was self-protection. The decision to publish his highly selective account and to use any information, no matter its relevance, that could distract or provide cover, irrespective of the consequences for others was the ultimate measure of the man. For me, as I left his home that day I appreciated fully that this particular corporate emperor had no clothes.

It was many years later that I learned of a postscript to the row of that day. In the days before publication, the book's authors, Brian Carey and Tom Lyons, and its publisher Penguin Ireland were placed under significant pressure not to proceed. Some friends of Seán FitzPatrick were sufficiently alarmed by how things had evolved that they used an intermediary to try to negotiate an eleventh-hour abandonment of the project. It was by then so advanced – publication was imminent – that what was offered had to have been substantial but no incentives would have persuaded either the journalists or their publisher to back out.

• • •

The day I appeared in front of the Oireachtas Banking Inquiry – July 30th, 2015 – three people were appearing in the courts in Dublin being sentenced to jail terms for various offences relating to their conduct as executives of Anglo Irish Bank. At the same time, in an adjoining court, the bank's former chairman and CEO, Seán FitzPatrick, sought leave to have charges against him dropped because of the publicity surrounding the case against his three former colleagues.

We can become cynical about clichés but one I subscribe to is the idea of the buck stopping with whomever is in charge. When I reflect on Anglo and my knowledge of what unfolded I always come back to the question of leadership, to the idea that those who run an organisation, no matter its size, are the greatest influence on its culture and, while modesty (real or otherwise) may demand that they are measured in how they take the plaudits in the good times; leaders cannot avoid the blame when things go wrong. It might at times seem unfair or unbalanced but it's just the way it is and there should be no escaping it.

During the lengthy delay ahead of my testimony in the Dáil that morning I sat alone in the ante-room as the legal arguments continued. I became strangely conscious of my surroundings. I know the Dáil well and had spent many interesting and sometimes productive hours there over the years but on this morning, from the moment I had come through the gates past a small gathering of photographers and reporters, I knew the circumstances were different. I had never before been in its precincts and been 'the story'. The focus was on me and not, as I had always experienced it previously, on the civil servant, minister, or even Taoiseach whom I was there to help guide through whatever was at hand.

I felt an overwhelming sense of isolation; I was troubled at finding myself so exposed, perplexed that, having always tried to conduct myself with probity, I was facing a day of questioning by parliamentarians where my integrity was most certainly, and in all the circumstances not unreasonably, precisely what they were going to challenge.

It was something that up to that point would have been simply beyond my imagining. I was cross as well, because I realised that I had missed signals of a culture in distress; there were signs of organisational fatigue that I should have identified. I could and should have seen them but I didn't. To that extent, the reason I was now facing a grilling at the hands of a group of our elected representatives was no one's fault but mine.

In the Dáil that morning, I felt trapped by events and circumstances as I waited to deal with the next stage in my personal Anglo odyssey. I knew it wouldn't be pleasant; it would be a public airing of discussions with different authorities I had already had many times in private since the bank's collapse. Yet, just a few miles away, in the Four Courts, the former executives were waiting to hear how long they would spend in jail.

Later, after my testimony was complete I was going to meet friends and family for dinner before, the following morning, leaving

Ireland for a few weeks holiday. Aoife Maguire, a single mother, was among the three executives going to jail. An assistant manager, she had deleted a number of client files that should have been sent to the Revenue, at least one of which belonged to a close connection of the bank's chairman, Seán FitzPatrick. It was a serious offence but I remembered that with all my experience I had allowed myself to be pressurised into becoming chair of the board's Risk and Compliance Committee and I wondered at the circumstances in which she had made that decision.

• • •

With leadership comes authority, responsibility, accountability, truthfulness and guts. Not, it would appear, in this case. Over more than a decade the legend of Seán FitzPatrick as an exceptional leader was rarely challenged either in Ireland or internationally. It was one he appeared outwardly to have little interest in but, as the plaudits became more common and more fulsome, that changed. Yet, when strength of character, something that's critical to leadership, was most needed, it appeared to be absent.

The reality is that Seán FitzPatrick had always needed acknowledgement but, over time, as the bank's legend grew, he became a praise junkie. I was one of the many dealers to whom he went for his hits, for the regular reassurance he seemed to need. In this way I contributed to his levitation, to that increasing sense he had of himself and of Anglo Irish defying gravity in Irish banking. I saw his gifts and they were many but through my membership of the 'fan club' I lost the perspective that could, perhaps, have slowed his adorative addiction. It is an unpleasant truth for me that I was among those who had helped to build his legend and, I was even close enough, for a period, to have been one of those who pushed its case.

There is one vignette which summed up his need. In 2004, as part of a formal celebration dinner to mark his almost 20 years as CEO, I helped to produce a video that, with testimonials from a cast of business luminaries, highlighted his achievements. While it was over the top, they were heady days when modesty and reserve were in short supply in Irish business. It was, however, illustrative of the deep seated cultural flaw within Anglo in which I was an active participant. I am certain that the Seán FitzPatrick I had first got to know a decade earlier would have cringed at that same event which celebrated his achievements so ostentatiously.

Anglo was not a Titanic but however simplistic the analogy may be, its waters were heavy with icebergs and the most senior people, including this board director over a six-year period, failed to be sufficiently vigilant. What shocked me perhaps more than anything was to see how the spiritual as well as the literal captain chose to use every available means to be first in the lifeboats.

SLEEPWALKING

Stewart Kenny was like some kind of corporate hippy when we first met to discuss Paddy Power bookmakers which he'd founded with John Corcoran and David Power. John had been the originator of the idea for the new business. It was 1989 and I had just left RTÉ. My memory is vague, though I do remember thinking that while I knew Stewart was the son of a Justice of the Supreme Court, his appearance was more of someone in trouble with the law than a serious businessman. Years later in an extensive interview on the creation of the business, Stewart generously praised me as an important influence on the establishment of the brand referring to my strengths as a strategist. We share the experience of falling into business rather than it being a real career choice but whatever influence I had in its early manifestation, Paddy Power Bookmakers was formative on my professional journey.

Stewart, John and David were very different men but had shared values and were determined to establish an Irish business that could compete with the big UK brands like Coral and Ladbrokes that had moved into the Irish market and were quickly growing market share.

David Power was both an on-course bookie and had a group of shops trading as Richard Power. David was old-school, in the best sense of that term, even as a young man. In those early days, in the few interactions we had, I remember his innate courtesy, quiet determination but confidence in what the brand could achieve and his utter belief in the genius of Stewart Kenny's natural gifts for marketing and promotion.

John Corcoran whom I didn't meet then, I knew to be the originator of the plan and someone who had real business savvy. Years later, shortly after I became Paddy Power chairman, I met John to tell him I wanted to shake-up the board and I thought the business, by then quoted in London and Dublin, needed to be freshened up and should shed one of its founding directors. I thought that should be him. Meetings like that are unpleasant but what made it more so was that John calmly offered reasons why he thought it was a mistake but said that he'd accept whatever decision I made. We replaced him as a director within a couple of months. A few years later, after an AGM, John, still a substantial shareholder, elbowed me to a quiet corner of the room to say he understood how difficult the process of exiting him from the board must have been but that he thought I'd done the right thing.

I got to know David Power well as he served on the board throughout my six years as its chair and what's interesting is how for all the 'suits' that adventured on and off the board over its first decade as a plc – and while I hate the idea of ever being one, I qualified – the standards of governance were set by the honesty and straightforwardness of its founders. The levels of reporting and diligence may occasionally have driven them crazy, especially Stewart, but they understood that there were expectations around being a quoted business that had to be met and they never shied from them. Ethics and old-fashioned honesty were deeply engrained in the Paddy Power way.

There was another important element of good fortune for the company as it began its transition from small private Irish company to public ownership and the phenomenal growth it was to experience. Like many emerging businesses, the three betting entrepreneurs took Paddy Power to a point where they needed institutional backing which came from Mercury Asset Management. The 'luck' was that its private equity division was led by that rare phenomenon then – a financier from the city of London whose head wasn't up his bottom and who genuinely believed that, while it was important that you made good returns on your investments, you should also have fun along the way.

In terms of the London investment community in the 1990s, Ian Armitage was a prince among, if not thieves, certainly generally superior City types who, back then, saw Dublin as a place to pick up businesses on the cheap before teaching the owners how to conduct themselves. The enterprise of the bookmaking trio warranted Mercury's institutional support, but where they maxed out was on its being Ian Armitage who was their guide to an IPO in late 2000.

I was to become chairman of its board a couple of years later and, while the market was more sophisticated, the underlying theme was driven by Paddy Power's marketing mantra of being fun, friendly and fair! This underpinned everything and with Stewart Kenny *conducting an increasingly sophisticated brand orchestra that was how Irish – and from the early 2000s English – punters saw it and experienced betting with Paddy Power. It really was fun and, time and again, Paddy Power demonstrated its fairness to customers in ways that drove the competition nuts.*

Still, in among all the positivity and real appreciation of how different it was, in every other respect Paddy Power was scaling heights of innovation that would ultimately lead it to where that clever and relatively genuine brand mantra became no more than a marketing relic of a bygone era. The underlying problem with the business was the nature of its business. Paddy Power (Flutter plc) is a phenomenal global success with revenues of around €5 billion.

VI
To Gamble Is To Lose

In 2004, two years into my term as chairman of Paddy Power plc, the board faced an unusual dilemma. The industry initiated discussions with the government to introduce machines called Fixed Odds Betting Terminals (FOBTs) across all betting shops in Ireland. This is a form of slot machine that allows players bet on the outcome of various events with fixed odds where the betting shop has a built-in advantage. They had been licensed in the UK since 2001 with a dramatic impact on revenues for the industry but also for the exchequer.

The industry lobby in Ireland, of which we were part, was tempting the government with eye-watering tax revenue numbers, pressuring it to consider licencing their introduction in Ireland. The problem was that there was early evidence in the UK of how addictive FOBTs were, representing the most accessible high street form of gambling with no thought required on the part of the customer. The impact on profitability would have been significant as would the benefit to the Irish exchequer but we were worried about what was emerging in the UK,

In 2004, the Paddy Power board, very deliberately and quietly, sanctioned Stewart Kenny to go behind the back of the industry to lobby government in Ireland against licencing FOBTs. Armed with the emerging evidence from the UK, the intent was to warn government of the societal damage the machines would do and that it should not sanction their introduction in Irish shops. It was successful.

This proactive move showed the Paddy Power board had the capacity to think of wider consequences than profit growth alone. The Irish government refused to sanction the move, so protecting society from one of the most egregious forms of gambling. The decision of the board to sanction a discreet lobby against the wider industry's push for FOBTs showed how profit could be relegated behind the welfare of society. For all that it was admirable, it was not consistent.

We were opening shops all across London at the same time and we made what seemed the only possible commercial decision which was to match the product offer of our bigger UK rivals. The argument – and it had merit – went that, as this was a licensed form of gambling in the UK, we wouldn't get customer footfall if we alone opened shops that had no FOBTs. While it was a sound commercial position to take, was it principled? We chose to put the welfare of Irish people ahead of profit and while the market circumstances in the UK were very different, reflecting back on it, we didn't do enough to address the imbalance. We might have been able to influence the industry or government in the UK to see the need for change but we didn't try.

Twelve years later, in 2016, years after I'd completed my board service, I chose to add my voice publicly to a lobby in the UK that wanted the Tory government to significantly lower the maximum FOBT stake from £100. By then the evidence of their harmfulness was incontestable. It would have been better if the machines were banned altogether but those leading the campaign knew that a drastic reduction in what could be spent by gamblers would ease the addiction problem.

In an Opinion article in the *Times* of London, I focused attention as much on the government as on the industry. In publicly backing the already well established campaign, I wrote of a *troubling partnership between government and industry*. I went harder still in an interview on the BBC's *Panorama* weeks later at a point where campaigning journalism across different media in the UK was increasing pressure on Westminster.

FOBT machines represented the most accessible high-street form of gambling, one that required no thought and, since their introduction in 2001, they had become a huge problem in the UK, particularly for certain socio-economic groups. Community leaders, social scientists and general practitioners started to document the machines' pervasiveness and perniciousness but not only were the betting giants earning huge profits from FOBTs, the exchequer was too.

The damage being done was such that, a decade after their introduction, they were dubbed the 'crack cocaine' of the industry not least because punters could stake up to £100 at a time and it was possible to lose as much as £18,000 in one hour. When I joined the lobby for change I knew that as a former chairman of one of the world's largest gambling companies, my intervention would give weight to the case. I wasn't known in the UK but Paddy Power certainly was so, as someone who had been its chairman for six years, my views garnered attention.

The industry – including Paddy Power Betfair – was desperately trying to protect the huge revenues that emanated from these machines and the UK government was its bedfellow. The UK Treasury had become just as addicted to the machines as many of their users, as by 2015, they were generating an estimated £500 million in tax revenue for the UK Revenue (HMRC). An unusual coalition of media interests across The Times, The Mail and The Guardian was resolute and unrelenting in highlighting the problem and gradually the government moved towards a reduction in the maximum stake.

Still, the Treasury's reluctance to lose the enormous tax revenues meant it was another three years before Theresa May's Conservative government acted on its intent to reduce the maximum stake from £100 to £2. Even then the industry launched a fierce rear-guard action to try to further stall the change and, with the support of the Treasury which was desperate to extract another six months of tax revenues, the cabinet announced a delay until autumn 2019. The Tory MP, Tracey Crouch, resigned as a minister prompting an immediate about face so the new regimen came into force as originally scheduled on April 1st, 2019.

• • •

When I first took a public position against the industry on the FOBT issue one institutional investor in Paddy Power contacted me to thank me for my intervention, expressing concerns at the direction of the sector. Some former colleagues were angry that, a decade after being its chair, I had chosen to act as I did. One senior figure, someone I knew well and whom I had respected, accused me of "treachery" , a charge repeated by others when later, in 2017, I called for changes around the regulation of TV advertising by gambling companies. I accept that it might appear inconsistent but I am not alone. The company's founder Stewart Kenny and others who, like me, profited from their involvement in the business, have come to despise elements of it and speak publicly about some of its worst practices.

It's not easy to challenge some fundamentals of an industry where you once had a leadership role. It leaves you exposed to the hypocrisy charge but the evidence of a global increase in problem gambling is incontrovertible, so if you understand its source and don't trust the industry then it seems important to highlight the problem. When I was involved with Paddy Power, its offer was promoted on the basis of being *Fun, Friendly and Fair* and, though it's easy to be cynical about marketing lines, the business was setting about ambitious growth with a genuine focus on providing a different, more 'fun-oriented' offer than others in the market.

The other constant with corporate ethics and the moral dilemma for business leaders is that the state is often ambivalent on the societal consequences that arise in certain sectors. The intense battle over Fixed Odds Betting Terminals in the UK wasn't the last frontier of this choice between private sector and exchequer financial rewards and the welfare of societies where gambling is prevalent. The real scourge, the most troubling phenomenon that has the potential for gambling to become one of the most consistently destructive forces in contemporary society is simply how the availability of core products has been massively extended by technology, particularly the ease of smartphone gambling. This is most pronounced among 18-24 year olds, which fact alone should be enough to see a co-ordinated, international, political response.

The last decade, with the inexorable rise of online and phone gambling, has seen a colossal increase in the value of gambling businesses across the world. This needs to be reined in by legislative controls as the industry has shown no interest in corralling its own profit ambition. Legislators should intervene but, with gargantuan tax revenues involved it may be that they are slow to do so. The appropriately named, 'Gambling Related Harm All Party Parliamentary Committee' in the UK, wants a £2 limit on online games gambling because of what it described as a public health crisis of gambling addiction.

This growth in online gambling needs strong legislative interventions because, short of them, its destructiveness appears unstoppable. In a world where almost everything is available on a phone, where human discernment has been blunted by the extraordinary ease of access to the consumer of those with anything to sell, stemming the growth of 24/7 gambling is the tallest of tall orders. Nonetheless, there are forces that could intervene to ameliorate its excesses.

• • •

When I first worked with Paddy Power, as a consultant in the late 1980s, phone betting meant using your landline to call a freephone number, speaking with someone who would then place your bet. Today the mobile apps of gambling companies are among the most sophisticated available in any business sector. Virus-like, gambling matures and mutates so that it is, today, always present, always easily available. The industry knows this but is not interested in any correction. The big players engage in platitudes while they invest resources in stretching ever further the potential for technology to expand their reach and deepen their hold on the punter's head space.

Writing autobiographically in *A Moveable Feast* about his time living in Paris in the early 1920s, the great American novelist, Ernest Hemingway, reflected on how gambling or 'racing' as he termed it had been a 'friend' to him and his wife. *We went racing many times that year – but it was not really racing either. It was gambling on horses. But we call it racing. 'Racing' never came between us, only people could do that; but for a long time, it stayed close to us like a demanding friend. That was a generous way to think of it. I, the one who was so righteous about people and their destructiveness, tolerated this friend that was the falsest, most beautiful, most exciting, vicious and demanding because she could be so profitable.*

Hemingway's account shows how the problem may have always been with us but developments in the industry since the start of the 21st century have accentuated its scale – considerably so. I was there at gambling's evolution into something that's now globally available 24/7. I was a leader in the global gambling business at that time.

Research suggests gambling is an inherently addictive activity. The US Psychiatric Association's classification system describes it as a 'gambling disorder' meaning it is now scientifically considered an addiction akin to alcohol or drug addiction. Professor of Behavioural Addiction at Nottingham Trent University, Mark Griffiths, argues that it's as destructive as any form of addictive behaviour and that regulation and legislation is needed. Colin Drummond, Professor of Addiction Psychiatry at King's College, London, has described it as *an inherently addictive activity; research increasingly uncovers the underlying processes of gambling dependents which has much in common with addiction to psychoactive drugs.*

It is not just that those with addictive tendencies or personalities may fall foul of the lure to gamble; it is that the product itself is addictive, 'inherently so' as Professor Drummond and many other experts argue. In waking up to the harmfulness of gambling and the growing threat it presents globally it needs to be viewed just as the tobacco industry was when the full scale of the health risk from smoking was clinically proven. The gambling industry does not want attention paid to this; it dislikes intensely any analogy with smoking; it's too potent, too reasonable a comparison.

In the last 20 years or so, gambling has been destigmatised and de-masculinised, becoming dramatically more accessible. The risk of addiction is now a global problem but its destructiveness is still not widely enough accepted. The dilemma for those in leadership in the industry is that of principle and it's one from which there is no escape. It is no less profound a challenge than that facing those involved in the manufacture and the sale of alcohol and cigarettes; arguably it is worse because the stigma is not as widely recognised.

• • •

In business, in commercial life, where profit is the motive, there is a challenge around the production and sale of goods that can be harmful to individuals, damage families or undermine social cohesion. In some sectors the problem is obvious but in others less so, though in most cases an involvement in advancing businesses that can do harm is passive and unthinking. This challenge isn't solely to do with products that are popularly understood to be addictive.

The ethical challenge in business is largely about the collective, whereas any issue that has an inherent moral difficulty is not; it has to be personal. Once you're aware of this dilemma, there's no escape. Wherever it occurs it demands attention but even when the issue appears stark, it's not always simple to resolve.

Practical considerations – like 'this is my job' or 'I need the work' – do arise, so it's reasonable for senior executives to hold reservations about what their company does but still rationalise their involvement. What's necessary however is to at least consider what it is you do and what the organisation does. I never undertook that assessment. As Paddy Power chairman, I failed to realise the uniquely destructive power of online gambling which the business was to the vanguard of developing during my time leading its board. The potential moral hazard never struck me. I never asked myself that fundamental question.

There are senior people in the gambling industry who have reconciled their involvement on the basis that they can help manage any societal risk from within. I know some who have made that choice; it was a reason Stewart Kenny stayed on the Paddy Power board as long as he did. It is personal so, whatever the sector, individuals will come to different conclusions about the appropriateness of the industry where they work. The critical point, however, is that decision-makers are conscious of the issue and do ask themselves if they're comfortable to be in a leadership position?

Over the last decade or so an involvement in an increasing number of market sectors carries this challenge. There are more industries where, irrespective of commercial value, the awkward, often stressful, question about whether the pursuit of profit could have the potential to do harm needs to be asked. This is not easy. Nor is it often a straightforward challenge with a yes or no answer but leadership needs its quotient of senior people who are willing to interrogate these deeper considerations as much as worry only about the commercial growth or the profit agenda .

• • •

Laterally, the existential threat posed by climate change has prompted debate around the idea that business has no wider responsibility to protect public good. The Friedman doctrine that 'the business of business is business', that its only purpose is to make profits, is under increasing attack. Leading business schools are bringing this wider perspective of the need for real socially responsible behaviours into the heart of business teaching. This isn't exactly new. The Greeks and Romans believed commerce should have a dual focus, the generation of profit and a contribution to the public good.

The days of doing whatever you want and engaging in public acts to balance the reputational books are over. Investing resources in doing good deeds under the old-fashioned Corporate Social Responsibility wheeze is no longer credible, companies now have to commit to the measurement of environmental and social activities as part of Integrated Reporting within the audit function. It seems the global investment community is embracing the importance of Environmental, Social and Corporate Governance (ESGs) and is making demands for change. The markets want to back businesses that are profitable while doing public good.

I was the first chairman of Mainstream Renewable Power which was founded by Irish energy entrepreneur Eddie O'Connor in 2008 and was sold, in 2021, for around €1 billion. I resigned from the board in 2011 when the noise around my involvement in Anglo Irish Bank was at its height and potentially damaging to Mainstream's reputation but re-joined in 2017. My involvement in the company's leadership cohort was centred on delivering strong shareholder returns but, uniquely in my experience, the very nature of the business purpose would benefit the planet and people.

Whatever about the markets seeking to back businesses like Mainstream that make a positive contribution to society, investors are starting to turn away from businesses where profits are made by producing products or services that are harmful to either people or the planet. This may have started with the growing concerns about the environment but it's gaining much wider traction. This is the critical axis; the emerging investor mantra means a deep reluctance to back businesses that do, or can do, public harm.

It is why the oil and gas industry is losing the confidence of the investment community. It refused to reform even when the evidence of a direct link between fossil fuel and environmental damage was clear. Its response to the overwhelming evidence of the damage its products are doing to the global environment is copybook corporate denial. In some cases they denied the evidence of reports they had themselves commissioned. In 1979 an Exxon Mobil report said that 'burning fossil fuels will cause dramatic environmental effects and the potential problem is great and urgent'.

It took decades for the tobacco industry to be brought to heel, but ultimately, with pay-outs of hundreds of billions dollars, it was forced to recognise the consequences of its wanton disregard of human health. The damage being done by the fossil fuel industry is a great deal more serious and the legal implications it now faces are enormous. The tobacco industry's malfeasance has cost it hundreds of billions of dollars in the US with more to follow and yet while people choose to smoke; we all need air to breathe.

Scientists and global experts have long been aware of the fossil fuel industry's size and economic importance so it's unsurprising that for decades, its leadership chose to ignore, or even challenge the science. It was unrealistic to expect the industry to reform, when its leaders, like their peers in the tobacco industry, were obsessed by profits and had no sense of a wider responsibility for public welfare .

My experience as chairman of Paddy Power tells me that's an error that's easily made. The vast exchequer sums generated in many of these sectors make getting legislative support for controls difficult. To date, some sectors that fail that test have legislative protection because governments are so desperate for the tax revenues that they generate. Gambling is one.

• • •

There's an increasing number of corporate areas where this dilemma is acute including the reach and scale of digital communications. Its sophistication makes understanding the privacy and personal security implications of our digitised world difficult. To a large extent, personal privacy, as it was known for generations, is dead. It is reasonable to suggest that, as the penetrative power of tech-enabled communications threatens even democratic elections, the advances in this sector carry a moral hazard for its leaders. Placing greater controls around its advance is critical but also complex.

Modern communications assists human progress, smartphones that enable social media can be transformational in addressing social issues. Over a decade ago I saw how Concern Worldwide ran a sophisticated mother and child scheme on a dedicated app for mothers in the vast Odisha province in eastern India. In a controlled manner, where people's welfare is enhanced, the positive power of a technology like the smartphone is profound; it can save many lives. The Covid-19 pandemic helped us understand more about the importance of mass-communication to billions of people in attempting to stem the spread of disease. It will be more so with future global health problems.

The challenge in this sector is around strategy and priorities but, perhaps most of all, it's around establishing limits. Those in leadership roles need to advocate hard self-regulation, clear definition about what is of public value or relevance so the basic entitlement of an individual to privacy isn't further undermined. Those businesses that choose to operate to a strict ethical standard will be led by women and men who applied the deeper personal challenge to their own decision-making about their involvement.

At one level, in most sectors, the consumer has to take personal responsibility for their choice. This is of course the case but it's not enough. Companies selling products that are potentially addictive know their customers are not one homogenous group. It would be nonsense to suggest that all consumers make rational decisions to purchase cigarettes or alcohol or to gamble when such inherently addictive products inhibit a percentage of consumers from behaving rationally. The key problem for anyone hooked on a product is the loss of capacity to self-regulate around its use. The number of sectors where this is a significant problem is increasing. Again, gambling is one.

• • •

The gambling sector is a particularly uncomfortable space. There have been some very limited moves to curb the risk of public harm but the monies being generated are so vast it makes progress quite slow. It is the single career involvement that most disappoints me, the one where everything about my life to that point should have made me more alive to how inadequate was our attention to gambling addiction.

When I become chairman of Paddy Power, I was in uber business mode. I was paid well to deliver value for the shareholders, something the board and management achieved. Key to that and to the long-term welfare of the business was the work we did on internet gambling. The achievement of that time remains central to the growth the business has enjoyed since the late 2000s.

My own leadership of the business contributed to the phenomenal commercial growth in a sector that's done great social damage. This is incontestable. I had the capacity and the status as chairman, to temper the growth. I could have sought to balance financial success with a commitment to an unrivalled ethical standard – made one conditional on the other. It wasn't just that I didn't choose to do so I failed to appreciate the need for the board to even consider the matter. The public good argument was never had.

The conduct of the Paddy Power board I chaired and each member's behaviour met any and every governance standard but it was much later that I came to realise that my own beliefs meant that I should never have become involved in the gambling industry. To have done so meant that I had to have suspended them in the pursuit of business success – my ego drove my behaviour without giving any great thought to the wider consequences.

Leadership often calls for taking hard decisions or having the courage to promote views that challenge the status quo. This is about me. I was the person in a leadership position at that important time. As chairman, I could have made the case for Paddy Power choosing to give sectoral leadership. I could have asked the board to adopt such radical thinking or attempted to mobilise the leadership team towards that outcome but, at no point, did I do anything of the sort. That was the real missed opportunity. It never even struck me because that part of my way of thinking had long before, subconsciously, been put out of harm's way for fear it would undermine the corporate me.

The development of the smartphone and its pervasiveness dramatically accentuated the range of gambling's appeal and made it considerably more difficult to control its growth. In the developed world the smartphone is like an extension of ourselves, an additional body part almost. The gambling industry is well aware of this and accesses customers all hours. We might be able to purchase alcohol online but we cannot consume it on the internet or over the phone. With gambling no such distinction is necessary and so millions spend large sums on the phone, engrossed in their own private gambling environment.

The underlying problem with gambling isn't new but controlling its excesses became a great deal more acute with the 'explosion' in online and phone use. I remember sometime in 2004 our then head of online gambling told a board meeting that a revolution in gambling was underway. Paddy Power's growth online was ahead of the global industry.

In the 1990s the business had invested in upgrading the retail units, making them more welcoming places for customers to visit to enjoy the gambling experience. We considered that a transformation but it was not. The shops might have been a great deal more comfortable but customers still had to be physically present during regulated opening hours, and they needed proof of ID in the event they were old enough to gamble.

It was another decade before the real transformation occurred one which meant that the customer could 'enjoy' the Paddy Power experience on their phone literally 24 hours a day, every day! This should have prompted debate on what this meant for problem-gambling which was already on a steep rise. It didn't. I wrote six chairman's statements in the annual report to shareholders and, other than the usual platitudes, at no time did I offer any substantive comment on the nature of our industry and on Paddy Power's wider societal responsibilities. Of course this was not for us alone to consider but that hardly meant we were exempt from thinking of the almost inevitable wider implications.

• • •

When I'd addressed the Oireachtas Banking Inquiry I said my tenure as a non-executive director of Anglo Irish Bank meant that during the boom, I had both been involved in *setting the menu and gorging at the table*. What I meant was that as a board member of a bank that had prepared tempting offers for clients, I myself had chosen from the menu more than I should. I never ordered what I couldn't afford but I had certainly, on occasion, enjoyed three courses when two would have sufficed. In the case of Paddy Power I had no such personal experience. I never even looked at the menu because I don't gamble.

Our own exposure to whatever it is we're promoting goes right to the heart of decision-making in business where a moral challenge is manifest. There's a test in some sectors for business leaders which involves asking would I purchase what we're selling? This hard, 'would I?' question becomes harder still when you apply it to your children or, as we get older, grandchildren. When I was Paddy Power chairman, I'd have been concerned if any of our children showed an interest in gambling yet I did see how easily our two sons and their peers flirted with it as it morphed into an online product. Even as schoolboys, they were tempted by offers that could, in other circumstances, have been gateway bets to the harder more addictive betting substances that the company I chaired and its competitors promoted with abandon.

In the heat of battle I donned my corporate warrior blinkers. Wider implications had to be ignored; increasing profits and shareholder value was the board's responsibility. We were consummately professional and squeaky clean across every governance matrix, but was it right to be influential in growing a business that I wouldn't have wanted knocking on my family's door? I knew, had to know, that it was a business that was profiting from its capacity to infiltrate the homes of thousands of others, so what if it had mine? It's a rhetorical question!

• • •

It would be reasonable for some to question my motives in how, years after earning considerable fees as Paddy Power chair and making strong gains through the sale of my shareholding, I chose to question the fundamentals. It would be reasonable to argue that it's easier to act and speak publicly now about online gambling, as I did about FOBTs in 2016, than to have acted when I had influence in the industry. Equally, it would be fair to assert that it's easy to dismiss those with experience who are troubled by the inexorable growth of online gambling as being 'spoilers' who choose to make trouble after the fact. To speak out now is easier but it's not easy.

It is the substance of the challenge that matters more than the circumstances in which it is made. When I first chose to question aspects of the industry's conduct there were no legacy issues from my six years as chairman, indeed I was asked to plug a short-term gap on the board in 2010, so there was never anything residual between me and the company, the opposite I believe.

When I joined the campaign on Fixed Odds Betting Terminals (FOBTs) in the UK and later raised concerns about online gambling and the absence of controls around advertising, this reflected only my growing awareness and concern at gambling's pervasiveness. It is also true that my insights are better informed and more considered as the uniquely harmful impact of digital gambling is now a great deal clearer. It's a global phenomenon and a global problem.

I wasn't alone in also being increasingly concerned by the huge growth in online gambling, something I'd observed in the Paddy Power incubator during my time as chairman. There was, within Paddy Power, a more powerful voice, that of its founder, Stewart Kenny, the inspiration behind the innovative, fun brand it was in its earliest manifestation.

I had first worked with Stewart in the early days of the business in the late 1980s. When, 20 years later, I retired from the board, Stewart and I remained close. Whatever about my discomfort over my time in charge of the board, Stewart had been Mr. Paddy Power for decades, so the challenge for him was more acute. It was also more difficult for him to extricate himself because he believed he could influence some change from within.

In 2016 Stewart resigned from the business he'd founded almost three decades previously. It was a couple of years later before he publicly acknowledged that his decision was on account of what he perceived to be the board's refusal to act decisively on the plight of gambling addicts. Specifically, he believed that the company had failed to do what was necessary to stop those most at risk of losing large sums of money.

The detail of this reveals something of the attitude that prevails in the industry. Sportsbet, Paddy Power's (Flutter plc's) Australian business, had run an innovative advertising campaign encouraging punters to take a break from gambling. It was successful and the company decided to scrap it. Stewart, encouraged by its success, had wanted Flutter to introduce similar initiatives in Ireland and the UK, so when the success of this campaign in Australia was followed by its abandonment, he resigned .

In autumn 2021, Sportsbet launched another similar campaign in Australia where gambling is virtually a national pastime. Around the same time, the parent company, Flutter plc, introduced a €500 cap on losses for Irish gamblers under the age of 25. It is hard to determine whether these kind of initiatives represent a contemporary form of the window-dressing prevalent in my time or flickers of real hope but globally, the industry needs to give priority to addressing its responsibility in this regard, really deepen and accelerate this work and accept any resulting diminution in profit if it's to halt the explosion in problem gambling. This was not about one incident or about just Flutter plc (Paddy Power) because it is, in fact, representative of a global industry that cannot be trusted to act responsibly.

Interestingly, the UK Companies Act explicitly recognises the moral challenge inherent in much decision-making when it states that directors must exercise independent judgement. A board operates as a collective, so a director who is concerned about something that's fundamental to the business will, at some point, either persuade his colleagues of the need to address that issue or accept a different outcome. In the event that they cannot do either, then they should leave the board. Stewart Kenny tried, failed and chose to leave. It was textbook!

• • •

The global gambling industry, worth an estimated $500 billion in 2021, is trapped by its huge commercial success on the one hand, amid incontrovertible evidence of the negative social impact of much of its offer on the other. It's an industry that surfs on the wave of technology to make its increasing product range more accessible to more people with no end in sight to the growth in profits. The industry regularly claims to be doing everything possible to promote the gambling 'offer' only to those who enjoy it but are not in any way addicted. Furthermore, the narrative is that those who display addictive tendencies are managed in a way that makes it more difficult to access the products. There is an absence of evidence to support these claims.

The industry unquestionably makes profits by producing problems for people so, as the global investment community becomes more fixated on Environmental, Social and Corporate Governance (ESGs), it will start to make demands for change, at least we must hope that it will do so. This could be the crucial axis; if the market is mobilising to turn away from industries that do public harm then it cannot continue to back gambling. The hope has to be that, just as the money men have turned away from the fossil fuel industry, more and more of them will look askance at the societal damage being done by gambling.

In my time as its chairman, the Paddy Power board 'worried' the problem of addiction like academics; a few times a year we would debate funding research into addiction or supporting agencies and self-help groups for those most affected, when really these initiatives represented nothing other than corporate conscience money. When new information prompted a more robust debate, we puffed out our corporate chest about how much more responsible were our behaviours than those of the pack. I suspect that was indeed the case, but that was a reflection on those others, not on us. This was the approach on my watch.

I controlled the board agenda and so for that period the

responsibility for our corporate indifference was mine. I was on a singular mission to support a brilliant executive team in making money for the shareholders. I was in corporate warrior mode, not consciously, but I gave no thought to any wider consequences of the ever-expanding reach of our product. Friedman would have approved: I led the board with a singular focus on maximising profits for the shareholders.

Digital-enabled gambling means the odds of social damage have narrowed considerably. It is neither truthful nor reasonable for the industry to argue that it's doing everything possible to ensure those who gamble excessively are policed and protected and without radical action the ongoing march of 24/7 gambling means increasing levels of addiction are inevitable.

The most worrying trend of all is one Stewart Kenny has been particularly vocal on for some time – how children are being drawn into the industry's web of gambling deceit. In 2019 a substantive piece of research in the UK found the industry wasn't policing sufficiently the access children under 16 had to online advertising by gambling companies. Ipsos MRBI, the respected international polling company, found that over 40,000 children followed gambling accounts online. The 2018 UK Gambling Commission study showed that almost half a million children between 11 and 16 bet regularly; that is more than those of a similar age-profile who have taken drugs, smoked or consumed alcohol.

While there's no evidence that children are being directly targeted by the established companies, research shows that little is being done to screen them out of gambling advertisements. The effect of this is that new generations are being groomed for the transition into the adult world of gambling adventure before the age of discernment. Different studies have shown little evidence that responsible gambling messages are promoted online. Adverts on TV and online also contain features likely to appeal to children.

In any consideration of problem-gambling we need to realise the pervasiveness of the product and how it's turbo-powered by sophisticated marketing. Advertising isn't just the means by which the younger generations are being teased into a world that can damage them before they've the capacity to understand; it is how those of any age who over-indulge find it almost impossible to escape the draw to continue. Across all age groups, all socio-economic groups in Ireland and Britain, attention needs to be paid to the unmistakable conclusion that, if we're going to tackle addiction, we need first to regulate advertising with an iron fist.

We need to address the scale of the challenge society is facing with all forms of gambling. It is not a question of banning it or restricting it to a point where the temptation to gamble can be removed. That is not possible, nothing approaching such a draconian approach is credible or necessary, but nor should it be acceptable to allow its online growth to continue unchecked. The research on its ills, the evidence of its power to infiltrate every corner of society and especially to appear attractive to young people before they are old enough to see its true colours, is compelling.

There's a need to address the pervasive influence of gambling across all demographics but especially with those who can least cope. Where an addictive disposition damages an individual and those close to them is when their need to keep doing whatever it is they're hooked on bleeds them of money (often not their own), of judgment, of self-respect and ultimately of hope. The increasing ease of access to an intoxicating range of gambling products is the principal reason why developed societies need to be alert and to intervene.

All the evidence is that the industry cannot be trusted to address the problem but nor, would it seem can legislators in most jurisdictions. The tax dollar is as much an incentive for governments to leave well enough alone as the pursuit of profit is for industry leadership. Given this, could it be that it is the financial market that will force the issue? Extraordinary as that might seem, it may be that its avowed interest in ESGs in other, perhaps more obvious sectors, will mean that to be consistent, the large institutions and the pension funds will be the source of the much needed correction.

There would be a great irony if, instead of governments protecting their citizens from exploitative businesses, it was the markets that were to turn on those companies, forcing them to change or to close. Not long ago that might have seemed fanciful but it's a lot less so now; it could just be that with an industry like gambling, the market's tail might need to wag the political dog.

• • •

Paddy Power is the business involvement that troubles me most. It is the one that highlights the difficulty of staying centred on ethics never mind personal decision-making in our professional lives. This 'hang-up' is not about others, it relates only to me because it's about only how some of my personal choices stack against my core beliefs. Considering all my roles, assessing behaviours across the spectrum of my career, was at times uncomfortable but never more so than in reviewing my tenure as chairman of Paddy Power.

Whatever about how I hadn't seen the corrosiveness of the Anglo culture, the commercial success of Paddy Power blinded my natural curiosity, heightened by my journalistic training, about how gambling really worked and, regrettably, it dulled my appreciation of how its reach would explode by being digitised. I'd embraced the role of chairman of Paddy Power and made a success of it. That success contributed to the growth of the company towards what it is today. How did I sleepwalk through such a process and how deep must the sleep have been for me to have sat, contented, at the helm for six years?

It was how I was then. It seems however that the corporate me had abandoned some points of principle but also strands of my natural curiosity that had always been so much part of me. I had adopted the corporate cloak of shareholder interest; it seemed to fit and for a long time I liked wearing it.

Something happened to this highly paid chairman of an already quite substantial plc., who adopted, as required, a singular mission to grow shareholder value. I think in these circumstances, once you stay on message and provide, legally and ethically, superior financial returns to the owners you're doing what you were hired to do. More than any other role, my chairmanship of Paddy Power plc manifest how I had become a 'corporate warrior', a term that would have filled my young journalist self with absolute horror.

It seems likely before Tracey Crouch resigned as a Minister in the Tory government in 2018 over its delay in acting on Fixed

Odds Betting Terminals that she asked herself the important 'what if?' question. She will have known people who were exposed to gambling's excesses, certainly constituents but perhaps even friends or family. It is a distinctly uncomfortable process, but it is the only way to test the appropriateness of what we do when we have leadership roles in certain areas of life. The discomfort is that it forces us to think more deeply about the wider consequences of what we do, to think of things way beyond success or money.

I and others chose to use our past careers and experience to promote the societal risks of gambling but Tracey Crouch jeopardised hers in real time by putting the welfare of the public ahead of her political ambition. Still, the damage to her professional career was nothing compared to the need she felt to stand up for what was right. She put it well at the time: *I couldn't take the responsibility of potentially not meeting people in the future because they'd taken their lives over these machines. I couldn't justify the delay to people like that.* It was a principled decision. Here was a young professional politician, a first-time minister in government, who chose the hard option that put the interests of people, of her community, ahead of her own professional advancement. She had already campaigned fearlessly for the legislative change, so she wasn't prepared to compromise, even over a delay of six months.

Those in leadership positions everywhere would benefit from doing the 'Crouch Test' occasionally. In her resignation letter to the Prime Minister, Theresa May, she reminded her party leader how, in her maiden speech outside No 10, Mrs. May had stressed her ambition to support vulnerable people against the power of big business. In politics, Tracey Crouch's determination represented a remarkable act of selflessness.

• • •

The myopia I suffered about gambling endured from my time as a consultant to the founders of Paddy Power in 1989 not just through my two terms as chairman from 2002 to 2006. It was only the Anglo trauma that prompted me to review my conduct across the range of my business experience. Indeed, in 2008 Nigel Northridge, who had replaced me as chairman, asked me to return to the Paddy

Power board for a short interim period, and I agreed. Not long after I'd returned to the board Brian Cowen became Taoiseach-in-waiting. Wrapping up the May 2008 board meeting, Nigel referred to the imminent change of political leadership before venturing that everyone was expecting my departure from business to work with the new Taoiseach, wishing me luck in the new phase of my professional life.

Immediately prior to that board meeting, the CEO Patrick Kennedy, who knew well my interest in politics and my belief in Brian Cowen had asked me if I had decided to make the change. I had but, as I said to Patrick, in spite of considerable engagement with Brian Cowen from the point at which he'd been elected leader of Fianna Fáil when *de facto* he became the country's new leader, the issue had never arisen. Still, I think he felt as sure as I was that the question would be asked and he certainly knew that I was already primed to move into the political world, somewhere I had long held a quiet ambition to work.

THE 12th MAN

Brian Cowen is in his early 60s. When he was approaching the landmark birthday of three score he suffered a serious stroke, so serious that, initially it appeared that he might not survive. Today, he lives at home in Tullamore, Co. Offaly. Once the most powerful political figure ever from the midlands of Ireland, he was elected as the country's twelfth Taoiseach (Prime Minister) after a stellar career projected him into that role unopposed at the age of 48. That was in 2008. We had become good friends about a decade earlier and remain so today.

I knew a number of his predecessors.

Charles Haughey was a Taoiseach and Leader of Fianna Fáil who divided opinion unlike any other; he was bright but mercurial, a man of vision and passion who loved Ireland but had also a fondness for fine things in life some of which should probably be beyond the reach of those in public life. It may be a bit trite to represent this dilemma by his ownership of an 18th century mansion in north Dublin and an island, Inishvickillane, off the southwest coast of Ireland but it makes the point. As it happened my professional dealings with him were book-ended by two very different experiences at his Dublin home, the first as a young reporter and the second, more than a decade later, as a communications consultant on a particular project for Fianna Fáil.

In my time in RTÉ I would have interviewed Charles Haughey a number of times, as I did the man, Garrett Fitzgerald, with whom he vied for the office of Taoiseach throughout the 1980s. Dr. Fitzgerald was very different to Mr. Haughey, an intellectual who, despite having few of the standard gifts needed for success in politics, twice became Taoiseach and was as much of a force for change throughout that period as his great rival. I spent a morning during one of the frequent general elections in the eighties, on the campaign trail with him and saw, up close, how the professorial awkwardness somehow translated into a real likeability wherever he went.

The next Fine Gael Taoiseach was John Bruton, one of two brothers who've had impressive careers in Irish politics and managed to sustain their status in public life. John and his brother Richard are intelligent, capable, low-key men, committed to being of public service. They generally behaved with dignity, something in short supply in other political quarters in the 1990s. I remember one occasion when Drury Communications erred on a piece of work it was doing for the Taoiseach's department when John Bruton was in office. The Fianna Fáil opposition sniffed blood and it would have been easy, and probably justifiable, for the consultants to be sacrificed but John Bruton knew it had been an honest mistake and went out of his way to handle the matter fairly and professionally.

Albert Reynolds, who preceded John Bruton as Taoiseach, was extremely likeable. He was straight-forward, capable, hard-working, and good company but, from what I had seen, was tough as old boots too. I was presenting Morning Ireland in May 1987 when a newspaper carried an interview with the German Finance Minister, Martin Bangemann, claiming that Reynolds, then Minister for Industry, had misrepresented his views on our forthcoming referendum on Europe. I called him at home at about 7a.m., explained the situation and he came into studio live at the end of the programme. I garrotted him which, given the circumstances, was no great feat of journalism but he took it, fessed up and without any drama simply addressed the frustration the government felt over the risk of the referendum not being carried. We were to work together for a short period when he was Finance Minister. It was productive, rewarding and often fun. My last formal meeting with Albert Reynolds was over lunch sometime in 1997 when he asked me to help run his campaign to be President. I wasn't interested. There were two reasons: I'd worked on a project at Queen's University, Belfast with Mary McAleese who was seeking the Fianna Fáil nomination and whom I admired and I suspected Albert was being 'played' by then Taoiseach, Bertie Ahern.

I had very little contact with Bertie Ahern. There were a few minor engagements, one in particular where a friend wanted him to use me for some communications advice in the early 1990s when he was Minister for Finance. It was an awkward meeting marked, I think, by a mutual disinterest, most probably even a shared disregard. When he became Taoiseach and was such an effective leader, I could both admire his achievement and wonder at how it had evolved. I never saw him as so many others clearly did, including friends on both sides of the Northern Ireland divide who stressed to me their great faith in him. I certainly saw enough to recognise his contribution to peace and to understand how skilful a politician he was but, for me, other doubts always lingered.

This was the line-up that Brian Cowen joined when on May 7th, 2008, he was elected Taoiseach and from Charles Haughey through to Bertie Ahern he knew all of them well. Brian had been a poll-topping representative of the people of Laois-Offaly when these five men were in power and had served in government under Albert Reynolds and Bertie Ahern. The 12th Taoiseach had an exceptional set of skills, a personality and years of cabinet experience that made him better equipped than any of his predecessors to provide outstanding leadership for the country. Almost three years later his government fell and he resigned from politics.

VII
Political Counsel

The comedian and satirist, Barry Murphy, a friend, does a monologue about Brian Cowen in which, as is often the case with political cartoonists and satirists, he takes one aspect of Brian's behaviour, exaggerates it and builds a fable that plays to a public view of the former Taoiseach that has deep roots. I've seen it a number of times. It always gets laughs, in part because of how it's performed but also because it reflects the public attitude, not just towards its subject, but public representatives generally. Barry's tale is harsh and unfair; it too simply picks on one destructive characteristic of an utterly decent man who achieved a great deal more than most but whose career also may exemplify how easily fame can turn to something less edifying.

The piece is uncomfortable to watch but the source material wasn't imagined. It is representative of what satirical writers do, take an important strand of behaviour in someone well-known and then make a serious point, creatively. In this way the unfairness is neutered. The satirist balances entertainment with the need to inform; after we've laughed maybe we should question whether there's a learning from it? One purpose of satire is to generate debate, to point out behaviours that need consideration in order to promote change so, when well-done, satire is more commentary on public life than humour. The real learning however is not for our public representatives, but for us all.

• • •

Brian Cowen was in his late 40s when he became Taoiseach. He had succeeded his father Ber as a TD at the age of 24, first serving in Cabinet at the age of 32. By the time he became Taoiseach, he had been minister of five different government departments and was widely considered one of the most capable and formidable political figures of his time. Just short of three years after his election to that office, he had resigned as Taoiseach and as Leader of Fianna Fáil with the party in such disarray that he chose not to seek re-election to the Dáil, despite being consistently one of the highest polling politicians in the history of the State. He was just 51.

I'm not sure he would agree with this analysis but I believe that, among the reasons Brian Cowen's career ended as it did, is the weight of responsibility he'd carried over such a lengthy period as much as the unprecedented circumstances in which he assumed office as Taoiseach. Brian's own inability to achieve a proper balance within his working life contributed to how under-powered he was at the very point when his professional battery most needed to be fully charged.

I was close to Brian Cowen for much of his career in government. It was a relationship that originated in a professional engagement but it changed to providing private counsel on political matters, irregularly at first but, over time, on a more consistent basis. Brian liked that I challenged him and gave him a non-Fianna Fáil perspective. I liked how his mind worked, his fearlessness but also his basic decency.

In spite of a public narrative, we were not friends at university. We first met in the early 1990s when I was hired to provide specialist advice to the Fianna Fáil parliamentary party. Then, after a short period of professional engagement, a friendship developed which deepened over time. It is one that I value to this day.

As his career strengthened I became a trusted source of counsel who understood his world but was not of it; someone who thought strategically, who had an understanding of politics and the management of difficult issues and someone whom he knew would never compromise on expressing an opinion. The more time I spent helping him the more I came to appreciate his intellectual brilliance, speed of thought, fairness, and personal warmth. I enjoyed being engaged in the political world and I liked his company. A coffee, a meal or a pint was nearly always stimulating but as neither of us is easily dissuaded of our opinions, argument was our constant companion.

There were two key drivers to Brian Cowen's political development, the factors that moulded not just his thought process but, critically, how he behaved professionally. Brian approached the role of an elected politician from an intellectual perspective. Those who worked with him in government, even many of those who were politically opposed to him, recognised this in him. In our dealings, whenever he would want counsel, almost no matter the issue, it had to be considered and debated intellectually before any consideration of the correct course of action.

The other notable feature was his focus on the public good. It was his principal motivation, rooted in the somewhat old-fashioned notion of the imperative for elected representatives to act always in the interests of the public. Stitched together, the intellectual rigour and the idea of service were what distinguished how he went about his business. Even in the midst of the economic and political crisis that enveloped his leadership, he never wavered in doing what he thought most needed to be done to limit the damage to the country. In many respects, though he had contributed to the crisis Ireland faced, it was those determining characteristics that whatever the perception, forged a decision-making that put Ireland first, at the expense of his party and most definitely to his own detriment.

What's not widely known about him is that Brian Cowen is a kind person. In political battle no quarter was asked or given but his first instinct was always to empathise with someone in difficulty or experiencing ill fortune. Like us all he could be bitter but it was rarely personal, something I witnessed frequently, even when he found himself ostracised by so many within the political environment. It's also worth acknowledging a better known feature of Brian Cowen, that when he felt secure in company he was great fun, a brilliant storyteller and such an accomplished mimic that you worried about how well he took you off in your absence.

Ours was never a standard friendship. I was to become for a period his primary private counsel, someone whom he turned to for advice from outside the civil service, government and the Fianna Fáil politburo, someone who challenged him to think beyond the immediate or the obvious. I never mixed in party circles, knew only a few of his parliamentary colleagues well, but increasingly I was someone whom he chose to count on to be straight and direct. Sometimes I was too direct and he certainly thought I betrayed a lack of political savvy when it came to party machinations, but Brian had the capacity to blend advice from different sources and make his own judgements.

While from the time I sold Drury Communications in 1999, the work was voluntary it could consume me. I had studied politics but it was my time as a journalist that had first piqued my attention and then fascinated me about political life. I believed I could have used my own skills in public life, something I regretted not doing, especially as I knew the principal reason was a cowardly fear of rejection. I admire the courage of nearly anyone, no matter their politics, who puts themselves before their fellow citizens for election. The only occasion I had the opportunity to do so, it was the wrong time and the wrong party.

• • •

In 1986 I was approached by a newly-formed political party, the Progressive Democrats, to stand as a candidate in the next General Election. I was 27 years old and established as a co-anchor on RTÉ radio's *Morning Ireland*. I loved being a journalist.

The Progressive Democrats was set up by a few high-profile, disaffected members of Fianna Fáil, but had failed to prise away another respected figure, David Andrews TD who had long been a critic of the Fianna Fáil leader, Charles Haughey. Securing David Andrews would have guaranteed the new party a seat in the Dún Laoghaire constituency on Dublin's southside. I suspect that when he chose not to jump ship, I was approached, presumably because I was becoming reasonably well-known as a broadcaster. I had done nothing else to warrant the approach, though my background would most likely also have pointed, however incorrectly, to my having a right-of-centre economic orientation.

I was flattered. It was about more than having my ego tickled though. I had an interest in representative politics and believed I could be good at it. I met with senior figures in the party a number of times. I did take time to consider the offer but after the first flush of excitement I knew I wasn't going to accept. The party's interest in me seemed to shift to the Dublin South constituency marking I think that the cooling was mutual and that, as the discussions had continued, the party heavyweights had come to see limitations in what I might offer so by the time I declined, their interest in me had probably already faded.

I never lost the appetite nor, for a long time, did I lack the self-belief that I had the wherewithal to have a career in politics. The only other occasions when I spoke seriously about it, or attempted to do so, was at various junctures with Brian Cowen who was utterly dismissive. Each and every time I raised it, he would ridicule the notion with his trademark roll of the eyes and a comment about how little I knew or that I 'wouldn't last a minute' though I'm not sure that was quite how he put it.

I remember on one occasion being so persistent that Brian threatened to bring me to a constituency meeting, laughing that *one of those will cure your delusion forever*! I realised that, for all the banter, if someone of his standing, someone who had got to know me well and used me as a private adviser, never took my interest seriously, never encouraged me to get involved then that was commentary enough. It meant the only political activity left was to enjoy working closely with him but even that was to prove limited in scope and opportunity.

• • •

When Brian Cowen was elected as Ireland's twelfth Taoiseach on May 7th, 2008, I wrote to Fianna Fáil applying for membership of the party. I had never been a member of any political party and had only ever voted once for Fianna Fáil. In the summer of 2008, my decision to seek party membership was born of a belief in Brian Cowen. I was sure that with a fair wind he could build the party into a left-of-centre force that would serve Ireland well as it headed towards the end of the new millennium's first decade. My optimism was based on a number of things: his intellect, his commitment to the ideal of public service, his experience, and his relative youth. The new Taoiseach was 48.

The confidence proved to be ill-founded, in large part because of the extraordinary events that followed but also because, just at the point where he most needed to be at the peak of his powers, he was worn out by his years of service. That is one part of my considered view of how things went awry for him. It is an assessment I think he might well dispute. There were other things too; a natural casualness and indiscipline hampered him though I would argue that, more destructive still, was a complete absence of ruthlessness. Brian Cowen had all the ingredients barring that real hardness – a mean streak – that great leaders need in order to achieve sustained success.

Brian Cowen was Taoiseach for just less than three years. In some respects, it's surprising he lasted as long as he did. It was, from the outset, a troubled premiership. Depending on your outlook, he was either unfortunate to assume power at the moment the state experienced its most acute socio-economic shock, or he took office when the reckless chickens he helped rear as Minister for Finance had come home to roost. The truth lies somewhere in between.

Even allowing for those circumstances, he had many of the skills to be a good leader but, by the time he assumed office, his once prodigious energy levels were flagging. That was in part to do with the demands of being to the forefront of national politics for so long but it was also to do with how Brian Cowen lived his life. Arguably, the overwhelming drag on his potential to succeed was an innate dislike of wielding power, as well as a softness in the political belly that decried his public image and was always likely to inhibit his prospects of success.

It would be an exaggeration to describe him as a 'reluctant' Taoiseach but nor was he overly enthusiastic about it. Certainly, I cannot recall him having ever expressed an absolute determination to secure the leadership. Some of his closest parliamentary colleagues would say it was always in his sights, in part motivated by bringing the honour to his beloved Offaly but that, at the same time, he never craved power. I think that while he liked the idea of the Cowen name on the roll-call of Fianna Fáil leaders it wasn't ever a fixation for him. I know his motivation was forged of public service, not of any personal, ego driven, need for power. Politics is one arena where really wanting power might well be a prerequisite to being successful at wielding it.

This is part of why Brian Cowen is so interesting; possessing neither the ruthlessness nor cunning of some predecessors, all he could do was to use every fibre of his intellectual capacity to ride out the violent storm that enveloped him, his government and the country over those final years. In that moment, Brian relied on his ability to understand complex issues and his sole motivation was to make decisions that served the public good, knowing, as he did, that his own career was heading for the rocks.

• • •

We had met first in 1991 when I was asked by Charles Haughey to prepare members of the Fianna Fáil parliamentary party for the planned televising of Dáil proceedings. I wasn't that long out of RTÉ, so I was surprised the Taoiseach and Fianna Fáil leader hired me to prepare the parliamentary party for this change in the conduct of parliamentary business. I was contacted by Mr. Haughey's press secretary and enforcer in chief, PJ Mara, who told me that Haughey had a *pain in his arse* dealing with his regular adviser and wanted me to take on the role, which probably meant that it was PJ who had the rectal discomfort and had persuaded the Taoiseach to give me the opportunity.

I trained most members of the parliamentary party for the imminent televising of proceedings in the Dáil chamber. The investment in honing the skills of TDs meant concentrated sessions with groups of four over about a three-month period. All but a handful of the parliamentary party took the training because TDs knew that if they opted out, only to underperform at some later point, there would be hell to pay with the party leader. I trained two people individually: Albert Reynolds who was Minister for Finance, and Charles Haughey himself. The sessions with Reynolds were in his ministerial office but with Haughey, they were conducted in the Dáil chamber.

These were done at night, much to the annoyance of the notoriously obdurate Superintendent Eamonn O'Donoghue. Management of the Dáil was his preserve and he hadn't much truck with anyone who chose to make things more difficult than they needed to be, nor did he care about the status of those who did. Mr.

Haughey's insistence on treating the Dáil chamber as his personal training room greatly irked the Superintendent.

One evening, the Taoiseach was delivering a mock script from his position in the chamber as I observed from the opposition benches. Suddenly, the main doors opened and with all the drama of a Shakespearean actor, Mr. O'Donoghue, framed by the doorway, suggested, quite firmly and not unreasonably, that it was late, and we needed to finish up. The masses would have paid a fortune to witness the salvo of abuse Haughey fired in the direction of the Superintendent of the House in reminding him, in no uncertain terms, who was Taoiseach.

There remains a lasting testament to my efforts to improve Charlie Haughey's delivery. The microphone at the Taoiseach's seat is higher than all the others in the chamber. This resulted from my complete frustration at trying to get him to lift his head when he was delivering a script. No amount of time improved this weakness so I determined the only solution was to get a taller microphone to reduce the extent to which, on camera, his head was tilted downwards as he addressed the chamber.

One of my training sessions with Albert Reynolds was scheduled for his office early on a Saturday morning. When I got there, he asked to defer the start so we could listen to the satirical radio programme, *Scrap Saturday* produced by Dermot Morgan, later Fr. Ted. It was a surreal experience. The minister asked if we could delay our work until after he had listened to the government of which he was a member, being played for laughs on radio. So it was that I sat with Albert Reynolds with a cup of tea and we laughed our way through Dermot's offering. I knew Dermot Morgan quite well, had the pleasure of playing in his 'celebrity' football team, but I never told him about this episode for fear he'd satirise the scene.

There was another interesting vignette. The weekend before Dáil proceedings were to be televised for the first time I was asked to meet Charles Haughey at his home in north Dublin. I'd been there once before when I interviewed him at his 18th century, Gandon-designed house in Kinsealy. On that first occasion I had only just finished my six months training in RTÉ and was sent to work on an election programme presented by Pat Kenny.

About a decade later, I was the hired help who had been tutoring him on how, as Taoiseach, he should behave when dealing with Dáil business now to be broadcast on television. The first broadcast was scheduled for budget day, January 30th, 1991, and the week before I was summoned to his office to review an array of suits that he was considering for the big event the following week. He was known to be particular about his appearance, especially on television. I remember assuring him that pretty much any of the suits would work well but that a blue shirt with a simple tie of one strong colour would be important. That was a mistake; I was then asked to be at his home in Kinsealy on Saturday morning.

When I arrived, I had company, an accomplished and well-known photographer, who knew Charles Haughey well and seemed less than surprised when dozens of blue shirts were put in front of us with proposed matching ties. All the Taoiseach wanted was that we would choose the best combination for the following Wednesday and, with that instruction, he left the room. The shirts were in boxes and most of them carried the initials CJH. It was years later that I realised I had probably been the one of the first people to see Charles Haughey's stash of the infamous Charvet shirts!

• • •

It was towards the end of the 1990s, with his appointment to the Department of Foreign Affairs, that my relationship with Brian Cowen changed and deepened. Brian had been a successful Minister for Labour, then Minister for Transport Energy and Communications before his two and a half years in Health between 1997 and 2000. It was the end of January 2000 when he was appointed to Foreign Affairs. I had worked professionally with him both training him as part of the Fianna Fáil parliamentary party but also during his tenure as Minister for Transport, Energy and Communications and on one project in the Department of Health.

Health had proved a difficult ministerial tenure but it was not without its achievements. It was on his initiative that a full review of national cardiac services was carried out leading to the establishment of a national cardio strategy. I had assisted him a little with this and the expert group he established was given the space to do its work, reported efficiently and recommended some significant changes to how cardio services were to be deployed nationally.

There were insights into his natural concern for the disadvantaged. The approach he took to the case of the Donegal woman, Bridget McCole, who'd contracted Hepatitis C through the Blood Transfusions Board's use of infected blood, was marked by his capacity, as a solicitor, to set aside the state's legal advice and see the state's primary responsibility to behave humanely. Brian focused considerable energy on improving mental health services both legislatively and in provision of additional resources and he was deeply moved by the plight of Parents for Justice over the state-sponsored removal of the organs of deceased children.

However difficult the Health portfolio was, it did increase public awareness of him. It was unmanaged however, because for all his complaints, often with cause, about his media portrayal, he steadfastly refused to countenance advice around his own profile. The media's presentation of him became dominated by clichéd features around a sometimes bedraggled appearance, grist to the mill of a metropolitan stereotype about presentation and behaviour.

Brian Cowen approved of the use of communications professionals only to assist in the management of issues relating to departmental business and strongly disapproved of the use of public funds to support personal profile management. There's a sensitivity in respect of this as his career was blighted, particularly over its final phase, by shocking presentation that could have been mitigated had he been more open to some degree of personal management.

Most political media recognised his intellect and his oratorical ability in Dáil Eireann but much of the media presentation of him was superficial and lazily constructed. Brian railed at this on occasion but most of the time he didn't care and he refused to countenance doing anything about it. I often tried to convince him of the importance of a managed profile, but he was disinclined, believing his work should allow people to appreciate him or not.

While this was in part admirable, his lack of concern for the importance of his own personal management contributed to the ease with which the emerging caricature of him around obduracy and moodiness took hold. With the increasing breadth of his experience, more people came to see and understand his political skills. Within politics and among the brighter and more open of those in the ditch, he was recognised as someone of exceptional ability.

There were personal traits that constrained him, but the greatest impediments were a lack of real focused ambition and the Fianna Fáil bridle that holds talent in check: the primacy of loyalty to the tribe over almost everything. It was a bridle Brian appeared happy to wear, his belief in and commitment to Fianna Fáil as an institution blinded him to some important issues that, if manifest elsewhere, would have driven him demented.

• • •

While he and Bertie Ahern were never close, Brian Cowen was a committed, senior member of Ahern's team and someone for whom 'loyalty' to the party and its leader were sacrosanct. While there were flecks of political chicanery about Ahern that he disliked and would never himself deploy, Brian believed Fianna Fáil's importance was subsidiary only to family and country. For him it was an honour to serve in government, one that was the prerogative of the Taoiseach alone to grant, so no matter what role he was asked to fulfil, Brian would always accept.

Towards the end of 1999 there were whispers of a possible move to Brussels but Bertie Ahern was really preparing the ground for appointing his Attorney General, David Byrne SC as Ireland's new Commissioner. The movement and intrigue nonetheless gave Brian the opportunity to pursue a change.

There would have been little appreciation then, even among political correspondents, of the breadth of his political interest across world affairs or the depth of his understanding of Northern Ireland. Bertie Ahern himself had grown into leadership in part through the peace process, earning the respect of the critical players in the North and building as strong a relationship with Tony Blair as that of his predecessor Albert Reynolds with John Major. The history of that period cannot give Ahern enough credit for what he achieved; one of his savvy decisions was moving Brian Cowen to Foreign Affairs.

It was Brian's choice but one Bertie Ahern was happy to support knowing that, at his shoulder, he'd have someone with a deep interest in and understanding of Northern Ireland, as well as a colleague ready to set aside his own ego in the pursuit of the right outcome. For Brian, while the political wisdom might have been that Iveagh House wasn't the best place from which to access the highest office, those whose counsel he valued thought otherwise. What was marked about those conversations was that he still refused to even think about planning a route to the leadership. It wasn't something he ever obsessed about or even planned for.

Brian Cowen was an exceptional Minister for Foreign Affairs. Former Fine Gael Taoiseach and Foreign Minister, Garret Fitzgerald, described him as the best ever in the history of the state. The Department itself, in the magnificent Iveagh House overlooking Dublin's Stephen's Green, was as alien to this rural Fianna Fáil man as it had been 'to the manor born' to his predecessor, the long-standing Dún Laoghaire TD, David Andrews. As a friend of Brian's father, Ber, David Andrews, whom I know well and respect, was delighted that Brian was succeeding him. David was just one of many TDs who saw him as the next leader of Fianna Fáil.

It was during this time that Brian and I started to meet more frequently. It was then that he used me more regularly for speechwriting; he knew I had a strong interest in world affairs and he thought me knowledgeable on Northern Ireland so, when he wanted a political speech, I invariably got summoned. Normally I'd get little notice, the ask would be to 'put some bite into this' and we'd then bat drafts backwards and forwards.

The greatest benefit of Brian Cowen's tenure as Minister for Foreign Affairs was how he supported the Taoiseach, Bertie Ahern, towards a resolution of the continuing difficulties in Northern Ireland. While he hadn't been directly involved in the negotiations leading to the establishment of the Good Friday Agreement in 1998, he'd long observed developments in the North with a diligence unmatched by his peers. Brian is a republican but a considered one, someone who always worked hard to understand events through the widest possible lens.

We shared a belief that understanding the depth of the injustice felt by the nationalist community – their lived experience over generations – was critical in any consideration of solutions. I knew that Brian invested time in understanding injustice not just in Ireland, but for all that we could relate to the depths of despair, neither of us could equate that hurt to an acceptance of violence as a justifiable means to its resolution. We understood its source but not its basis, its motivation but not its course of action. By this time the extremes of the bloodshed were over but I had personal experiences of little more than a decade previously that informed my thinking when he and I talked about the issues he was working hard to resolve with officials and those on all sides of history.

No issue was of more importance to him than a permanent end to violence on the island so, while, in his previous ministries, he had limited involvement in Northern Ireland policy, he had made sure to keep himself informed. Partly for that reason, Albert Reynolds and Bertie Ahern saw him as wise and balanced counsel on the North. Importantly, as attested by Seamus Mallon, a pivotal figure in the resolution of the long-running crisis, Brian was also admired and trusted in the North. Mine was no more than an additional perspective, but one that, through real and recent experience, saw Northern Ireland's unique tapestry as it was and how Brian saw it too.

There were some Foreign Affairs highlights. Ireland's membership of the UN Security Council including a period as its chair allowed Brian Cowen to demonstrate his wider political knowledge and capacity. Seasoned mandarins like Dermot Gallagher and Richard Ryan admired his intelligence and grasp of detail and thrived in an atmosphere where the minister trusted them, worked closely with them but vested responsibility in them. Whether it was delicate and complex global issues or events in Northern Ireland, the most senior and battle-hardened among them realised they had a gifted man in Iveagh House.

Ireland only holds a position on the Security Council about once every 20 years so it was remarkable that during Brian Cowen's term in Foreign Affairs, Ireland was its chair at the moment the US government, supported by the UK, chose to carry out attacks on Afghanistan in response to the terrorist attacks on the Twin Towers in New York a month earlier. It was a period of immense global tension laced with points of real drama.

Brian Cowen's full account of 9/11 itself, one of the most dramatic events in modern history when terrorists commandeered several planes and deliberately plunged them into the Twin Towers in New York and the Pentagon in Washington, properly rests with Brian himself to tell. The bones of it are that on that fateful day he was in Palestine for a meeting with Yasser Arafat, Head of the PLO.

To many Arabs, Arafat transcended the Palestinian cause and represented their wider needs across the world. It was extraordinary that the occasion of Brian's meeting with him was to coincide with the catastrophic events in the United States. Almost 3,000 innocent people were killed and 6,000 injured. The source of the attack was unconnected to Yasser Arafat or the PLO but it was a moment of grave tension between, in the most general sense of the term, the Arab world, and the West.

When Yasser Arafat addressed the world from right outside his base, the remarks were unambiguous. They appeared heartfelt as he said he found it difficult to speak about what had just happened, describing the events as an attack on all human beings. Visibly shocked, Arafat said he would be sending condolences to President Bush and the American people because what had happened had touched his heart, the hearts of all Palestinians.

As a student of world affairs, Brian appreciated the enormity of being in that place with the leader of the Palestinian people in that moment. Circumstance had dictated that, on the day of the most audacious, brutal terrorist attack of modern times, he was with the man who personified more than any other one individual, the resistance of the Palestinians, and elements of the wider Arab world to their oppression in the Middle East.

VIII
The Ahern Conundrum

The argument that during his time as Finance Minister, Brian Cowen and Fianna Fáil had exclusively sown the seeds of national recklessness that germinated into Ireland's acute economic crisis of 2010 to 2012 is questionable. There was wider political ineptitude on display than just on the government benches. The difference in economic policy emphasis between Fianna Fáil and Fine Gael was negligible but the former's economic management in government was, from 1997, influenced by the fact that its partner in government was the Progressive Democrats. There was too a uniquely Fianna Fáil relationship with the property sector – not of the tent at the race meeting caricature – one rooted in tax-based incentives that was to prove difficult to break.

When Brian Cowen succeeded Charlie McCreevy in 2004 the economy was still growing, there was some emerging comment on its property dependence but in expressing concerns to the Central Bank international agencies like the IMF and the OECD were reasonably guarded; not many countries had reduced public debt as a percentage of GDP from 88% to 24% in a dozen years. It was to be 2006 before their views hardened and started to become public.

The consistency in growth rates, year on year, the realisation of all but full employment in the early years of the new millennium masked some fundamental weaknesses or certainly obscured to most observers the scale of the risks. The primary consideration was the make-up of the economy; low personal and corporate tax rates and the sustained low interest rates made Ireland especially vulnerable to any global economic crisis. The second was the property sector which by the time Brian Cowen became Finance Minister resembled an economic juggernaut that had, in part, been facilitated by tax schemes which had well passed any value they may have had.

When he assumed the Finance portfolio, the Fianna Fáil led administration continued to lean heavily towards a pro-business, liberal market view and any amendments he made came too late. Brian had long been a senior member of cabinet but he privately felt that Fianna Fáil had drifted away from its natural economic disposition and that the benefits of Ireland's phenomenal economic success weren't being widely or deeply enough felt across society.

Brian Cowen could certainly have immediately addressed the property based tax incentives but he hesitated, choosing in 2004, to instead initiate a review of all tax incentive schemes across industry estimated to cost the exchequer around €8bn annually. Not all of these schemes had been initiated by Fianna Fáil but the delay in taking action was, symbolically at least, material to the approaching two decades of turmoil that would follow for the party. Critically, deferring hard decisions in the early years of an administration brings the next turn of the electoral wheel closer, compromising a government's willingness to act.

Brian was the one Fianna Fáil politician who was powerful enough to have taken a radically different view and to have hoped that overtime colleagues and then the voters would have followed. Instead, upon assuming control of the public finances the economic miracle of the time seemed to dull his appreciation of the need to correct that flaw; I believe he had been determined to provide a more conservative political management of the public finances but even that predisposition couldn't protect him. That, within a couple of years, a general election loomed made it politically a great deal more difficult to make economic decisions that would be unpopular. That is not right but it is politics.

It's easy to be critical but the country was in the grip of such a mania that if Brian Cowen had attempted to change fiscal tack at that point it would have been catastrophic electorally for Fianna Fáil. In the long term, the country could have benefited from a significant economic change of course but the way Ireland saw itself in that moment, meant that neither he nor Fianna Fáil would not have been thanked for it. Even when politically it was becoming clear that the spectacular growth was weakening, the people weren't ready to hear it; those who had gained most weren't persuadable that there was trouble on the horizon. That is not to excuse the failure to act. The best political leadership finds a way to do the right thing even in circumstances where it is not popular; politically this may perhaps have been the first big moment where Brian Cowen's sharpest political instincts went missing.

This, rather than his oversight of the economic crisis that would later engulf the government he led, is, arguably, the main stain upon Brian Cowen's political legacy. I believe it is his greatest regret. Here was the politician with the skills as well as the disposition to rid the party of any association with wealth and vested interests, to place it sufficiently to the left of the economic median line to make a difference, politically and for society. With more time in charge, in less dramatically challenging economic circumstances, it is possible that he would have realised that ambition.

• • •

Those close to Brian Cowen saw the inevitability of his leadership more clearly than he did. For some years, I believed he should move politically against Bertie Ahern. Brian saw no grounds for such a precipitous act; his legal training and sense of fairness meant no matter how strenuously I made the case, he wouldn't countenance it. Over and above everything else, he believed Bertie Ahern's leadership on the North meant only something the Americans might call 'serious crimes or misdemeanours' would justify anything other than continued support of him. Brian also protested to me at various points that he wasn't even sure he wanted the job.

It's hard to know if this reservation was real or just a defence against those few, like me, who wanted him to move against Bertie Ahern, but it's likely that he himself was unsure. Brian Cowen has a great sense of history, a respect for tradition and a deep sense of place. Were he to become leader of Fianna Fáil, it would be about the connection of such office to the Cowen family and its importance for Offaly and for rural Ireland. Those perspectives are what would have motivated him to ever assume the leadership, making the circumstances of realising it, all the more important. Equally, such concerns would have made him more guarded about any pursuit of the leadership of the party and the country.

While there may well have been an element of self-deprecation about it, I believe that Brian was also concerned about one feature of leadership that he knew would be challenging for him. The public persona of the Offaly pugilist was at odds with his true character. In political debate he could devastate those in the opposite corner but leadership in politics demands more. Political leaders need a capacity to be clinical and cunning and to be absolutely ruthless in the corridors of power, as much with their own as those on the opposition benches. For all the pugilism of his debating style, none of those other traits are natural to him.

Brian Cowen knew that with leadership came the responsibility of hiring and firing; it would be his first task were he to become party leader, and that was something that filled him with dread. To have to make tough decisions about the careers of colleagues, progressing some and stalling, if not sending into reverse, the careers of others was not a responsibility he wanted but it came with the job. Brian is highly sensitive to people's circumstances to the point where making cold judgements, based solely on political needs, was always going to be hard.

Brian Cowen and Albert Reynolds were in personal style and disposition quite alike but Albert Reynolds had no great difficulty with the consequences for colleagues who had to be disappointed at the time of appointments. It was never personal; it was absolutely critical to being a successful political leader that you made appointments based on having the best possible team around you. In contrast, when it came to choosing a cabinet, Brian was always going to be tortured by the personal consequences for those he would overlook or worse, those whom he felt he should stand down from office. This proved so.

Overall, Brian Cowen's character and wide experience warranted the weight of expectation people had of him. The Department of Finance was the last piece in the career jigsaw that would position him as perfectly equipped to lead Fianna Fáil and the country. As he assumed the role of Minister for Finance, the great conundrum was his apparent indifference to pushing on towards assuming the leadership and his reluctance to disturb the status of the man who then was Taoiseach.

There's little doubt the largest part of that reluctance was a wish not to disturb the tribe, a belief that any pre-emptive move against Bertie Ahern would be antithetical to how Fianna Fáil did its business, but the hesitancy may also have betrayed doubts about his personal desire to lead. Whenever a full and thorough assessment of Brian Cowen's political career is undertaken it should include consideration of whether his interests and those of the country would have been better served by him playing a senior role but not to have taken the leadership position. It's a curious thing about politics that leadership skills are rarely tested until it is for real. Curious may be an understatement as stable, secure, civic society is so dependent on effective political stewardship.

There are those in any walk of life for whom being in charge is natural, easy almost, but for others the change from a senior role, even being number two, to the top job proves unwise. It's not necessarily the case that this applied to Brian Cowen but it is true that he was never remotely fixated on being leader. Certainly, this was not a case of a talented and experienced politician craving the leadership so, while there were elements of being in charge that were never going to be easy for him, the fundamental question is whether, without a burning desire to lead, could he – or anyone – be good at it?

• • •

One of the considerations around leadership is the importance of a leadership team and the suitability of individuals to different roles within any leadership 'hierarchy'. In organisations that respect the importance of leadership, it is unlikely to have a single source. In May 2019, I attended the launch of Séamus Mallon's memoir. Séamus was one of Ireland's foremost political leaders, though he was someone who never actually led either his party or any administration, being Deputy Leader of the SDLP between 1979 and 2001 and Deputy First Minister of Northern Ireland from 1998 to 2001. That the word 'deputy' prefaced the titles that followed cannot diminish the sense of Séamus Mallon as a political leader; he gave decades of leadership in politics across his local community, Northern Ireland, the island and beyond. Séamus was the public figure whom I most admired.

We knew each other quite well during my years in RTÉ and then reconnected later in different circumstances, but always it was the consistency of his approach to the task of improving Ireland, of recalibrating it politically and socially, that shone through. In 2019 Séamus Mallon chose Brian Cowen to launch 'A Shared Home Place', his book of reflections on his life in politics, explaining that he selected Brian because of *the low-key consistency with which he always put the interests of everyone on the island*. That spoke volumes. This legendary Irish constitutionalist recognised in Brian Cowen that powerful sense of service without the need for public affirmation.

I know it to be true of both men. What had always struck me, from when I first met him as a very young journalist, was Séamus Mallon's 'mettle', his stubbornness on points of principle and his determination to see things through, no matter how long the journey. These were the features that were hard to ignore, his grim determination in the midst of the dire circumstances of the latter half of 20th century Northern Ireland, his sense of public service and his commitment to his own people.

My consistent impression was of a man of dogged belief in the rightness of his peaceful, constitutionalist, nationalism. The night of his book-launch he spoke with firmness about what Ireland needed to do to forge a bright tomorrow for future generations. That vision seemed to me a broader contemporary version of what he'd espoused when I first got to know him in the early 1980s, a politics that was rooted in courage, brotherhood, compassion, forgiveness and wisdom.

There was no one other person in public life who seemed quite so determined to place the people's interests above everything and who did so without the need for affirmation. Séamus' Irish jersey was woven of modest but resilient cloth, he eschewed the trappings that are sometimes on offer to people of high achievement and he never lost focus on the need to serve his community. Séamus Mallon's sense of community was circular from the people of the border town of his birth in Markethill, then the wider constituency of South Armagh, the nationalist people of Northern Ireland, all its people, every Irish person and then right back to Markethill.

One great casualty of his and John Hume's tireless work towards ending the bloodshed in Northern Ireland and the dawn of the new peace, was the decline of their own political party the SDLP. In 1999 Séamus approached me, through a mutual friend Tom Kelly, to see if I would carry out a strategic review of the party. The SDLP was in the early stages of decline. It was an interesting task. I spent quite a bit of time over the next three months travelling around the North meeting people at all levels within the party before I presented my report to its Annual Conference that December.

The report was solid if unexceptional. I considered the proposed actions to be realisable but, to many, the recommendations which covered an overhaul of party structures as well as a 'brand' repositioning seemed radical. It may be that the report was overly ambitious in parts; certainly, few of its recommendations were ever implemented. This wasn't a great surprise. Party leader John Hume saw no great need for reform and the concentration of the party's principal actors was so intensely focused on the wider political needs that it was always likely to be put to one side. The SDLP's decline was, by then, already deeply embedded.

Two decades into the 21st century, there are acute signs that Fianna Fáil is in a sharp decline, perhaps not as serious as that which faced the SDLP 20 years ago, but one that needs urgent attention if it is to have any prospect of retaining its status as the preeminent political party in Ireland on its centenary. For Irish people of a certain age, Fianna Fáil has always been the dominant political force. It remains an important presence in Irish life but its organisational powers and its relevance are waning. The intensity of the debate around its political leadership, generally engendered by personal ambition, misses the real problem, that organisationally it is suffering from a curious mix of neglect and incompetence.

The party has been an institution in Irish public life since its foundation in 1926 but it has failed to adjust to contemporary Ireland and to the emergence of Sinn Féin as a force in constitutional politics. The 'hit' Fianna Fáil took by being in power at the time of the economic collapse contributed to the party's difficulties but this really only accentuated and accelerated a pre-existing problem. It was not the root cause. Unlike another great Irish phenomenon, the GAA, Fianna Fáil has failed to modernise and without urgent attention to its purpose its power will continue to erode. It might be time for the party's leadership to imagine what to them might still be the unimaginable!

While the SDLP continued to serve people locally, its leadership committed itself fully to the wider achievement of peace for everyone on the island at a cost to much of the party's grassroots endeavours which had served it so well. The party elders left the community door ajar, failing to appreciate the scale of Sinn Féin's activism as it transitioned towards constitutional politics. Understandably Hume and Mallon were consumed by pursuing a new beginning for Northern Ireland but the cost to their party was to prove enormous.

There was no easy solution. Over time the SDLP became more organisationally compromised while the longer the troubles continued, the more time Sinn Féin had to build its support for the exclusively constitutional road it would later choose.

Séamus Mallon saw it then; he knew the SDLP's very survival was under threat and while it has managed a degree of revival under Colum Eastwood, its best days are likely behind it. In part that is about circumstances and a natural post-conflict evolution of political representation, a consequence of a troubled society evolving into one that's less so, one where the political middle-ground is dominated by divisive social issues. It is that social dimension which had given oxygen to the SDLP in its formative years before, decades later, Sinn Féin unhooked its side-car from the Provisional IRA and became the huge political engine it is today.

While there's so much to be celebrated about what Séamus Mallon and John Hume achieved, so much that every Irish person and future generations should be grateful for, to this hurler on the political ditch, the flawed organisational structure undercut the party's potential to adapt and grow with the radical changed circumstances of 21st century Ireland.

It's to be hoped that the younger generation on this island, born into the new 'normality' of peace and relative social stability, will know enough to appreciate how valuable that is, how hard won it was, and how it will need their constant attention to endure. Within that learning they should know that Séamus Mallon was an exceptional political figure whose contribution to securing Ireland's peace is immeasurable, someone described as *simply the most courageous political leader I have ever met* by Andy Pollak, *Irish Times* journalist in Belfast in the 1980s who co-wrote Seamus' book.

• • •

With Brian Cowen in the Department of Finance our discussions were exclusively about politics and I made sure they were dominated by the leadership of Bertie Ahern. As more evidence emerged of erratic behaviour by the Taoiseach some of it financial, I started to really bug Brian about his party leader. It often takes an 'outsider' to see things as they are; if anyone had nagged me then about Seán FitzPatrick's character as I did Brian about Bertie Ahern, I'd have been just as dismissive. It's ironic that I was so convinced of what I considered questionable conduct in an arena where I was an observer on the edges of the action but, at the same time, I failed to see the errant behaviour in a business where I was a director. Often the closer to the centre we are, the more difficult it is to have perspective.

In 2005, in the midst of this continuing argument, a Bertie Ahern – led government appointed me as chairman of the RTÉ Authority, sending me back to the organisation where my professional life had started. It was to prove short-lived, so short that there was little of note that could be achieved. It was interesting nonetheless in giving me a brief insight into the immense challenge of public service broadcasting in a digitised, social-media dominated world.

The Director General was Cathal Goan, a colleague from my time there as a journalist in the 1980s. Cathal was a hugely committed, determined and talented public servant; our relationship was very positive. We wanted to set about some radical change, aimed at ensuring the public service remit dominated its purpose. I believed, and the new board agreed, that the organisation might have too many responsibilities and too many diverse strings to its bow, some of which had evolved over time and may not have been strictly appropriate to its primary mission. We had hired international consultants to undertake a review when comments made by the Taoiseach, unwittingly placed me in a very awkward situation.

It was January 2006 and in an interview with Setanta TV Bertie Ahern said the government thought the forthcoming Ryder Cup Matches, to be held in Kildare that September, should be available free-to-air on RTÉ. I was Ryder Cup's principal adviser in Ireland and I was chairman of RTÉ, a role I wouldn't have accepted the previous summer if an agreement hadn't already been in place where Sky, host broadcasters to the event, were allowing RTÉ show Ryder Cup highlights each evening. I could not have taken the role if that issue had not been already resolved. The Taoiseach's comments got traction and I felt that even the perception of my having a conflict of interest meant I should resign, which is what I did.

What happened was unfortunate but it was absent any political motivation. I know from others that the possibility of political influence is never far away from membership of state boards; even in my short time on the Authority I witnessed the threatening wag of a ministerial finger over an important editorial decision. Cathal Goan and I managed the issue firmly and stilled the wagging finger, managing, in the process, to both preserve RTÉ's editorial independence and, as it happens, the reputation of the politician in question.

• • •

My discussions with Brian Cowen about Bertie Ahern gradually became more fractious as I remained fixed on the need for him to ask pertinent questions of the party leader. Stubbornness is something we share but, ironically, it was Brian's steadfastness about politicians never compromising the implied contract they form with their constituents that allowed me to be so obstinate on the issue. There was increasing evidence that Bertie Ahern had questions to answer, ones that seemed more and more compelling. Brian complained that my fixation on his refusal to move was tiresome, betraying, he thought, a lack of understanding of how the party did its business.

Bertie Ahern's achievements in Northern Ireland were immense. With the support of a talented group of civil servants, he established a strong relationship with the British and the political cadre in Northern Ireland, allowing him to build on the achievements of his predecessor, Albert Reynolds. It's undeniable that in addressing the longest-running, most fundamental, political challenge Ireland has ever faced, his leadership was exceptional.

None of this deflected me as I continued to press him about Bertie Ahern. As a political purist, he was troubled by the rumours. Brian believed you were elected by the people to act for the people and nothing, no matter how seemingly inconsequential, could ever be allowed to dilute the purity of that contract.

While I believed the substance of the rumours that ran counter to that fundamental, there was also a tactical element to my pushing Brian to act. While I thought it was in the country's interests that he moved against Bertie Ahern, I also believed it would benefit his career. Brian remained resolute; without certainty of serious misbehaviour on Ahern's part, there were no grounds for making any move. I was struck by the depth of his belief in party loyalty and his continuing denial that the leadership was something he wanted, though I and others close to him didn't really believe him.

On March 20th, 2008, Gráinne Carruth, Bertie Ahern's former secretary, broke down while giving evidence to the Mahon Tribunal at Dublin Castle. She was trying to explain large cash transactions, some of which were in pounds sterling, that she had managed on the Taoiseach's behalf. In the process she blew apart any remaining credence people were prepared to give Bertie Ahern's narrative. Brian Cowen was in the Far East on his way back from St Patrick's Day duties. Within hours we spoke on the phone. We discussed the relevant details of the Tribunal and he sought time to take soundings.

When we spoke again later that day, he'd resolved to act on his return; there were now real concerns that Bertie Ahern was undermining the office of Taoiseach and gambling with Fianna Fáil's reputation just to prolong his time in charge. Loyalty to the party leader was important to Brian but it was secondary to protecting the party and, as the evidence built up, his axis of loyalty shifted. Brian Cowen knew Grainne Carruth's testimony changed everything; the evidence of inappropriate behaviours that he believed needed to predicate any political move against his leader had now been delivered.

There was another consideration, something Brian impressed upon me when we first spoke that day. He was shocked by what Gráinne Carruth had gone through at the Tribunal, horrified that someone who was effectively in service to Bertie Ahern had been left to face the public humiliation that Gráinne Carruth had experienced. It was anathema to him that anyone in a position of responsibility would leave a colleague as exposed as the Taoiseach had left his former PA.

This, as much as how damaging the nature of the evidence was to Fianna Fáil, upset him. Brian always believed senior people must be prepared to take responsibility for their actions, something he was to display at the end of his own political career. What those in leadership positions should never do, by his code, was leave a subordinate to take the flak for an error of their making.

We should be able to assume integrity and probity on the part of those in public office. It may go against much public discourse, but since the establishment of the state the overwhelming majority of those in political life have given us reason to be so presumptive. While some have undermined confidence in that most basic expectation, and the backdrop to Brian Cowen's time was pockmarked by some high profile cases of impropriety involving figures in both Fianna Fáil and Fine Gael, those public representatives who have devalued their contract with the public are in a small minority.

Brian set up a meeting with Bertie Ahern for the early afternoon of March 27th, the day after his return. We arranged to meet for lunch just ahead of that and Brian asked me to prepare a note covering how best he would approach the meeting. The then imminent Lisbon Treaty Referendum meant that there could be no possibility of Bertie Ahern remaining in power with the attendant risk that people would use that plebiscite as a means of registering a protest vote against him and his government. Gráinne Carruth's evidence in Dublin Castle meant that the political die was cast.

Almost a decade later when I appeared at the Banking Inquiry, the state investigation into its financial collapse, an issue was raised about that meeting between Brian Cowen and Bertie Ahern on March 27th, 2008.

• • •

Ahead of my appearance at the inquiry I chose to pay little or no attention to the testimony of other witnesses. This was deliberate; I didn't want my own account to be influenced by the narrative of others. I was confident in what I knew. I felt that reading the evidence of others could compromise me; that my testimony could be informed, in part, by things I learned through the account of others rather than my own memory of events at the time.

My account to the inquiry was clear and consistent. It may have been unsatisfactory to some but it was accurate and truthful. In the midst of a set of questions from Eoghan Murphy TD, he asked if Brian Cowen and I had interacted between the phone conversation we'd had when he was away in the Far East and his March 27th meeting with Bertie Ahern on his return. I confirmed that we'd met when he was on his way to the meeting with the Taoiseach and also that I'd spoken with him directly after it had ended.

Throughout the hours of testimony, the atmosphere in the room had been quiet. Most of the time that you're being questioned by one committee member, the others are only partially engaged. The atmosphere changed at that moment. It wasn't exactly high drama but there was some muttering as a few of the committee seemed to switch back to my evidence.

I had confirmed to Eoghan Murphy that Brian Cowen and I had met before he went to see Bertie Ahern yet, throughout my testimony I had said that Brian and I never discussed Anglo. We hadn't but when I answered Eoghan Murphy, I had not been aware that in his account to the inquiry, a fortnight earlier, Bertie Ahern had referenced that a meeting he'd had that day with Brian Cowen was about the banks including Anglo Irish.

Eoghan Murphy's questioning of me was reasonable, given Bertie Ahern's evidence a fortnight earlier. The committee knew I was still an Anglo Irish board member at that time and now, in my testimony, I had confirmed that I'd had lunch with Brian Cowen on his way to his meeting with the Taoiseach and that he had called me immediately on its conclusion. There appeared to be an inconsistency. I had stressed that Brian Cowen and I never discussed issues where there could be a conflict of interest but my evidence confirmed that he and I had met before and spoken after a meeting he'd had with the

Taoiseach, a meeting which Bertie Ahern had, in his evidence, said was about banking.

Until that moment I had no idea what Bertie Ahern had testified. The conflict in our accounts was pretty stark but that didn't mean that they weren't both accurate. I knew of only one issue the two men had met to discuss but I never revealed it to the inquiry because I wasn't asked. I simply reaffirmed that Brian Cowen and I had not discussed banking and that it had nothing to do with why we had met before his meeting with Bertie Ahern and why Brian had called me immediately on its conclusion. I repeated that point a number of times including after Bertie Ahern's testimony was brought to my attention.

I chose not to offer up the reason why I had prepared Brian for that meeting because it had no relevance to the proceedings and because no one asked me. Reading Bertie Ahern's evidence subsequently it was clear that he had, perhaps not unreasonably, focused on where the committee's interest lay. His account of that meeting came in response to questioning by Senator Susan O'Keeffe; he continually referenced how Brian had come to his home to discuss the precipitous fall in the Anglo Irish share price over St Patrick's weekend of 2008. Unsurprisingly, no one asked him had they discussed anything else of import which meant that each of us, in our evidence, gave accounts of the same event that were markedly different.

I knew that banking was not the reason Brian Cowen had called the Taoiseach from Malaysia to arrange a meeting for the day after he returned. Brian had asked me to prepare a briefing note and we had met for lunch on his way to meet the Taoiseach. I still have the note setting out the reasons why Mr. Ahern had to resign which was the only issue we'd discussed over lunch and it was the only issue Brian called me about after their meeting had ended.

It may be that they discussed the banking situation as Bertie Ahern testified, but if they did, Brian made no reference to it when he called me to confirm Bertie Ahern's agreement to resign. Why would he? We had a clear understanding on such matters. The purpose of our meeting, the work I had done over the previous 48 hours, was exclusively focused on preparing Brian for a meeting with Bertie Ahern where he would present him with a political *fait accompli*. It went to plan as Brian had explained to me and to a very few others on its conclusion.

In our phone conversation after he left the Taoiseach, Brian said Bertie Ahern had agreed to stand down but wanted time to inform family and close friends. The announcement was made on April 2nd.

I wasn't pressed at the Inquiry on what was so important – if not banking – about the meeting that I had to brief Brian Cowen ahead of it and necessitated him calling me on its conclusion. I chose not to reveal the reason but if other committee members had pursued the apparent conflict I'd have been obliged to do so. It may be that it suited the committee to leave the matter 'hang', with the confusion and apparent conflict in my evidence giving more oxygen to the false, predetermined narrative that fed a political agenda.

• • •

Over the weeks between Bertie Ahern announcing his retirement and leaving office I spent a great deal of time in the Department of Finance. Brian's move there in autumn 2004 had changed our relationship. I was active in business in a number of different sectors so, unlike his time in Iveagh House when we'd discuss Northern Ireland, international affairs or Ireland's commitment to Development Aid, once he took over in Finance, our meetings focused purely on politics, well away from departmental matters. That was the unconscious backdrop that had seen me move into a more directional mode, or at least attempt to do so, around his own political career. This included repeated attempts to get him focussed on personal management.

Finance also brought a greater level of public scrutiny for him as a minister. Once you assume the office that controls public spending and frames the national budget, every citizen has a stake in who you are and how you do the job. Brian saw how the media was changing, becoming more intrusive but he remained dismissive of the need for personal management. Editorial standards had changed; the increasing influence of British tabloids, the outsourcing of editorial oversight in one of the largest broadsheets with a reduction in critical high value resources, were contributory factors. So too with social media; its emphasis on instant comment diminished the importance of consideration or reflection.

Brian hated the manic melting pot of contemporary media. His DNA was designed for public service and so, for all his ability and intelligence, his personal ambition was restrained and, as a result, his interest in any form of managed profile was limited. By this point he was displaying signs of pretty acute professional wear and tear. A serious, though as yet undiagnosed, sleep apnoea was taking its toll, as was the lack of attention to his personal well-being. I knew how resistant he was to any profile-management but this same resistance was being displayed around his own welfare not just how the public might perceive him. The importance of only one is debatable.

Once Brian was confirmed as Bertie Ahern's successor that changed, he wanted my input on lots of things including, as previously when at Foreign Affairs, on speeches he had to give as incoming leader of Fianna Fáil and Taoiseach. The interregnum was lengthy because of Bertie Ahern's odd request that he be allowed fulfil an invitation to address the Joint Houses in Washington before leaving office.

During this period, in the middle of April, former President and Fianna Fáil grandee, Patrick Hillery died. Brian was asked by the family to give the graveside oration at his funeral. He saw the former President as someone who represented the values of the Fianna Fáil he had so admired as a young man. The lineage of Lemass, Lynch, and Reynolds was part of what he wanted Fianna Fáil to recover under his leadership. The graveside oration would allow him to re-establish some basic principles of Fianna Fáil as a party of the people, rooted in community and in the welfare of everyone.

Paddy Hillery may have held the highest office in the land twice and been a TD at the age of 28, had also served as European Commissioner, but, first and foremost, he was a medical doctor, something I chose to reference early in the oration that I scripted for Brian. The Hippocratic oath taken by all medical practitioners captured what Brian considered fundamental to political life, certainly to those representing Fianna Fáil. So, in his eulogy to President Hillery in April 2008, he reflected: *I will remember that there is an art to medicine as well as science and that warmth, sympathy and understanding may outweigh the surgeon's knife or the chemist's drug. I will remember that I remain a member of society with special obligations to all my fellow human beings.* Brian Cowen believed absolutely in this as a basic tenet of political representation.

Over the weeks of the transition, I was one of a small team that met frequently with him to consider the wide range of political and policy issues facing him as he became Taoiseach. Brian's closest lieutenant was Gerry Steadman, a career civil servant who'd worked as his special adviser in the Department of Health, Foreign Affairs and Finance. Gerry was smart, civil service savvy, with a work ethic and a sense of humour – a vital component if you wanted to work around Brian Cowen.

Joe Lennon had joined him in Finance about two months previously to establish some order around his schedule and manage his political needs. A former Government Press Secretary of standing, Joe was experienced, hard-working and extremely capable with other important characteristics that were good for Brian, including being calm and low-key. Joe had left the role of government adviser two years earlier to join the crisis-hit HSE, but Brian's increasingly troubled media image had prompted me to recommend that he recruit Joe to Finance. Months later, Joe Lennon found himself back at the frontline, only with a new man in the office of Taoiseach.

I was in the Department so often over those weeks that Secretary General, David Doyle, offered some typically caustic comment about my 'moving in', as he offered to organise a 'cubbyhole' near reception so I could more easily support the Taoiseach-in-waiting. I was working with Brian's team on political issues, drafting notes and speeches in support of his work. I helped him to recruit Peter Clinch from UCD as his Economics and Policy Adviser while his Press Secretary, Eoghan Ó Neachtain and script writer, Brian Murphy, completed his inner sanctum.

I was part of it but my work was strictly political and was done *pro bono* as it had been for years but, for the first time, I had expectations and ambitions to be involved formally. The conversation I anticipated and hoped for never happened. I believed that I could add value so I was sure Brian would ask me to be at the centre of political operations, that he should do. I knew he valued my independence and directness, so I was confident he'd ask me to work with him as Taoiseach but his hand never reached out for my shoulder.

There were already excellent people *in situ* but I still expected Brian would ask me to take a key role. I thought I would be good at it and had, however arrogantly, presumed he wouldn't have considered this next phase of his career without me beside him. I assumed the discussion would be about the nature of my role, not about whether there would be one. Over the weeks of the interregnum, where I spent a considerable amount of time debating many political issues with him, I waited patiently for him to ask me if I would work with him. I had rehearsed the one word answer frequently but the question was never posed.

IX

The 12th Taoiseach

Brian Cowen's political CV was uniquely shaped, more diverse and demanding than any other Taoiseach in the history of the State including Charles Haughey who'd been considered young when he became Taoiseach at 54. Brian was 48. The economic ministries early in his career had been followed by a couple of years in the Department of Health, then Foreign Affairs before his four years in Finance. No previous Taoiseach had the breadth of cabinet experience and, while he'd performed better in some than others, arguably no one before him had displayed a capacity to deal with such diverse issues.

The office of Taoiseach should, in some respects, be one of the easiest to hold. The scale of responsibility is great but if you choose the best people in your Cabinet and then manage them well, you should be able to concentrate time and energy on what's now colloquially termed the 'big picture'. Three things were to militate against this for Brian Cowen. The first was that Noel Dempsey and Dermot Ahern excepted, he was short on deep cabinet experience. The second was the sheer enormity of the economic tsunami that engulfed the country. The third was Brian's own natural disposition which leans towards detail rather than ideas.

Within weeks the flush of success had washed through and was being replaced by anxiety over the scale of the issues he faced and a realisation, unstated but recognized, that Fianna Fáil, as the senior party in government, was shorn of experience. Charlie McCreevy was still in Brussels; Albert Reynolds had retired, and Bertie Ahern was finishing out his time on the backbenches.

This meant that significant personnel change was inevitable. Brian Lenihan, a bright and talented man who had been long overlooked, was appointed to Finance and Mary Coughlan was made

Tánaiste. These appointments highlighted a serious and genuine attempt to build a new-look Fianna Fáil, but domestic and global events conspired to render the timing of such boldness, disastrous.

Brian Cowen's conservatism around political life meant he had certain principles that were immutable. In my time working with him professionally and advising him personally I know that he would never countenance briefing against a colleague. The same core value which wouldn't allow him to really consider the case for a *putsch* against Bertie Ahern, applied to never using outside influence to shape a prospective government decision.

The political traditionalist in him regarded membership of a cabinet as a position of the most extreme privilege that bore immense responsibility. Few things angered him more than those who failed to understand the values unique to cabinet membership; there was, for example, one senior party figure, who in Brian's time as a minister, regularly briefed the media on government business. It drove him crazy. When he established his cabinet he stressed these values but sought to encourage a free and open debate among ministers, believing that expertise and opinion were accumulated, so matters before cabinet could be explored to arrive at an agreed position.

What all of this contributed to was a more collaborative than directional style of leadership that he himself profiled as being about a Taoiseach who would be a 'first among equals' based on his confidence in the wisdom of cabinet colleagues. Within months of assuming the leadership, Brian Cowen and others at cabinet were to see evidence of behaviours in the new Finance Minister – especially a determination to act unilaterally – that may have explained, in part, the reluctance of Brian's predecessors to appoint Brian Lenihan to cabinet.

Later, when the pressures facing the new government became more intense, Mr. Lenihan's shocking cancer diagnosis and its devastating course, added considerably to the difficulty between the two men. Brian Cowen's primary concern was his colleague's health, but it seemed the more serious his condition became, the more determined Brian Lenihan was to continue to do things his way. The Finance Minister's resolve was admirable but even the gravity of his illness couldn't alter the frustration of the Taoiseach and other cabinet members at his determination to act alone. While Brian made a number of attempts to address this with him, the situation meant that he couldn't resolve the problem as some believed he must and that he would, most likely, have done in different circumstances.

• • •

In the early part of his term as Taoiseach I continued to assist with some strategic political considerations and speech-writing. I always saw his approach to speeches as emblematic of his political management. Writing for him was fun but also frustrating. The idea of creating images and making bold or broad statements wasn't natural to him; no matter the subject, it needed to be explained, and normally in great detail. The way he wrote, his standard way of speaking, betrayed more than a pedantic approach to communications; it epitomised the challenge for Brian in finding a modus for leading government.

In private conversation, he could discuss issues broadly and suggest ideas eloquently. Brian read widely but in the professional political world, perhaps influenced by his training as a solicitor, he tended to shut down that natural capacity. I felt that throughout his career his predominant instinct to cover each and every base was born for fear that without attending to the detail, important considerations could be missed. It was a feature of his struggle as Taoiseach which was magnified by the scale of the financial crisis and his sense that the Minister for Finance was not working with him or his cabinet colleagues.

This problem of over-managing became more acute as the months of his leadership passed and he allowed himself to be weighed down by even small problems with different ministers, with worries about his own choices and, understandably, the increasing scale and complexity of the country's economic travails. The pressures on him were growing and beginning to take a toll, which meant those of us close to him started to focus on other things. We thought Brian's tendency to micro-management was increasing, that he was failing to lift his head and see the broader issues the Taoiseach must both understand and address. Some of his concerns were well-founded but he needed to accept them, apportion responsibility and lead his team with everyone knowing their role and that he would hold them directly accountable.

This was the start of Brian Cowen's political demise. There was a gathering pall over the government and, while it wouldn't have been obvious then, it was to prove to be the point at which Brian's natural pessimism started to emerge. More worryingly for those closest to him, it was the beginning of a descent into a moroseness that at times seemed to consume him. There was a tension between how Brian lived and the pressure of leading the country. A renewed effort was made to streamline the demands on him but to little effect; over his 25 years in politics, Brian had travelled to and from Tullamore daily. There were rare occasions when he stayed in Dublin and, as a minister, he'd always had a Garda driver but nevertheless such a long commute at the start and end of most days took its toll.

The acute sleep apnoea, his poor diet, a lack of exercise, and his preference for a pint at the end of many of his working days, all meant tiredness was his constant companion. While these were contributing factors to his fatigue, some became amplified in elements of public discourse to levels that bore no relationship to the reality. They became the easy fodder with which to feed elements of the media that was anxious to portray the simplistic caricature as though it was a reality.

I believe that worry, though camouflaged, was a significant inhibitor for Brian. The public saw someone who exuded confidence and assertiveness in media interviews, in the Dáil chamber or any form of public debate, but Brian was a lot less sure of himself and had always been a worrier. I am too, but men of our generation aren't always open to acknowledge the shadow presence of anxiety. It is a big part of the human condition which, unmanaged, is destructive of confidence and spirit. With the ascent to leadership of the country and of Fianna Fáil, that part of Brian's natural disposition fed a decreasing self-confidence. When, by the end of 2008, the economic storm clouds on the national and global horizon had moved directly overhead, this drag on his spirit had become problematic, seriously so in my opinion.

While my own work and my professional woes were of no consequence when compared to the scale of the responsibilities Brian Cowen long carried, on a human level I could relate to his difficulty. The worry gene is one I'd inherited but managed largely unseen. In business I worked tirelessly to hide it, deliberately exuding the constant vibe of confidence that's essential to success. When you're bathed in it, however conditional or fleeting, you feel the need to sustain the impression of a 'bullet-proof' persona no matter how at odds it is with your reality. It then becomes an essential. It certainly was in the largely male world of Irish business across my generation where so-called emotional weakness is frowned upon and an aura of confidence is critical to survival.

Politics is no different and Brian's circumstances saw anxiety emerge and begin to dominate. The lack of heavyweight political colleagues fuelled a vortex of uncertainty and angst. Over the next 18 months, as Ireland slid inexorably into an economic abyss, Brian was to become more isolated or at least experience a profound sense of isolation. While he would be loath to admit to pessimism being his default position, I believe that it is, as it is for many of us.

While I could relate to this, I wasn't Taoiseach. The destructive power of my own demons allowed me to empathise with him but nothing could allow me to really access the enormity of his challenge. There were elements of his schedule and his lifestyle which were accentuating the difficulty of being in office at such a tough moment; the marked obsession with detail meant that while he tried valiantly, his natural instinct made it difficult for him to move above the minutiae of the job.

• • •

That Brian Cowen didn't govern as effectively as he might have done and his ultimate political demise were due to a multiplicity of factors. There was a myriad of issues, a complex set of circumstances, bad timing and ill-luck, but a great deal of it was just about his own nature, always acknowledging that elements of his make-up, particularly the worry gene, were the most difficult things of all to manage.

The obsession with detail, its natural pull was, in part, due to a personal reserve, an embedded conservatism around keeping things grounded in a reality. It has its place but the great downside for those in leadership is that it keeps ambition quarantined. Brian would shy away from painting bold political narratives because he'd be concerned that they couldn't be delivered. Politically, he was of the realist not the impressionist school; careful and cautious rather than bold and imaginative. That's not necessarily all bad.

In the United Kingdom, the wilful warping of truth by those who led the 2016 Brexit campaign is a stark example of the dangers of broad and colourful brushwork. Senior political figures deliberately falsified the narrative to promote a future to suit their narrow self-interested political objectives, centred on the bewildering notion that the UK would be better off economically and socially outside a community of nations it had been part of for almost 50 years. The outcome showed the power of feeling over thought, of instinct over consideration. The gut reaction of a small majority of UK voters was to support something that most rational analysis considered economically reckless. The Brexit landscape was impressionist in scale and colour but it was a forgery, the post-impressionism of Trump in the USA, even more so.

Brian Cowen abhorred that kind of politics but in politics impressionism does have appeal and value. People need to be led by imagining how their society and their lives can be made better, to believe in a brighter future where even a considered ambition is presented in a manner that's attractive and stimulates public confidence. The everyday – the world of realism – was what Brian carried with him: it was his life experience and what he felt comfortable articulating, explaining, even campaigning about. Whatever brush he had in hand, facts and truth were on his palette.

In some circumstances he could be a brilliant orator, especially if the subject stirred him and the audience was in any way familiar. When he most needed to engage the public, acknowledge failures, stress the scale of the economic peril but appeal directly to the people of Ireland by also creating images of a brighter future by pulling together, his conservatism manacled him. In the midst of the financial crisis I was among a small number who tried to convince him of the need for him to address the nation but his reticence prevailed.

Fate decreed that when he assumed the position of leader, not long after he became Taoiseach in May 2008, the economic circumstances made it extraordinarily difficult for him to rise above the everyday. Furthermore, reality for large numbers of Irish people over the coming years was so bleak that almost everyone went into survival mode and that included the Taoiseach. It's perverse that, at a time when the nation most needed leadership based on realism, on hard, practical, unexciting management, the man whose natural disposition and skill-set made him tailor-made for just that job, couldn't align the political stars to make it happen.

• • •

Strangely, in 2007, he had played a large part in tilting the political fates in a manner that would later prove so unhelpful to the interests of Fianna Fáil and, indeed, his own. In the election of 2007, Brian Cowen's direct intervention in a seriously faltering campaign saved Fianna Fáil from almost certain defeat. It was the ultimate pyrrhic victory. Being in government in that subsequent period did irreparable damage to Fianna Fáil, benefited Fine Gael and presaged the end of Brian Cowen's political career.

More than anyone else in Fianna Fáil, Brian Cowen's actions in the last week of the 2007 election campaign put his party back in government but at some cost; aligning events so he became Taoiseach just as Ireland experienced a cataclysmic economic meltdown. It finished his career.

That election had been called at a time of declining support for the government parties of Fianna Fáil and the Progressive Democrats; in fact, the junior party was receiving the last rites. Issues around the probity of Bertie Ahern at the Mahon Tribunal, were to the fore and opinion polls consistently pointed to the real possibility that Fianna Fáil would be defeated. Then, with ten days to go in the campaign, Brian Cowen led a dramatic electoral response, checking Fine Gael's run at government and securing a new mandate for Fianna Fáil. Events would prove it to be a poisoned political chalice, not the mantle of government that he had succeeded in prising away from Enda Kenny and Fine Gael's grasp.

On Sunday April 29th, 2007, Brian and I met to prepare for

an interview on RTÉ's *This Week* programme and for a meeting with Bertie Ahern where he wanted to impress upon him that he shouldn't electioneer outside North Dublin for the final week of campaigning. To his credit, Bertie Ahern was electorally savvy and a big enough man to recognise the political reality.

So it was that Brian Cowen made three crucial interventions over those few days. He did an exceptional radio interview, he pressed his party leader on limiting the range of his electioneering and he helped to prepare Bertie Ahern for the televised Leaders' debate in which the Fianna Fáil leader surprised many commentators by comfortably out-performing Fine Gael leader Enda Kenny. Fine Gael lost an election that had been theirs to win; it was to prove a fortuitous roll of the political dice.

• • •

A year later, in the summer of 2008, the bubbles of global economic disorder were becoming more violent and there were early signs that the timing of Brian Cowen's ascendency to leadership could hardly have been worse. Few were more aware of this than Brian himself. The worry lines became deeper, fed in part by his naturally pessimistic disposition.

I kept pressing him to take a wider lens. When any leader is embattled, it is natural to become defensive. In those early months, I and his professional advisers believed he needed to set wider political objectives that could resonate with the public. I, in particular, was pushing him to get wider economic and private sector advice and, after long consideration, he accepted there was merit in establishing a small group to provide different perspectives on socio-economic issues.

Brian saw the value but his natural reserve meant he was concerned at how it would function and how it might be perceived. I understood that anxiety so we agreed, if it was to proceed at all, that anyone selected could see it only as an occasional sounding board for the Taoiseach to use as he saw fit. I reassured him that we'd involve only those who would have something to offer; a small group and that no one who sought or needed public affirmation would be even considered.

Early that summer we had an initial meeting with three individuals. Alan Gray, the widely-respected economist was chosen because of his intellect and measured manner but also because he and Brian had positive experience of working together. We both admired and trusted Alan as we did the industrialist Gary McGann who was an experienced if quite low-key senior business figure. The third was Seán FitzPatrick, whom Brian had met once or twice only but he accepted my advice that he should be included.

I've often thought since of that list and the discussions he and I had around that meeting – banking was so far from our minds that it never even occurred to us that Gary McGann and Seán FitzPatrick were on the board of Anglo Irish or that Alan Gray was a Director of the Central Bank. Alan was a leading economist; Gary a respected industrialist and then CEO of Smurfit Kappa plc.; Seán FitzPatrick was my 'pick', as it were. The first and, as it turned out, only meeting of the group with Brian was delayed because he wanted certainty that everyone would understand the rules of engagement.

That meeting at my home covered a lengthy agenda that Alan Gray had prepared. Banking was not on it. That meeting, as well as the nine holes of golf and dinner that followed, had absolutely nothing to do with anything that later evolved into the Irish financial services crisis. There was no discussion at any point about banking, never mind Anglo Irish Bank.

The previous March I had acted as a conduit for a call from Seán FitzPatrick to Brian who was then Minister for Finance. The approach was entirely proper. Seán FitzPatrick, as the chairman of a bank, justifiably used my known access to the minister in this way to raise a commercial concern that was relevant to his department. Brian was particular about procedure and as he later explained, arising from the call with Seán FitzPatrick, he spoke first with the Central Bank governor who then dealt directly with bank officials. I neither offered nor was asked my opinion and, at all times, boundaries were maintained and respected as Brian ensured the matter was dealt with by the Central Bank.

Politics is a ruthless business where political advantage often takes precedence over acting responsibly. I understood how it served the narrative of Brian Cowen's political foes to suggest that he and I may have acted in consort to the benefit of Anglo Irish Bank. Presented in a particular way, certain events were intrigue-laden elements in a story that could put Brian in a bad light. They were grist to the political mill.

Typically, there was little interest in details that undermined any other version. The facts around the 'notorious' Druids Glen scenario that July didn't suggest subterfuge. After our meeting we had nine holes of golf, a pint in the public bar where Brian met and spoke with Sinn Féin TD, Caoimhghín Ó Caoláin, who was attending a wedding, before having dinner in the main restaurant where our group included his Garda driver. Somehow in the midst of all this it was presumed that something underhand was afoot. The facts received little attention because they didn't suit the screenplay based on stratagem and duplicity.

Bizarrely, a separate charge against me was what opposition parties described as my 'unparalleled access' to Brian Cowen during that time. The very same people who wanted to know why I was in his office so frequently, wanted the public to believe that, notwithstanding such unlimited access, I still chose to involve him in under-hand dealings through discussions on a golf course and in a public bar and restaurant.

Given the febrile political and public mood of the time it may not be surprising that the colourful narrative took hold, that such a wildly inaccurate portrayal of events gained traction. Multiple failures contributed to the economic collapse that damaged the welfare of many in our society. The idea of it being down to some conspiracy of interests was appealing. The public and the body politic were hurting as never before and therefore the need to lay the blame somewhere was strong and deep. It was also rich political material with which to damage an already badly-wounded Taoiseach and it played to the appetite across some elements for a sensationalist, simplistic, reasoning on events that were of national interest.

Much of this lacked thorough analysis, in part because some of the principal characters were either legally prohibited from talking or were too scared to do so, meaning mis-information and half-truths prevailed. I knew the interest in me was largely political and that truth becomes compromised in the rush to portray and understand any catastrophic failure of human endeavour like that of the scale of the Irish banking crisis. Nonetheless, the media's interest in evidence-based commentary was limited.

The boring reality is that what happened involved no political conspiracy of vested interests or any secret management of personal interests between 'high-flying' business figures with political influence and 'suspect' senior politicians. The truth is a great deal less Hollywood. A considered analysis would start with an acknowledgment that in early summer 2008 no one in Ireland thought that the Irish banks, including Anglo, were at risk of collapse. There was a worldwide liquidity problem but few looking at the situation then imagined anything approaching what ultimately happened.

Patrick Honohan, who was Governor of the Central Bank from 2009 to 2015, was an economics professor in Trinity College Dublin then and met Finance Minister Brian Lenihan early that summer. The minister was seeking views of informed people from outside the department. Years later, reflecting on the meeting, Professor Honohan said they discussed the tax shortfall, rising social welfare costs, increasing unemployment and the bleak outlook for the property market, but, he said *banks didn't come up at all*.

The wider agenda Alan Gray had prepared for our meeting in early July covered the same areas the Minister for Finance had spoken about privately with Professor Honohan. As with that meeting when our group met in the first days of July 2008, banks were not an agenda item and did not come up at all.

Only one person at that meeting held the position of Taoiseach. I know of no one in politics who thinks Brian Cowen capable of compromising that office or the public interest by being party to any private discussions about a private enterprise. When I challenged the members of the Oireachtas Banking Inquiry on that very point – on the uniform view across the political spectrum of Brian's integrity – not one person demurred. I've spoken privately with senior members of Fine Gael who acknowledged as much. For all the political capital made of those events, no one has ever expressed anything other than certainty around Brian Cowen's integrity and commitment to public office.

Brian Cowen accepted responsibility for decisions made both as Minister for Finance and Taoiseach that, in the former case, contributed to the scale of the emerging problem and in the latter, did not ease elements of the crisis as other steps might have done. The tangential material is a media opioid, no more, but it damaged him unfairly and, in the process, undermined public confidence in politics and in the conduct of public life. The fall from office of the 12th holder of the office of Taoiseach warrants closer attention.

X
Free Fall

The idea that Brian Cowen acted defensively, or out of self-preservation during the period of the financial crisis is not borne out by the facts. When the balloon went up he made choices that were in the national interest, knowing they would damage Fianna Fáil and end his own political career. In time a more considered perspective on his final years in public life will show that, in managing the crisis that holed Ireland below the economic waterline, he put his own career and the interests of his party aside in trying to correct or at least ameliorate a situation that bordered on impossible. Brian took unpopular decisions, some of which carried an inherent admission of his own failings, knowing they were necessary but also that they would end his career and could leave him exposed to public ridicule.

It would be easy to dismiss these actions as being late and being the decisions someone makes when they've no other choice. In politics, acknowledgement of failure is rare, particularly when you're still at the helm. A politician's instinct is normally self-preservation, irrespective of the scale and gravity of any situation. Brian took the opposite approach for which history should record him credit. That's the argument: it's about a sense of fairness within an overall narrative where his leadership faced a most daunting test and, in the round, was found wanting.

This more balanced assessment can come only with time. It is for others to provide. A decade on, the atmosphere is calmer but not yet sufficiently so to allow the important deep analysis best done by political historians. It needs the application of an unbiased critical assessment by those not compromised by having been present for much of his time in office and who provided contemporaneous analysis.

The economic analysis will have to consider how the Irish

economy grew rapidly over the decade from the mid-1990s that saw huge investment in infrastructure and public services as well as a reduction in public debt as a percentage of GDP from around 85% to 24% in 2007. Those who argue that Fianna Fáil under successive Ministers for Finance Bertie Ahern, Charlie McCreevy and Brian Cowen were driving the economic juggernaut – branded the Celtic Tiger – over the cliff need to review the politics of the period.

Over his four years as Finance Minister, Brian's budgets were consistently criticised by all the opposition parties as 'not giving people enough' or that the levels of public spending were 'totally insufficient'. In the general election of May 2007, the manifestoes of all parties reflected confidence in the condition of the Irish economy.

Brian Cowen's term as Taoiseach was as shattering of a stellar political career as it was unexpected; his intellect and political qualities meant he should and could have been a significant political figure for many more years. While a number of elements conspired against that, perhaps the primary consideration is that he never displayed the obsession with power that is considered an imperative for successful leadership in most walks of life, particularly politics.

It is also the case that, allowing for everything else, the turn of history's wheel meant that, whatever his capacities, it was a perilous time to assume leadership of his party and his country. The banking sector was lending excessively, the Financial Regulator and the Central Bank were not diligent and the boards of banks weren't attentive enough or sufficiently questioning of what their executives were doing. Property and development lending were past excessive levels and when this domestic cocktail was subsumed by a global financial crisis of a scale previously unseen, Ireland was 'shot'.

Brian Cowen, for all his political gifts, is not as he seems to many and certainly he is not as he has been profiled. At heart he is quite reserved, shy even, and like many men who grew up in Ireland in the 1960s, he's slow to acknowledge to himself, never mind anyone else, any personal weaknesses lest in doing so he betray self-doubt or provide opponents with material to undermine him. It's regrettable that the rules of the political game don't allow for anything other than the pretence of perfection or certainty especially when, as the greatest threat to success is often lurking within your own ranks, to do so would be the career equivalent of white water rafting.

These were the principal reasons Brian Cowen's political career ended as it did. It is fair to presume, even allowing for the absence of any obsession to lead, that if the economic collapse hadn't occurred, he'd have prevailed as a major figure in Irish public life for longer, but it's also possible that the end would still have been premature and, if so, that it would have been influenced by personal factors as much as by professional ones. That may often be the case but with Brian it is a more pronounced consideration.

Working with professional athletes I've seen how short, highly intense, careers build pressures that most of us don't experience and there's a sense of that in political life too. The concertina nature of a career in politics may not be as acute as in professional football but, in Brian Cowen's case, I've long believed the pressure of his length of service in government contributed to his challenge when he became Taoiseach. While his exit from politics was premature and discombobulating, Brian had by then spent almost 30 years in the frontline of Irish politics with more than half of that in government.

The absence of any robust independent analysis of some important issues in the reality of how political life works, short-changes us all as citizens. There is no area of life more important to the welfare of society than politics. We need excellence in public representation and in government so a means of permanent and ongoing evaluation of how our democracy functions would be in the public interest and might, over time, build greater confidence in how the citizens' interests are represented. It would also enhance decision-making around the career development of all those – permanent and elected – within politics who are there to serve the public good.

Critical to any rational, non-partisan, assessment of Brian Cowen's career should be consideration of all the factors around why it was that he failed to fulfil his potential. Some considered understanding of what happened to stall and then end his political journey might better inform future decision-makers about political leadership. The review could start by asking if 13 years in different, mainly senior and challenging cabinet positions, is the ideal preparation for someone taking over as Taoiseach or if, in such circumstances, there is a real risk of institutional fatigue as well as intellectual and emotional burn-out?

Brian Cowen isn't the only rural Taoiseach who had long years of public service when he assumed leadership of the country. Enda Kenny, from Mayo, who succeeded him had also followed his father as a TD at the age of 24, but the most marked difference was that when he succeeded Brian he had only once served in cabinet as Minister for Tourism for two and a half years.

When he assumed the top position, Albert Reynolds, a Longford TD, had served half the time in cabinet that Brian Cowen had and yet, in more standard times, Brian's battle-fatigue might have had little or no impact. There's rarely any consideration given to the career circumstances of those we thrust into political leadership which, given that it's the most important job in any society, is perplexing.

When the domestic and global economic situation at the time of assuming leadership is cataclysmic – in this case on an unprecedented scale in modern times – the potential for failure is heightened. When you add a lack of attention to personal welfare there is, statistically, a smaller chance still of performance meeting potential.

I've seen situations throughout my professional life where people much less able than Brian Cowen, dealing with circumstances a fraction as demanding, couldn't function and failed to meet the standards of work expected of them or that they'd have expected of themselves. In many large consulting, accountancy and legal practices, partners get a six-month paid sabbatical after ten years work so they can recharge their batteries. It's a practice the New Zealand All Blacks adopted to allow some of their most hard-worked international players feel refreshed ahead of a particularly important competitive period.

This issue warrants attention. It's obvious that the sabbatical idea is problematic in electoral politics but dismissing the very real problem of fatigue, would simply represent an extension of our generally unenlightened approach to political life. As citizens we fail to value as we should the well-being of professional politicians who need to be functioning at optimum levels for the welfare of society. What could possibly be more important? I'm not sure that Brian Cowen would agree with this emphasis but I believe it was a significant contributor to his relative under-performance as Taoiseach. Again, some of it was the extraordinary circumstances of the time, some of it was his own fault but there is, nonetheless, an issue of substance around our expectations and treatment of those in political leadership.

In any large business the appointment of a senior executive to a leadership role would be predicated on a full evaluation process including their health and wellbeing. I believe that if such an approach was taken to the appointment of those selected for the most senior political positions, Brian Cowen would probably not have been cleared to take the role of Taoiseach in 2008. This would not have been because of any skills or experience deficit. In fact in respect of those essentials he was gifted, but any thorough assessment would likely have found that his energy levels were so drained that, far from being fit for the top job, what he most needed was a good break from the frontline.

Such an assessment is standard practice in the awarding of leadership positions in many areas of life yet not, it seems, with the most important position of all. Why? Because it's not the norm elsewhere or because it's never been the norm here? Those are not good enough reasons for it not to be an absolutely essential part of the process in choosing someone to be the elected leader of the country. The idea of 'fitness for office' covers other critical considerations which the Oireachtas is equipped to establish and where Brian Cowen met every conceivable test, but the more generic sense of the term should have some weight in determining the more basic and critical capacity of any candidate for such a responsible position.

On the one occasion that we discussed this issue a few years ago, Brian dismissed it as completely impractical in politics but to ignore the principle seems to me unwise. It goes right to the heart of the value we place on political life and the interests of those whom we elect to represent us. Their welfare is ours but in our persistently negative and corrosive outlook on politics much of our behaviour undermines the institutions but especially the characters on whose judgment and actions we depend. To undertake any radical overhaul of some critical, if practical, elements of how politics is conducted would not be straightforward, but surely it would be worthwhile. The alternative seems to me that we continue to adopt our largely unenlightened approach to political life.

● ● ●

There's a wider challenge too. In a secure democratic society, politicians should be revered but in most countries it's a blood sport. The consequences of political decision-making dwarf those taken in most every other walk of life. The pressure all politicians face in today's world of instant gratification, where the citizen has become a 'customer' of those whom they elect rather than an active participant in the civic society of which parliament is just one part, is unsustainable.

When we're thrust into a leadership role, no matter its scale or prominence, to be an effective leader we have to be in the best possible personal shape to have hope of success. That includes being comfortable with the conditions of leadership which, for someone as private and reserved as Brian Cowen, would always have demanded a considerable adjustment. The personality of the leader is critical to determining their success or otherwise. Brian Cowen may have had a reputation as a tough man from Offaly but that bears no relation to how he is or how he conducted himself professionally.

That analysis is not to put a gloss on what followed but it must be worthwhile to better understand how someone with a surplus of the skills and relevant experience, may always have been unlikely to be able to do the job as it needed to be done. How can that have happened and what, as we reflect on it a decade on, can we learn from that experience to limit the chances of similar circumstances arising again in the future?

The old cliché about people getting the politicians they deserve is facile but there is, within our outlook on politics and our treatment of those whom we ask to represent us, an institutionalised indifference to their welfare. While their welfare is our welfare, our behaviour as citizens seems a denial of that truth. We refuse to see it that way; society's capacity to challenge, distrust, ridicule and display hostility towards politicians has increased. It's unsophisticated and it's unintelligent. We want it both ways.

Most elected politicians are well-intentioned and hard-working but somehow our expectations of them have become skewed to such an extent that nearly all the commentary is within the moment and is often sectional and emotional rather than long-term and analytical. The former might make for good copy or rowdy debate on radio or across social media but the weakness of so much of what passes for analysis is that it's designed to meet the expectations of the 'baying public' or boost revenues, rather than dealing with the facts.

The body politic itself needs to mature too, needs to be more respectful and balanced. It is unrealistic to expect the public to be more informed, empathetic and understanding of politicians if all they witness is a political class that cannibalises itself. Not one politician in the Oireachtas believed Brian Cowen would ever act against the public interest but nor did any of them declare that publicly, when not only he but the whole profession would have benefited had someone of stature chosen to do so.

Citizens shouldn't be fed information or opinions that suit a political agenda but which their political sponsor knows to be highly unlikely or even suspects to be untrue. The trade, in cheap, vacuous and often untrue political capital across the Irish political marketplace, something that Brian Cowen himself deployed on occasion, needs to stop. It is generally pitiful and it's nearly always unnecessary. This behaviour is particularly unhelpful in moving the needle of public respect for political life in the right direction.

Day-to-day political skirmishes are one thing but when substantive issues become platforms for political make-believe or petty insults, they become acts of political self-harm that serve only to narrow the vein of public support for and belief in political life that's critical to its welfare. It is society, the public, that nourishes politics not the other way around. Without the public's support for how political life is organised and those in whom it entrusts its management, our system of governance is open to attack.

This is why the behaviour of our elected representatives matters so much, it is why if they want the respect they need and largely deserve then they need to proactively conduct their affairs in less febrile manner. It's only then that politicians can legitimately turn to how their world is analysed and presented by others.

It is strange, however, that the same people, including some media commentators, who argue for the need to protect our athletes from being overused because of the pressure of top-flight competition, cannot seem to appreciate that Leinster House and its surrounds are considerably more demanding of body and soul than Thomond Park, Croke Park or the Aviva Stadium. No athlete has ever had to bear the responsibility that goes with being Taoiseach or a senior government minister. No club or county manager in the GAA, no international manager in any sport, no performer in the arts or media has ever faced the sustained and weighty pressure that senior politicians do.

Overall we need to find more balance in our commentary on politics including a greater recognition that most public representatives want to be of service and do work hard towards that end. Some of this is about how the media functions today but as much, if not more, it is about the conduct of politics itself.

Brian Cowen had the most challenging job, the most demanding career, of anyone I ever worked or shared ideas with but also the one where success, achievement and certainly, admiration, is most elusive. I saw politics on these islands at reasonably close quarters as a journalist where, by career definition, the task is to find fault, to question and to probe. Later I worked with senior political figures across the political spectrum, most of them in government striving to be the best servants of public welfare that they could be.

It is sad but not that surprising that Brian's leadership during the financial crisis is seen through the haze of clumsy public pronouncements, informed reports of a generally gloomy disposition, one distressed morning radio interview and few apparent efforts to quell a growing public alarm over the state of the nation. The haze was one Brian Cowen himself had largely created and, as the crisis deepened, however bad his profile, it appeared from the side-lines that the effort required to rectify it seemed beyond him.

With the Irish economy in crisis and his political career with it, at that point it was as if a fatalism set in around his leadership. Brian recognised that the critics had now too much material with which to harm him, that the loss of public confidence was at levels which made his position irretrievable but, more than any other consideration, Brian Cowen knew Ireland's economic back was against the wall and that alone was what needed his full attention.

I believe that in time, a considered assessment of his leadership will show that for all the visible chaos, hard decisions were taken and without a thought of anything other than the public interest. I know people, not all of whom were Fianna Fáil colleagues who worked closely with him over that last grim year, who say that his pursuit of the best for Ireland was remorseless. One former senior colleague likened his leadership to the captain going down with the ship: *it may not be the greatest accolade, but facing what he was, Brian put the country first, his party a distant second and as for his own career he did nothing that would have made it any more salvageable.* It may be worth noting that the ship, while badly damaged, didn't sink and that its new captain, Enda Kenny, found on taking command that it was not just seaworthy but, in large measure through the grim determination of his predecessor, had been set on the right course towards a return to calmer waters.

• • •

In 2017 Brian Cowen was offered an honorary degree by the National University of Ireland. I was one of those whom he consulted about it. Brian, an NUI law graduate, was unsure of the wisdom of it, as was I. So we debated whether he should accept the honour, given the inevitable attention it would draw at a time when life was gradually settling into a more agreeable pattern for him. My chief reservation was that there was little he could say that would deliver even a modicum of public rehabilitation, but others argued, with some merit, that in accepting the award he would have a rare opportunity to place certain matters on the record.

So it was that in July of that year I found myself back in speech-writing mode. It was as though nothing had changed as we argued over the same old considerations of length and detail. I provided a 12 to 15 minute script that was broad in its observations, drew on imagery and especially the ideas of the poet-philosopher John O'Donohue whose writings we both admire. Brian used most of it but only as part of speech that ran to over 40 minutes which drew criticism both for its length and its obduracy.

Some of the criticism was reasonable but most of it was a predictable, lazy, anti-intellectual commentary. Opening his address, Brian Cowen referenced John O'Donohue on how he wrote that *politics seems devoid of vision and is becoming more and more synonymous with economics*. I don't think Brian regrets his actions once Ireland hit the economic rocks. I believe he knows that when the water was flowing over the sides, he remained on deck doing everything possible in that moment to keep it afloat, certain that his career was over. I also believe that, in all the circumstances, most of his actions of that time were correct, all were principled and certainly were executed to the best of his ability.

I suspect that the regret lies elsewhere, that the twitch of his left-of-centre economic instincts hadn't been stronger, sufficient to force him towards a fundamental correction during his time as Minister for Finance. Ireland was so juiced up on its economic miracle then that there would have been great political risk in attempting this but that risk, calculated and thought through, isn't something that should have prevented him from establishing and articulating a vision for a different economic approach that would, in time, deliver a different and better-balanced society. When he emphasised John O'Donohue's view that vision is critical to effective leadership and when he publicly regretted its omission from his own time in political charge, I believe it is to that point in history and in his political career that he was referring.

Brian reveres those who, over the centuries, thought deeply about life to better understand human endeavour and he placed special value on John O'Donohue's insights into contemporary Irish life. In his speech to the NUI in July 2017 he read: *In the Western Christian tradition, we gave a huge role to intellect and to will. The intellect was used to find out what the goal or object was; the will then drove it along the linear track towards it. This model of human sensibility brought us much beauty, but its neglect of the imagination has also cost us dearly. A human life can have everything including status, reputation and achievement, but if the imagination is not awakened, all these will lack presence and depth.*

It may have passed most commentators by, but I believe this carefully chosen emphasis was one of the more important things for Brian Cowen to have acknowledged in reflecting on his political career in Dublin on July 26th, 2017. It is hard not to reflect that, in the widest sense of what vision might entail, all those thrust into positions of leadership, all those who are part of a leadership cohort in their lives, should consider its import.

'BALL BEARINGS'

Liam Brady and Kevin Moran brought me into the world of professional sport back in 1989. I continue to work as a sports management professional, representing footballers in the UK as a registered FA Intermediary and working with clubs and different sports associations. Much of the work is no different to any other area of business and the highs and the lows are generally self-induced in professional sport, as elsewhere. One interesting feature however is the prevalence of fame junkies, the hangers-on who, though they have nothing to offer, desperately need to be close to the action.

Liam Brady warned me of this phenomenon the first time we met. In encouraging me to take the role as commercial adviser to the Irish World Cup squad for the 1990 Finals, he offered the sage advice to always be wary of the 'jersey touchers'. The explanation, born of weary experience, was that some people want to get close to famous people, be their 'friends' for no other reason than that they are famous. I was wary. Instinctively so. On account of that warning, while I worked with some exceptionally talented, high-profile people in different fields I chose not to hang around their 'scene'. Any friendships made were low-key and not about what the individuals had achieved.

The most dramatic example of 'jersey touching' in Irish sport, one that has had ruinous consequences for football in Ireland, was the 15 year tenure of John Delaney as CEO of the Football Association of Ireland. I've worked with administrators in different sporting organisations at home and abroad who were talented, hardworking, driven to progress the interests of their sport and knew that, as far as possible, they should stay out of public view. Sports fans dislike the referee who wants to dominate the narrative but in Ireland, at a critical juncture for the development of football, we allowed the FAI to be run by someone with a penchant for self-promotion.

The travails of the association, particularly since 2010, reflect a deep cultural malaise within the game, where outdated organisational structures are used to keep control in the hands of largely, though not exclusively, malleable committee men for whom match tickets and the occasional trip overseas are the height of their ambition for their sport.

Over the same period, I had engagement with CEOs at Leinster and Munster Rugby – in Mick Dawson and Garrett Fitzgerald – who dealt with everything in a professional business-like manner consistent with my dealings with Philip Browne, CEO of the Irish Rugby Football Union. We didn't always agree and there were initiatives with some that didn't work or couldn't advance but, on those occasions, there was no drama, intrigue or 'after taste' as was always the case with John Delaney even when, in the earliest years of his tenure I had tried to work with him a number of times. What was noticeable too was the absence of these rugby union executives from anything approaching the players' inner sanctum or in the media except when it was necessary in the conduct of their work. They were CEOs of high profile businesses but they understood the difference between being a player and an administrator.

This low-key approach to governance and management is even more acute in the GAA. Gaelic games has transitioned brilliantly to compete in a fast moving, contemporary world of popular social engagement across all forms of entertainment including sport. In the presentation of its competitive offer, the GAA is as good as any sports federation anywhere but in organisational terms, I suspect it's considerably better than most. In the extensive dealings I had with it over a three or four year period, none of its executives, most especially Páraic Duffy, its Director General for a decade from 2008, had any interest other than in doing their job. They were excellent administrators with no need of celebrity.

Yet, in Abbotstown in west Dublin, the administration in Ireland of the world's most popular sport fell into the hands of someone whose motivations for taking the role were, from the very outset, so questionable it should have ruled him out. In the early years, John Delaney was known to like mixing with the players in that harmless, if childish, sense of 'jersey touching' that many athletes find irritating. That was only the start as displaying his great need for recognition, it morphed into a belief that he himself had similar celebrity status, that, like the players, his profile meant both the media and fans wanted his time, his company. The legend grew and with it attention to the needs of the sport vanished in thick clouds of wastefulness, intrigue and celebrity. Irish football, as they say, 'went down the pan!'

XI

Regression

The Chief Executive of the Football Association of Ireland (FAI) between 2005 and 2019 was John Delaney. Over that time he was easily the highest paid executive in Irish sport and in spite of Ireland being one of the smaller nations in the world, one of the highest paid executives in world football. When he was forced to resign, the Association and the sport it had been his responsibility to nurture and develop had debts of over €55 million. John Delaney's remuneration, his terms and conditions and the frequency with which his contract of employment was renegotiated and improved were all at the discretion of the board, the composition of which he controlled. That is inherently wrong but it's what happened. I know from experience how corrosive a controlling management style can be. I have the T-shirt.

Football has been the only constant in my 30 years involvement in professional sport. The FAI has been part of that experience, initially through my work with the Irish international squad then in different types of engagement from negotiating a renewal of the Eircom sponsorship for the association to being Ireland's first UEFA-registered player agent, building a proposal for reform of the domestic senior game on an all-island basis and representing international players and, once, the manager of the international team.

I like and follow most team sports but football, or soccer, is my sport. Apart from the emotional attachment, I like its unparalleled power for good across communities, societies and nations. It is, at once, the most monied sport on the planet and the one that's the most accessible because it costs nothing to play. Many legends of the game have come from very poor backgrounds yet it's now so popular that it attracts huge financial resources that, if well used, can facilitate many wonderous things. It also means, as one of the most respected executives in English football once said to me, that the game attracts characters and influences that are destructive of its core values.

While that observation related to the edgier parts of the UK football industry – like the preponderance of agents – in Irish football the last two decades have witnessed destructive behaviours in the governance of the sport. Laterally, in part inadvertently propped up by private money, and inadequately supervised nationally and by UEFA, John Delaney had 15 years where he was able to do great damage to the game he always professed to love.

I gained a great deal from the years I played the game, almost as much from those involved in coaching with my sons' club, Greystones Utd and I've worked with great people in senior and schoolboy clubs as well as being privileged to work with the exceptional squad of players that took Ireland (and me, for work no less!) to consecutive World Cup Finals in 1990 in Italy and 1994 in the USA.

The timing of my unintended move into professional sport coincided with my decision to establish my PR business, Drury Communications, in 1989. Kevin Moran contacted me on behalf of the Irish football squad that was on the point of qualifying for the 1990 World Cup Finals. Kevin had been ahead of me in UCD from which he'd become a key member of the legendary Dublin Gaelic football side of the 1970s before joining Manchester United. I had played football with one of his siblings but the timing of his approach, just as I was in the throes of establishing my own business, made me resistant to even consider the idea.

My lack of interest seemed only to convince Kevin that I was the right person to manage the squad's commercial interests. They were different times. Top players earned well but nothing like the levels now, so there was real value for them in generating additional off-field income, even as part of a squad initiative. While I was a sports-lover, I wasn't minded to take on the challenge so I declined. A few weeks later Kevin contacted me to ask if I would reconsider, as another member of the player's committee, Liam Brady, would like to discuss it with me 'over a pint'. Kevin was a star but Liam was mega and I fell for it. Jersey-toucher!

Today it would qualify as entrapment. Football was my thing and Liam Brady was a football deity. We met on a Monday evening and, two pints later, I had not only pretty much committed to managing the players commercial interests for the anticipated 1990 World Cup Finals in Italy but also to manage Liam's testimonial. Quite how or why I don't know but we immediately struck up a trust and so started my involvement in the murky world of professional football and a lasting friendship with Liam.

• • •

Billy Murphy, whom I had so recently persuaded to leave what was then Ireland's premier PR firm, Murray Consultants, to join Drury Communications, was initially nonplussed. Murrays was largely a corporate 'house' but Billy had a number of the less interesting consumer accounts. I had in part persuaded him to join me by saying we would focus exclusively on corporate work. We'd agreed not to do consumer PR for fear it would dilute the seriousness of the corporate 'pitch' and now I wanted to bolt on football!

Billy shared my interest in most sports but I suspect in that moment he wondered about the wisdom of his decision to leave the sanctuary of Murrays to join his friend's questionable new enterprise. Billy had more to lose; he'd made the commitment to join me in the knowledge that I knew about as much about public relations as he did about nuclear physics. Ultimately though, we were young men who believed that if our business venture didn't work out, I'd be able to return to journalism and he would find sanctuary in another PR company.

Ten years later it was Billy Murphy who led the MBO that bought me out of Drury Communications, becoming its CEO and later its chairman, always guiding the business expertly into what is now its fourth decade of success. There isn't a more trusted and respected communications adviser in Ireland but, it's a little known fact that, in the early years of the sports company, he more than 'dabbled' in it. In truth he had little choice as we ran the two things in parallel so we had to switch from preparing a plc board for an angst-laden AGM to presenting to some FMCG brand on the value of sponsoring the Irish football team.

Billy's accomplishments in corporate public relations are immense but when he wants to regale an audience with tales of notable exploits, he's as likely to recall his involvement in some episode from the earliest stages of the sports business. My favourite is his, doubtless exaggerated, account of negotiating the terms of Tony Cascarino's transfer to Aston Villa in the home of the then Villa chairman, the notorious, 'Deadly Doug' Ellis.

In that first period I was responsible for what was known as the *Players' Pool* reporting to a four-man committee of senior players Kevin Moran, Liam Brady, Ray Houghton and Frank Stapleton. The 1990 World Cup in Italy was Ireland's first appearance at the finals and, while we made excellent money for the players and profited the business too, at the very start of our work things nearly came unstuck. Our endeavours were met with a fierce response from the FAI's principal sponsor, Opel (General Motors) but our management of it broke new ground for professional athletes in Ireland. It didn't do us any harm either, we worked with the squad again in 1994 for the US World Cup.

The Football Association had an existing sponsorship agreement with Opel, the management of which had irritated the squad during the 1988 European Championships in Germany. We saw no reason why players should be obliged to do promotional work for Opel. The players had no contract of employment with the FAI and received no financial gain for promoting Opel or any sponsor of the association. Their playing contracts with clubs could oblige them to promote the club sponsors but not, I believed, a national association which had no contract with its players and simply paid them a match fee. The first recommendation we made to the players' committee was to challenge this and the committee readily agreed.

It seemed to me that, irrespective of what the Opel sponsorship agreement said, the FAI could not bind players to perform promotional duties for its sponsors. They were not its employees. Confident of what we could achieve, sensing it was a special group of men, we decided that we should press ahead with an ambitious plan to put their interests at the heart of a sponsorship platform in opposition to the association-centred model. Drury Sports

Management was the first sports management agency in Ireland, so such areas of tension and at times conflict were inevitable.

We were sure Opel would challenge anything we might do that could undermine its sponsorship and we were hoping it might, in the process, be clumsy enough to give our initiative some profile and commercial impetus. Equally, we had to have our alternative plan thought through; we needed a business that would become the lead sponsor of the players, just as Opel was the primary sponsor of the FAI. We needed a brand we could rely on to fight the probable response of Opel and/or the FAI.

The Irish Permanent Building Society (a forerunner of ILP) was the standout candidate. It had deep pockets, its Marketing Director, Enda Hogan had an appetite for high profile sponsorship and the courage to take on perceived sacred cows. It had an extensive mortgage business and a national branch network, meaning it could derive real value from a relationship with the squad. I was certain Opel's contract would have left them exposed, for as the FAI had no contracts of employment with the players, it would have been virtually impossible for the association to bind them contractually to its sponsors. While my friend and former coach, Tony O'Neill, was then FAI General Secretary, I resisted the temptation to ask him but my instinct was that we were on solid ground.

We put a detailed sponsorship plan and budget together for the Irish Permanent that was approved by the players' committee. The company signed it and we went into planning mode in the full knowledge of what was likely to unfold. We targeted the final qualifying match against Northern Ireland in Dublin as the evening when we would launch the sponsorship and through it announce to the Irish public, the establishment of the *Players' Pool*.

A critical piece of this was to develop a separate brand identity for the *Players' Pool* so we could offer it as part of the marketing inventory to sponsors and licence products without recourse to the FAI logo. Only Billy Murphy and I, the squad members and senior people in the Irish Permanent knew what was afoot. In April 1989, Ireland beat Spain 1-0 at Lansdowne Road in Dublin, taking the decisive step to qualification for the following year's World Cup Finals but it was the following October that a home victory over

Northern Ireland confirmed the outcome. That evening as fans left the stadium, they were met at each main junction with giant 48 sheet posters of the squad wearing green t-shirts with the Irish Permanent emblazoned across them. The top of the posters read 'Irish Permanent – Proud Sponsors of the Irish Footballers' with the newly developed *Players' Pool* logo neatly positioned on one side.

We went for a few pints. On a night of high achievement and excitement for Irish sport, acting on the players' behalf, we had launched a scud missile into the FAI's commercial turf. It had detonated, people coming into the pub were talking about the 48-sheet posters and we knew that just down the road, in the stadium, the FAI and Opel would be consulting over the strange marketing campaign that appeared to have the imprimatur of the Irish squad. I wondered what poor Tony O'Neill would make of it all – apart from the undoubted irritation of having his post-match pints interrupted by the inevitability of Opel CEO, Arnold O'Byrne in his ear, demanding to know what he was going to do.

I also suspected that Tony would, privately, be laughing at the audacity of it and particularly at how we'd managed to 'blindside' all the key stakeholders, including him. That was to be the theme of the next 24 hours, how we'd managed to get a squad photograph in that formal way promotional shots are taken for sponsors, but with them wearing Irish Permanent branded T-shirts without anyone knowing about it? Well, almost no one!

The photo had been taken right under the FAI's noses at the end of a training session weeks previously. The great Charlie O'Leary, long-time bagman for the team and Mick Byrne, the team physio and general confidant of many players had been included in the *Players' Pool* and had been briefed to commandeer Jack Charlton and his assistant Maurice Setters at the end of a session, while we quickly distributed the T-shirts before a well-known sports photographer organised and took the photo.

Billy Murphy and the Irish Permanent's Marketing Manager, Philip Murray, replaced the missing John Byrne and David Kelly whose heads were then 'photo-shopped' onto the lads' torsos, though the fact that this was at least a dozen years before 'photo-shopping' meant even a cursory look at the 48 sheet posters revealed the production sleight of hand. Getting the photo done that day took about 15 minutes but the impact of that one shot and the use we made of it were profound. Our decision to establish the *Players' Pool* as a legal entity and its initial sponsorship by the Irish Permanent had driven the proverbial coach and four through the presumed entitlement of a national association to contract players to its sponsors.

When Tony O'Neill and I talked about it the next day, he was his usual droll self, blaming me, exactly as I'd expected, for having destroyed his post-match libation and wondering, momentarily, how the hell we'd taken the photo before quickly saying that, actually, 'he'd much rather not know'. It was no surprise to learn that Opel had gone apoplectic and he thought it would end up in court. That was as we'd expected. The smart thing for Opel to have done would have been to ignore it but, as large organisations and institutions often do, they over-reacted, in the process giving oxygen to the guerrilla tactics of the Irish Permanent.

It was a case-study in how not to handle such a scenario. In the moment of corporate *hubris*, the aggrieved party often forgets who they are and how little people care about their 'problem'. It was to prove a textbook over-reaction by a management that treated what could have been a good sparring session like it was a world title bout. That's exactly how Opel behaved with the result that it drew huge public attention to the player cause – and more sponsors to the *Players' Pool*.

When we found ourselves facing a legal battle with Opel in the High Court, the determination and single mindedness of this group of footballers became apparent. Opel tried to go after my business, in the hope that the players might want to avoid the hassle of a case or that some of them might break ranks but, when legal counsel advised that we would need to demonstrate just how united the players were, Frank Stapleton took responsibility for making sure every member of the squad had signed an affidavit within days. That was no easy feat with a squad of players scattered across the UK but it was done. We were not going to be left exposed – the players stood behind us and when it came to the court date, members of the players' committee rode into town!

The matter was settled by counsel. Opel later attempted to argue that it had 'won', but by what measure they reached that conclusion was hard to fathom. The settlement meant the *Players' Pool* continued with absolutely no restrictions; the Irish Permanent deal was completely unaffected and we continued to build a portfolio of commercial interests that worked with the players with no connection or recourse to the FAI. The extensive publicity around the case lifted public awareness of how the international players were organised to work as a unit and gave the *Players' Pool* extensive brand exposure. New sponsors came seeking us out. Over the six years covering the 1990 and 1994 World Cups, the *Players' Pool* used its own logo, engaged with the Irish Permanent exactly as per its original contract and recruited more sponsors, some attracted on foot of the publicity surrounding the case that Opel had taken.

The acknowledgement of the players' entitlement to contract independently established legal precedent. The Irish Permanent deal had established that right and led to significant change in how the association would contract in the future with its primary sponsors. From that point forward, no commitments were entered into with sponsors that involved players without clauses requiring any involvement of the players to be explicitly agreed in advance. Today, part of player remuneration by the association incorporates a controlled use of the squad and individual players by its main sponsors.

The Irish Permanent built a strong association through its relationship with Irish football over those years without any engagement with the FAI. This demonstrated powerfully that in sport value is centred on the key assets which is generally the athletes rather than the federation or association that governs them. Without athletes bound in, as Opel's contract could have done, the aspired brand benefit is hard to achieve. Opel continued to support the FAI but, going forward, it had certain player benefits included contractually, and those revenues now came to the *Players' Pool*, managed by Drury Sports Management. Throughout the 1990s independent market research showed huge public awareness of the Irish Permanent as a sponsor of Irish football.

There was another interesting difference in the approach of

the two corporates. The CEO of Opel, Arnold O'Byrne, always personalised the company's investment in Irish football and he broke a golden rule of effective sponsorship by not keeping the correct distance between the sponsor and the athletes. Mr. O'Byrne failed to appreciate that providing financial support didn't entitle you to blend into the squad. It seemed that, short of training or matches, wherever the players were gathered, he was there too.

In 1990, Charlie Haughey as Taoiseach, had been a national laughing-stock when he did a lap of the Olympic Stadium in Rome after our World Cup Quarter Final defeat to Italy. He had form in this regard, having joined Tour de France winner, Stephen Roche, on the Champs-Élysées in 1987. Mr. O'Byrne suffered from the same malady. In contrast, the senior executives of the Irish Permanent and other *Players' Pool* sponsors met with the players quietly, away from the limelight, knowing that sponsorship is a transaction that offers no entitlement to be part of public acknowledgement of success.

'Jersey touching' was prevalent then, the FAI's commercial director during those glory years always had multiple photos of himself in every match programme; it was perhaps a portent of what was to come with more serious repercussions for Irish football. When the FAI fell under the leadership of John Delaney it had a CEO who was so self-absorbed that he considered himself as important as the players.

● ● ●

John Delaney wasn't known outside football when he assumed leadership of the FAI in 2005. My dealings with him prior to his appointment were enough for me to know that a large part of his ambition was as much about raising his profile as it was the welfare of the sport. Even in his early honorary roles he'd craved public attention, something that should have disqualified him as CEO but that's not how Irish sport was governed then.

We first had contact when I worked on the re-negotiation of the Eircom sponsorship and I thought him unremarkable until, at the time of the appointment of Fran Rooney as CEO, we had a discussion which suggested a high level of calculation and personal ambition. I believed he influenced the choice of Rooney suspecting that it would fail, which would allow him to prepare his own status so he could move into the role. It's exactly what happened, Delaney moved from Honorary Treasurer to acting CEO knowing he could manoeuvre himself into the position on a full-time basis. I saw his scheming then but came to see his capacity for maliciousness over time. There were efforts to undermine the legitimate interests of my sports management business but, more importantly, he set about trying to crush the careers of two hugely important figures in Irish football, men who were clients and are friends.

Brian Kerr is an unusual man in professional football; he's well-read and has opinions on lots of things which he isn't slow to offer. In the early years of the sports management business I hardly knew him. On the few occasions we'd met I liked him, his bubbly infectious manner and his forthrightness. Our professional relationship came after his success with the Irish under-age teams, a success that remains standout, not just in Ireland. Few associations, including our neighbours in England, have achieved what our youth teams did under Brian.

We were bronze medallists at the 1997 World Youth Championships and in 1998 Ireland won the European Championships at both Under-16 and Under-18 level. In 1999, we again qualified for the World Youth Championships and were knocked out on penalties by the eventual winners, Nigeria. Brian Kerr guided us to the Finals again in 2003, before being appointed manager of the senior team. The achievements had been noted by other, larger, more powerful football nations that wondered how Ireland was now consistently sitting with them at the top table? There were some exceptional young players but not enough to explain the phenomenon, especially as it was sustained for almost a decade.

It was around then that Brian Kerr asked me to represent him. What was more remarkable was that he was achieving success with the youth teams while he was Technical Director of the FAI, where he was thinking about and planning the long-term development of the sport in Ireland. Brian was doing two jobs excellently at once but his efforts represented, even then, a silo of excellence in a centre of mediocrity. In spite of the remarkable things he was doing, there had never been any discussions about the value he could contribute to the overall welfare of Irish football.

The majority of our football legislators were then, as they are to this day, men (unfortunately, almost exclusively so) most of whom have a classically narrow perspective around the game and their importance to it. They served on committees to protect their club or their league's interests and, in many cases, their own personal benefits. John Delaney used a form of old style parochialism to better protect the powerbase of the CEO and those closest to him. This culture of cliquish comradeship was the corrosive source that allowed the organisation to rot from the inside out, resulting in its effective demise 15 years after he'd been appointed CEO in 2004. John Delaney was far from the reformist he claimed to be, he was a protectionist who believed power had an inestimable value; his mission was to build his own base and protect it at all costs.

Brian Kerr was appointed manager of the senior international team before Delaney took over as CEO, but the day Brian was appointed, he rang me to warn that his support for the appointment was heavily conditional. It wasn't so much that his teeth were gritted, they were padlocked shut. The message was clear; he believed the FAI should have appointed someone of international stature but while he was underwhelmed by the outcome, he would support it, for now! Even clearer was the sense that Brian would have to perform miracles to hold on to his position because John Delaney wouldn't give him anything like the same latitude others before him had enjoyed or, as we were to discover, those who were to follow.

So it proved; after one and a half unsuccessful campaigns, Brian was despatched; thrown out to fend for himself having worked full-time with the association since 1996. I protested at this treatment of someone who had done so much for the game, but Delaney boasted that not only would there be no role for Brian, that there would be no compensation either. With his trademark arrogance he said Brian would receive nothing as he wasn't terminating his contract but choosing not to exercise the option on an extension.

A few weeks later, my arguments well prepared, I met him and set out where this would go if he didn't change his stance. Within an hour I'd agreed a reasonable settlement for Brian on condition that no one was to know of it, early evidence of Delaney's penchant for smoke and mirrors. Internally, the message was that Brian Kerr had been removed at no cost to the FAI, so while he was agreeing a sizeable enough settlement, it was essential to his standing, that this would not be known. It represented how he would use FAI resources to attempt to side-line and silence those, like Brian, with a public standing and a voice that he feared could damage his interests.

That the Kerr era didn't last was, in part, down to that old managerial cocktail of some questionable decision-making, what some believed was a tendency towards tactical conservatism, and just rank bad luck. Brian contributed to some of the negativity as his relationship with the football media showed signs of strain. This was to an extent orchestrated by elements in the FAI that built a sense of negativity around their own manager; some were actively briefing against him in a display of corporate self-harming. I couldn't seem to manage Brian's media profile constructively. My distaste for what was going on was so acute I couldn't provide the calm, considered management Brian needed.

At one point I tried to address the problem but succeeded only in making things worse. It was autumn 2005, with Brian's position perilous as the media campaign against him was turning many of the football public against him. I went on evening radio with Matt Cooper who is knowledgeable about football. I made the case for Brian but, in the midst of the interview, I referred to the squad as being 'not the most talented' we'd ever had. It was a schoolboy error and within an hour I was fielding calls from reporters who wanted to know why I'd chosen to criticise the squad. The FAI had gone into overdrive about how Brian Kerr's agent had chosen to attack Ireland's international players.

We were at a war of sorts so the tactic was legitimate, no matter how disingenuous it was to have taken one sentence out of context and presented it as though the manager's 'man' was attempting to push the critique from him onto his players. I was embarrassed but also furious with myself. No one was interested in reviewing the full interview or in acknowledging that, however clumsy it may have been, what I'd said was still correct. That was 2005 and a further 15 years on, no Irish squad, other than that Mick McCarthy led to the

2002 World Cup, has even come close to the quality Jack Charlton managed between 1988 and 1994.

The undermining of Brian Kerr's position was relentless and began to grind him down. We'd become close but I couldn't seem to help him deal with the sense he had of being slowly suffocated. I should have done a better job of protecting him. I had got to the point where you become useless as an adviser, I was feeling his angst and upset. I was empathising with him rather than challenging him to get beyond it and even his great friends Noel O'Reilly and Gerry Smith were finding it difficult to get him to temper his anger at what he saw as the unfairness of it all. The inner-sanctum voice that always preached calm was Chris Hughton, measured and sensible, but as he wasn't living in the 'hood' like the rest of us he appreciated that it was difficult to understand the depth of malevolence involved.

Brian Kerr was dumped because John Delaney wanted box office. When he assumed power in December 2004, he'd have wanted Pierce Brosnan to be the manager, but the man in charge was more Brendan Gleeson. Short of his bringing the squad to heights only one Irish squad had achieved, Brian's position was under threat from the moment he was appointed. Paranoia is an unhealthy state, but when Brian Kerr sensed the FAI closing in on him he wasn't imagining it. I was there; you could smell it, as some key executives and high-ranking committee men disgraced themselves in their rush to win the praise and gratitude of Delaney. There are few more stark examples of a CEO discarding valuable intellectual capital, of wilfully casting aside one of the organisation's greatest assets than when Brian Kerr was ushered out of Irish football in October 2005.

Brian's treatment by his employers was shocking on a number of levels. It could be argued that, at senior level, his teams failed to produce consistently and in some critical matches had become overly defensive of early leads with, as a result, games that should have been won being drawn, but the line between success and failure at international level is even finer than in the club game.

Brian's problem was the determination with which John Delaney set out to undermine him perhaps most evident in his actions just as Ireland was preparing for a crucial competitive match. The CEO claimed that Brian had threatened the integrity of the association's contract with its principal sponsor, Eircom. The board was told that Eircom was extremely angry over a serious breach of the sponsorship agreement which Delaney said represented a failure by Brian to respect the needs and entitlements of the sponsor. The truth was very different.

In the week before Ireland played a crucial, 'must-win' World Cup qualifying match against France in September 2005, Brian had attended a photo shoot for the sports charity GOAL to mark its annual sports jersey day. The match with France was days away so he could have done without having to attend but he'd long supported GOAL. For this reason he made time to attend. Brian's aversion to wearing English club shirts was well known so the organiser handed him a St Patrick's Athletic jersey. The next day when the photograph appeared in the papers, the problem emerged. St. Pat's had a new sponsor whose brand was on the front of the shirt. It was a telecoms company which, given that the FAI's principal sponsor was Eircom, was slightly embarrassing, but nothing more than that; an unintentional error made in a good cause which could have been dealt with as such.

That's not how John Delaney saw it. The CEO and his acolytes swooped on it. I was contacted to say the FAI sponsor, Eircom, was furious that Brian had brought the commercial agreement into disrepute and that there could be serious consequences, including the risk to the sponsorship itself. I was immediately suspicious. I had been a senior member of the advisory team to Tony O'Reilly's Valentia consortium that won a lengthy takeover battle for control of Eircom in 2001, so my relationship with the FAI sponsor was anything but standard. I soon discovered that the FAI's presentation of the facts was groundless.

Eircom's Head of Retail, Cathal Magee, told me they fully understood the circumstances and had expressed immediate support for Brian whom Eircom loved having as the team's manager. Unaware that I knew the true position, John Delaney had a letter couriered to Brian in which he set out alleged concerns of its main sponsor and sought an explanation by return. Given that the manager was preparing his team for a crucial world cup qualifying match against France days later, it showed the lengths the FAI's CEO would go to in order to damage him.

In a move that was more deliberately undermining of his country's interests than Thierry Henry's handball in Paris four years later, the CEO behaved in a manner that was harmful to our prospects of qualifying for the World Cup Finals. Delaney had placed a noose around Brian's neck and was about to kick open the trap door. Professional football is, as the cliché says, a results business so, not qualifying for the World Cup Finals had left him exposed; with a supportive CEO, the option for an extension could well have been activated, the atmosphere of the previous 18 months wouldn't have been so negative and there might, then, have been a very different outcome.

• • •

Many of the bigger decisions John Delaney took as CEO of the FAI were led by self-interest and self-protection. The welfare of the game was secondary. Delaney's governance of football was rooted in a dated model of his father's time, where supplicant members and club representatives across the committee structure, were given office to protect and insulate him. It worked brilliantly and allowed him to hold power, absent of any real scrutiny for 15 years. The consequences of what prevailed will take that length of time to correct, maybe longer.

Irish football has been grossly mis-managed. Its finances are precarious since the construction of the Aviva stadium, the domestic game has been allowed to wither over a period of expansion across almost every other sport. We have stuttered through two European qualifiers, despite UEFA making it more difficult not to get to Finals than to qualify and we haven't reached a World Cup Finals or had any success at under-age levels over all that time. In spite of this, John Delaney's contract was extended regularly by a compliant board.

The unconscionable salary, the perks and the enormous ego might all have been overlooked, if everywhere you saw a game that was thriving, you saw innovation, some success but, unlike football associations in other, including less economically advantaged countries, and, unlike the GAA at home, none of this was evident during the Delaney era.

One of John Delaney's great skills was how he claimed anything successful had been his inspiration but everything that went wrong was the fault of others. There were plenty of examples but the best known was how he claimed Stephen Staunton was his inspired selection as Ireland manager in 2005 but then, when it turned out to be the disaster everyone had feared, he acted as though he hadn't anything to do with his selection. There are other similar tales but there's little doubt that his greatest feat of conjuring was how he managed to distance himself from Pat Hickey when the OCI Chief was incarcerated in Brazil. Until the moment of his arrest, John Delaney told anyone who would listen how friendly he and Pat Hickey were but when the OCI chief got embroiled in a controversy that was to end his career, John Delaney chose to walk away, protesting that the relationship had, in fact, never been that close. The Abbotstown cock could be heard crowing its head off!

• • •

Packie Bonner and I have been friends since his playing career ended. I'd been his agent for most of his time with Celtic and my company Platinum One had managed his testimonial. As happened with some of those I've represented in sport, the relationship gradually and naturally changed from client to friend.

In December 2010 he rang me and said he needed to meet urgently as John Delaney had told him his contract as Technical Director would not be renewed and the FAI was letting him go. Packie had an illustrious career for Ireland, earning 80 caps and he had succeeded Brian Kerr in the position of Technical Director. Towards the end of his club career, Packie had studied business and he was capable across a range of metrics, all of which helped him further develop Brian's considerable work on a long-term Technical Plan for the FAI. The two men were close; Brian wanted to continue to assist the work of the Technical Department and Packie welcomed his support.

Packie Bonner believed his playing career should be of little relevance to his position within the FAI, that he had to demonstrate a capacity to do the job, working hard to prove himself, perhaps to excess on occasion. There was no doubting his focus on improving the work of the association at all levels, but the harder he worked the more he exposed failings elsewhere. I had long warned him that the more often I heard people talk about him as being a CEO-in-waiting or, worse, as someone who aspired to the position, the more at risk he would be.

We met within an hour. When he explained the nature of the discussion with John Delaney I knew it had gone beyond a point where I could help, so I called Donal Spring, a former Irish international rugby player who is an even more effective and rougher opponent on matters of employment law than he'd been at the end of the line out. It was some weeks later that a settlement was reached – one Delaney, true to form, had said at the outset would never be forthcoming – and Packie's departure from the FAI was confirmed.

The association's loss of Packie meant, as had been the case with Brian Kerr, that more intellectual capital was lost to the development of the sport. The emergence and cultivation of talent is dependent on technical knowledge something Packie Bonner and Brian Kerr had in abundance. It is sad that these two men, who wanted nothing more than to contribute to the development of Irish football, were effectively frog marched from the building by a CEO who saw them as a threat to his sphere of influence. There was hardly a whisper of discontent from any of the keepers of the flame within the FAI or from those of influence externally.

The media knew the true narrative. Politicians, the agencies of the state all knew this was another case of Delaney clearing the FAI of any possible opposition. There was silence. Virtually no one spoke out. Unfortunately, as a result of what Donal Spring managed to achieve, nor could Packie Bonner. When even someone of Packie's stature could be neutered, it's easy to see how many hard-working football people, and there were quite a number, with no national profile had been unceremoniously removed for showing anything approaching disloyalty to the FAI supremo.

• • •

When the FAI replaced Brian Kerr as Manager, John Delaney personally chose to back one of our best-ever defenders but a managerial neophyte, Steve Staunton, to improve matters. He was to be supported in a consultancy role by England's Bobby Robson but this didn't proceed because Robson became seriously ill. The appointment of Staunton was bewildering. I knew him well, he had been a client of mine; a decent person and a wonderful footballer, but he had no relevant experience. It was a truly bizarre, a complete managerial rookie was chosen to replace someone who'd just gained experience at senior level to augment his decade of success with the under-age teams.

The decision to appoint Staunton was akin to turning your back to the dartboard before, blindfolded, throwing your only dart over your shoulder and still hoping for a bullseye. Even then, the FAI was Delaney's personal playroom and, if that's how he chose to play darts, there was no other child brave enough to challenge him. Steve Staunton's reign lasted just under two years and with standard chameleon quality, when it ended in tears, the FAI CEO denied that it had been his choice.

Then, in February 2008, the FAI announced its new manager would be the legendary, if ageing, Giovanni Trapattoni. While knowledgeable commentators wondered about the conservative tactics of Trapattoni's teams there was widespread recognition of his experience and reasonable record of success. In fact he'd have been the type of appointment that would have made the replacement of Brian Kerr more credible but, with Trapattoni, the real story wasn't the timing of the appointment but how it was funded.

John Delaney revealed that Denis O'Brien, the Irish businessman, had offered to support Irish football by providing funding to allow the FAI to recruit the long-promised management team of 'international calibre'. Delaney told Denis O'Brien's radio station, Newstalk, in March 2018 that he believed O'Brien's millions were an *extraordinary contribution*. They were indeed but the fundamental question is about national sporting organisations being funded by private individuals and, most especially, how any such investment is used. This is not about Denis O'Brien being prepared to offer funds to the FAI but how that money was to be used. Why did the FAI consider it right that a private individual would fund the salaries of some of its most senior staff? Why did UEFA or indeed the government not question this?

In a small country with limited resources, the funding by private interests of different sports should be welcome but only provided it's focused on capital projects or community welfare initiatives which the relevant federation cannot afford. Philanthropy that contributes to necessary infrastructure or innovative non-core programmes to help develop the sport has an important place but the release of public funding to large sports bodies should be predicated on the federation being able to cover its own general overhead. Otherwise there's a risk that, however well-intentioned, private sector support of payroll costs could help to camouflage significant gaps in the business model or to obscure serious financial neglect.

As a member of FIFA, the FAI has a wide range of obligations, one of which is to field a senior team in international competition; to do that effectively it needs to employ a qualified management team. It is an absolutely basic requirement of its business. That it manifestly couldn't do so without the support of a wealthy benefactor signalled the FAI was financially troubled. However, the transmission of that distress signal wasn't clear, in part because, courtesy of Denis O'Brien's generosity, the association could afford to bankroll a high profile and expensive senior management team.

• • •

While most of Platinum One's work in football was in player representation, in the mid-2000s my colleague, Eamon McLoughlin, pressed me to widen our role within the sport. It was both sensible and timely and was to lead to some of the more challenging and exciting work we did. It also gave us further insights into the mindset of the leadership of the FAI. To say that it was hostile towards us would be something of an understatement.

In 2007 we were awarded a contract to manage the pre-season training camp for FC Barcelona. The mechanics show this work isn't for the fainthearted. To secure Barca's agreement we had to display not just a competence to provide what it needed but we had to pay a massive upfront fee plus cover the costs involved in preparing a training set-up that would meet the requirements of one of the giants of European football.

The facility was the hotel on the Old Course at St Andrews, Scotland which sat across the road from pitches in St. Andrew's University. Top clubs needed everything on the one site so players can walk to and from training. The training pitches were not of the right standard so, to make the plan feasible, we had to pay for them to be significantly up-graded, with the university granting us exclusive rights each summer for three years.

We had acquired a small Edinburgh-based sports management business owned by former Scottish and British & Irish Lions legends Gavin and Scott Hastings. This meant we had a core team *in situ* that allowed Eamon to drive the project from Dublin. The contract with FC Barcelona granted us two friendly fixtures to generate revenues that would, we hoped, cover our costs and, all going well, see us return a profit. The two matches were against Dundee United at Tannadice which had a small capacity of 14,000 and the principal game against Hearts which, in order to have any hope of making a return on our investment, meant staging it at Murrayfield, the home of Scottish rugby.

The first match at Tannadice was remarkable for a number of reasons, most notably that in the second half, Barca manager, Frank Rijkaard gave a debut to Thierry Henry. The French striker scored in the 90th minute to win the game which meant that he both made his debut and scored his first Barcelona goal in a match promoted by Platinum One. This was a nice little coup for us but one that would be surpassed in Dublin a couple of years later.

The second match that summer saw the largest crowd ever to attend a football match in Scotland's capital city, Edinburgh. More than 57,000 fans saw, on this occasion, two of the goals being scored by another, more established, Barcelona star, Ronaldinho. The huge turnout meant the Scottish Rugby Union earned a large payday in midsummer and, despite the less than advantageous terms, Platinum One, as promoter, made a return on its investment. The case Eamon McLoughlin had made for this move into football appeared to be borne out but, unfortunately, we had overstretched on our ambition.

The following summer, 2008, with Pep Guardiola in charge of Barcelona, we were again appointed and brought the club back to St. Andrews. We had factored in the likelihood of a significant reduction in the number of fans and our financial exposure with Barcelona was more modest so, while we didn't make a profit, nor did we lose money on the 2008 version of what had been so successful the previous year. Eamon and I were now focused on trying to replicate the idea in Ireland.

In 2009 we contracted Real Madrid to undertake a ten-day training camp at Carton House in Co. Kildare. Again, as with Barcelona in 2007, we had to agree terms with Madrid that were financially demanding, especially when we learned that the one friendly match which was part of our contract, would not be sanctioned for the Aviva stadium in south Dublin. The finances were challenging but our experience with Barcelona in Edinburgh and a packed Murrayfield meant we pushed forward with Madrid in the belief that we could make it happen.

In part the motivation was to replicate in Dublin what we had done in the Scottish capital. Eamon and I were determined to bring the world's most famous football club to our hometown. The FAI owned the Aviva Stadium with the IRFU and, as financing its half of the loan repayments was already problematic, we thought the prospect of a sizeable payday from our proposed match with Real Madrid would appeal. In each of the previous two years we'd paid the Scottish Rugby Union very substantial fees for the use of Murrayfield.

The FAI could have done with the revenue but I was told by stadium management that John Delaney had expressly ruled out any football event promoted by Platinum One being staged at the 50,000 capacity stadium. In explaining this to me there was no attempt to dress it up as anything other than a blanket ban on our having access to the stadium. John Delaney didn't like me or my business and there was no point in appealing the decision. This meant that in bringing the biggest club in the world to Ireland for a ten-day training camp the only way we could replicate what we'd done in Scotland was to host the mighty Real Madrid in a small municipal stadium in Tallaght in west Dublin with a capacity of 6,000.

We were determined not to lose the opportunity. Eamon and I refused to believe it couldn't be made to happen; how often do you get the opportunity to work with a club like Real Madrid? The stubbornness that sometimes got me into commercial difficulties also helped me on occasion. Madrid did ask why we weren't staging the match at the Aviva so we told them and that might have helped in negotiating hard with them a deal that, as with Barcelona's second year in Edinburgh, gave us confidence that we wouldn't lose money. It also helped that by then Real Madrid had visited Carton House and knew it offered the ideal surroundings in which to prepare for the La Liga season.

We just resolved to make it work. With the support of South Dublin County Council we got agreement to double the capacity with an additional 6,000 temporary seats and, with Ticketmaster, we worked out a ticketing model that gave us a chance. We scaled back our financial expectations but, even still, would have to charge €65 a ticket to make even a modest return. It was an extraordinarily high ticket price for a pre-season friendly but, once it was confirmed that Cristiano Ronaldo would be in the Real Madrid squad, the demand was such that we could have sold three times the number of tickets – even at the exorbitant €65. The average ticket price for Hearts v Barca in Edinburgh two years previously had been c.€20.

So it was that, on July 20th, 2009, 11,000 paying fans, many of them wearing Shamrock Rovers shirts, packed into a transformed Tallaght Stadium to see the Galacticos narrowly beat a Rovers team that was, to go on and experience great success, becoming the first Irish club to qualify for the group stages of European competition. The Real Madrid side was packed with some of Europe's greatest players, including the scorer of the only goal that evening, Karem Benzema, who just as Thierry Henry had done with Barcelona in Murrayfield, made his debut and scored his first goal in a Platinum One match.

Benzema has enjoyed a stellar decade with Madrid but he was only the support act that July evening as the star attraction was Cristiano Ronaldo who'd left Manchester United that summer. This sporting phenomenon, one of the game's greatest-ever players, who went on to play 292 matches in a Real Madrid shirt, did so for the first time in this Platinum One promoted pre-season game against Shamrock Rovers. It remains a highlight on the corporate CV. Commercially it worked for us, but only just. The more important consideration was to see how, when different parties critical to making something different, something of real scale, happen for the wider good, they can pull together to defeat the odds.

To make it at all viable, we had to turn Tallaght stadium from a 6,000 seater stadium to almost twice that for one night. This required time and energy from public officials, private interests and from Shamrock Rovers. We had to ensure the safe and secure movement of people and traffic on the night with a shopping centre across the road that had to continue business, almost as usual, all of which meant we were heavily dependent on the local council officials and the Gardaí to ensure it could be a success. The effort from so many different stakeholders was immense, way beyond what could reasonably have been expected, but it was in large part what made the project so memorable.

It was 'full-on' right up to kick off and we had to pull favours from places and people that, consistently we found, wanted only for the event to succeed. Few people were aware of the utter indifference of the Football Association. Eamon and I most certainly were. It became an additional motivation; it made us more determined to succeed so when the odds were beaten, the real pleasure was in achieving an outcome that left all but the most cynical, and certain senior people in the FAI, thrilled by its success.

John Delaney didn't attend the match that he should and could have co-hosted at a packed Aviva Stadium, generating hundreds of thousands in much needed revenue in the process. The problem was that for him to have done so would have meant elevating a business and its owner when he was, in fact, determined to undermine me at every possible turn.

• • •

In 2014, the businessman Denis O'Brien appeared in a video about John Delaney, which was made by the media group that Mr. O'Brien then owned. It was about Delaney's stewardship of Irish football with the gloriously under-stated title, 'John the Baptist'.

In it O'Brien extolled John Delaney's qualities, offering the opinion that Mr. Delaney *could run anything, UEFA, FIFA, any business*. The praise was so fulsome it was hard not to think the real John the Baptist fortunate to have his name associated with that of the FAI boss.

John Delaney's father, Joe, also featured and referenced his son's *great wisdom*. When Joe Delaney held the position of FAI Treasurer during the 1994 World Cup, he'd been involved in ticket-dealing that had gone badly wrong. Joe was trying to access more tickets for Irish fans through a well-known 'scalper' and to his credit, when this fan-centred initiative went awry, he paid IR£110,000 to cover the FAI's shortfall. There was, therefore, a certain irony when more than 20 years later, his son, as CEO, revealed that he'd made a six figure loan to the FAI.

Is it any wonder that back in the mid-1990s writing about that strange saga involving Joe Delaney and the ticket tout, exotically known as 'George the Greek', *Irish Times* journalist Gerry Thornley began his report, *Like a drunk in an alleyway, the FAI lurches from one crisis to another*? It is or should be alarming that for most of the last quarter of a century, the drunken organisation has been allowed to continue on its stumbling way; the havoc wreaked was of such scale that the damage is not limited to any alleyway. Shocking levels of neglect mean Irish football's main arterial routes are weak and dreadfully incapacitated.

It's been painful to watch the disintegration of any semblance of order within the governance of the sport. Across the island, football has the potential to be a hugely positive societal force. It is rich also in the resources of exceptional men and women who want to contribute to its development in just the same way as the GAA, through volunteers and excellent central management, has made its contemporary offer more relevant to more people. Irish rugby has progressed too, just on a smaller scale, and hockey and cricket too gain numbers amid increasing interest.

Interestingly, all those sports are played on an all-island basis, whereas both internationally and with the domestic professional club game, football has two of everything, including decades of largely poor administration. While other sports have grown and developed over recent years, football in Ireland, certainly in the 15 years of John Delany's tenure, has regressed. Seriously so.

The Delaney approach stultified growth and development; his stewardship of Abbottstown was such that it undermined those who showed any hint of independence. The labyrinthine committee structure aided this; the FAI Council was distended, comprising, with some notable exceptions, appointees who fed Delaney's needs with little care for or interest in the nourishment of the sport.

Over time, more committees were populated by more football vagrants to whom the FAI supremo threw scraps in return for propping up his regime. Most, but not all, were harmless but others participated knowingly in the FAI's uniquely twisted version of snakes and ladders where the snakes seemed to ascend the ladders with consummate ease whereas those with something to offer slid helplessly to the bottom.

The administration of football in Ireland has never been strong. My experience, back to my early twenties is that, with few exceptions, there's been a real absence of grown-ups around its governance. The leadership of John Delaney and the warped corporate culture he promoted have been calamitous for the sport. It is an egregious example of how a form of leadership where the primary orientation is about oneself, can devastate the progress of an organisation.

• • •

When Delaney was eventually forced out, the FAI had debts of €55m. The organisational chaos and the huge indebtedness pales in comparison to the collapse of Anglo Irish Bank or the scale of losses of the whole Irish banking sector years earlier but, within its own small theatre, the FAI figures were staggering. Analysed systemically, while the consequences of a failure of leadership in a sports organisation don't compare to the collapse of a country's banking system, there are parallels. The conditions which allowed the abuse of responsibility take hold were similar, a leader on a singular mission centred on the realisation of his own ambition. Everything other than that person's overriding purpose to retain control, informed by a twisted belief that they alone can take the organisation forward, is secondary. Invariably in these situations, a necessary condition is to build a largely unquestioning inner circle that, however unwittingly, can facilitate the process. Thus over time the organisational culture is corroded to facilitate the singular mission that prohibits organisational achievement unless it belongs to him. I know how it's done. As I've said, I have the T-shirt.

XII

Identity Crisis

Jonathan Sexton was doing what he has always done best, training as though he was playing a World Cup Final. It was Friday morning January 25th, 2013, and the Irish squad was preparing for the upcoming Six Nations. The Ireland and Leinster out half's reputation as a trainer is legendary: competitive, argumentative, obstreperous to the point of driving many of his club and international teammates nuts. I've heard some of them complain at the relentlessness of how he strives for perfection in every circumstance. This morning would have been no different except, as he trained, concentrating on every detail, he carried the drumbeat of a brief phone conversation he'd had just before the session had started.

The call had been to the IRFU CEO, Philip Browne, to advise him that he would not be signing the new contract that was on offer but instead would be going to France to join Racing Metro in Paris on a two-year deal from the start of the new season. In typical Sexton fashion, he chose to make the call himself and, while it had been courteous if to-the-point, what had surprised him a little was that there was no apparent push-back or even a request for more time. As he trained that morning this bothered him and all the time he half-expected to be called aside and asked to delay the decision. It was a most unusual case. The call he made to the Union's boss wasn't one last attempt to bounce the IRFU into meeting our demands but, with that crushing honesty of his, when Johnny revealed his hurt at the Union accepting that he was leaving, he left it open to that interpretation.

The previous evening we sat together in a quiet corner of the lounge in Carton House where the camp was based. It was clear the IRFU wouldn't shift its position materially. Racing Metro was looking for an answer to the final offer it had made to secure his services. I had spoken again that afternoon with Leinster coach Joe Schmidt who was doing everything possible to ensure his prized asset wouldn't be lured away. Joe had phoned me to outline those final efforts just as I was preparing to travel from Dublin to meet Johnny but, despite his best efforts, there appeared no willingness within the Union to make an exception. That the Union was being inflexible was neither unusual nor surprising but, in this case, the financial offer of Racing Metro was such that its reluctance was perhaps understandable.

The behaviour of most organisations reflects the outlook of those in charge. The Irish Rugby Football Union remains somewhat 'establishment', so while it has come quite a distance over the decades since professionalism, it isn't enthusiastically pro-player. There are positive features, changes that have served the game well but the governance of the sport can still display a sense of superiority particularly manifest in its upper echelons. Throughout the decade or so that I represented many of its top players, the Union's treatment of them often betrayed a failure to fully appreciate the fundamental of all professional sport, that without the athletes you have nothing.

This was in part the influence of some former internationals who saw themselves as guardians of what they regarded as rugby's glorious past, but more of it was about a not unreasonable fear of the future. Most of those in charge believed rugby had to steer a professional course dramatically different to football and player contracts being negotiated by agents was just one example of the kind of football influence they didn't like.

There was then a reluctance to put the players at the centre of everything. There was a belief that any marked increase in player wages could not be supported by the game's finances whereas, across global sport, there is no proven correlation between the professional athletes being highly paid and those paying them running into financial problems. In most sports it is at the lower levels, where the standard doesn't warrant the remuneration, that the more acute financial problems arise.

The IRFU was in a difficult place. Caught between the draw of the past and the still relatively new and scary demands of professional sport, the result was an unsurprising general failure to be proactive and assertive enough. I had been representing rugby players for over a decade, starting with Shane Horgan, Denis Hickie and Gordon D'Arcy, at a time when rugby was still in its infancy as a professional sport. While this was no longer the case by the time I started to work with Jonathan Sexton, the sport was still grappling with the challenges of professionalism – and not just in Ireland.

When it came to reviewing his playing contract, the IRFU conducted its business as it generally did: slowly! It appeared to have a sense that Johnny wouldn't be going anywhere, based on both his special relationship with Joe Schmidt at Leinster and that his fiancée, Laura, was a schoolteacher in Dublin. These were the principal reasons the Union thought him an unlikely flight risk. There was a certain credence to that assessment but, ultimately, it was a miscalculation, one that imbued the Union with too much confidence that he would stay.

This also played to Johnny's deep sense of being taken for granted, a feeling that had its origins in how slow his career had been to ignite. It was only at the end of the 2009 season, with Argentine, Felipe Contepomi, a permanent fixture at out-half for Leinster, ruled out by injury that, the by then 24-year old Sexton, emerged from central casting. The impact was immediate but despite the success of those next years, his low pay level to that point allowed the IRFU to offer large increases which still left him behind his peers. The couple of years when he was playing All-Ireland League for St. Mary's while his contemporaries were regulars with Leinster and beginning their international careers, had depressed his future earnings and he knew it.

Given the extraordinary deal that was to take him to France, it is moot as to whether tactics around the negotiations would have mattered. What the case highlighted was the flaw in the global structure of rugby union. There is a fault line running through the structures of professional rugby that needs to be addressed if the game is to realise its full potential. Change is essential, and across those territories where the game is most popular, it is imperative that the power over player contracts is vested where the asset value should reside. This is becoming urgent but will remain only an interesting debate, unless all the stakeholders accept the idea of players as tradable assets.

• • •

When the announcement came that Johnny was leaving Leinster, the Union had one obvious fall-guy to target. Once the statement was issued, the word spread that I'd influenced, even pushed, Johnny to go to Racing Metro. It wasn't the first time this clumsy archaic tactic was used but it was insulting to the player. Suggesting that I'd told Irish rugby's star player what to do, simply reinforced the doubts Johnny had then about how he was regarded.

I had just done my job. Starting in late summer 2012, as the contract discussions continued with the Union, I had suggested to the player that we would explore other options. That was agreed. It was early autumn before I had established that a number of French clubs were interested. The Top 14 appealed to Johnny as it should to any player who wants to test himself. I travelled to Racing Metro in Paris twice, first on a recce to review the training facilities, the options for accommodation and to have preliminary discussions with the coaches. I prepared a report for Johnny that we then discussed in his home one evening. We considered every aspect of the possible move other than the financial considerations.

In three decades I've never recommended to any professional athlete that they make a career choice based on finance alone nor have I ever allowed it to be the dominant consideration. My job is to provide a holistic appraisal of the options for the player. At this point, other than having researched market values in France, the discussions I'd had with Jonathan Sexton were exclusively about rugby and living in Paris.

A year earlier I'd been in Paris with Seán O'Brien for discussions with Michael Cheika about Seán moving to Stade Francais. It went well but my overriding concern was that I felt Seán, who loved being able to commute from Dublin to his place of sanctuary in the Tullow countryside, might struggle to adapt to living in Paris. No financial package would allow any professional sportsman or woman perform to the optimum if they're unhappy with where they're living. On the afternoon before we returned home I asked Seán to walk around the neighbourhood on his own for an hour, just so he could absorb some sense of Paris as a place to live.

When the agent does their work properly, attention is paid to the wider environment the player would experience if they moved club. Around the same time that I was managing Johnny Sexton's prospective move, we were working on the potential transfer of a 17-year-old footballer in the UK. The boy was a fantastic prospect from a small city who had a number of London clubs and one top overseas club that wanted to sign him. The big clubs would all have paid him more money and our agency fee would have reflected that, but there was an outlier option, a smaller club not playing in the Premier League but with a phenomenal coaching team. The club was ambitious, had a great record for bringing young players through, and, importantly, it was located in a small city.

The agent must try to match more than just the player with the club, they must think of how the person would settle in the wider environment, especially when the player is young and short of life experience. This player was a quiet, almost introverted, young man who was close to his family so we recommended the smaller, lower-ranked, club. We outlined to him and his parents that, while he would earn less money, he would be more secure and that we believed it would benefit his development. We were confident it was the best option and so it proved. Within a few years he was playing in the FA Premier League where he is now an established, highly-paid, star for a huge club in, as it happens, a big city.

This is a big part of where good advisers earn their keep, any failure to take a rounded approach to include the non-playing considerations, represents a disservice to the client. While Seán O'Brien was understandably attracted to the idea of playing Top 14 under Michael Cheika, I had reservations that he would settle into life in Paris. I guessed Seán had them too but sometimes the player needs to know that it's all right to allow non-sporting or non-financial considerations influence their decision. There is never certainty about these calls but the job is to consider every angle and, in this case, the biggest one was whether living in Paris would be right for him. While he had to examine the rugby dimension, I needed him to consider Stade Francais in that broader context.

I knew Seán quite well so, in getting him to consider life in Paris, I was pretty sure of the answer and certainly, if my instincts were correct, it meant there was little chance that Stade Francais could be right for him, irrespective of rugby or financial considerations. Johnny Sexton was different. He was 27, he and Laura were getting married in the summer before any move, and they both thought living in Paris would be exciting. There were other non-French players at the club some of whom he knew. That would help make the transition easier.

My second visit to Racing Metro was in late December 2012 and this time Johnny travelled too. It was largely about meeting the coaches and directly hearing their outlook for the club over the two-year term that was under consideration. That meeting went well and, in the evening, we went to the home of the owner, Jacky Lorenzetti, for dinner. He is an interesting man, quite warm but, even in a social context, business-like in his demeanour, so there seemed an easy mutual respect between the two principals from when they first met. They were both high-achievers, focused, highly motivated men. Kindred spirits of sorts, over dinner they seemed to establish a good personal relationship.

Johnny left first thing the next morning. I stayed in order to conduct the final negotiations with Jacky Lorenzetti. This was unusual. It would rarely happen in football that you'd be dealing with the owner of the club but I liked it because he was business-like and we were able to move things quickly towards a conclusion. The final thing – at least it's the last thing that agents should discuss in negotiations – is their own remuneration, and so when I'd everything sorted for Johnny, I told Mr. Lorenzetti what agency fee I expected.

There was silence for a few moments before he said he thought it was 'high', which meant that it wasn't, so when I finished my defence, he sighed and said, *bloody English agents*. I looked at him, said nothing but, in a slow, deliberate manner, got up from the table and went to my coat. I was silent as I rummaged in my pocket to find my passport which I then threw on the table in front of him and, in mock rage, said *bloody French; Je suis Irlandais!* As I retook my seat, he got up and in silence went over to his desk, opened a few drawers before coming back to the table, throwing his passport in front of me saying *et moi? Je suis Suisse!* We laughed, he agreed to my 'ask' and we shook hands, which meant I was flying back to Dublin in the knowledge that Ireland's most prized rugby union player had an exceptional offer to play in France which would leave him with a big decision to make.

The offer reportedly made Johnny Sexton the world's highest paid player – quite how anyone could be certain is beyond me – but, as it stood, it certainly put him among the most highly paid players in world rugby. The IRFU's position seemed set. There was no openness to amending its position or working with me to find a solution. Once I had finalised Racing Metro's offer it meant the choreography had changed, the only deal for him to stay would mean Johnny accepting considerably less than what was on offer in France. That was a real prospect but the movement the Union had made already proved to be its upper limit. To compromise is not something organisations flushed with their own importance find easy, but when that is as much a façade to cover an institutional insecurity, it makes a resolution even less likely and so things drifted as the Union continued to believe its best player would not leave.

That was the backdrop to my sitting in Carton House with Johnny that evening in late January. This was the moment where the starkness of a choice that he'd never really thought he'd face had fully crystallised. The Racing offer was hugely attractive on a range of levels and he felt genuine excitement at playing in France. Still, he loved Leinster and particularly loved playing under Joe Schmidt so, however it panned out, he couldn't lose. Only the very top players find themselves in such an enviable position.

That evening I again reprised the essentials with him. It was a huge club in the Top 14. It was Paris. Joe Schmidt would likely become the Ireland coach which meant he could be playing club rugby in France but still working with him at international level. Any idea that he would be 'blackballed' by Ireland for moving overseas was laughable; that was a matter of principle for the Union only provided the player in question wasn't your most important player. Separately we'd talked about the opportunity to learn French and I had suggested that playing a number of years in the Top 14 would be a big positive if he at all aspired to working as a coach when his playing career was over.

That evening, as we sat in Carton, the detailed assessment was already done. Joe Schmidt was doing his best to magic up a solution but I knew that, while Johnny was excited at the prospect of France, he was still hoping for the Union to change its stance. Most great athletes retain an element of romanticism throughout their careers; they're always dreaming great things and, for all his toughness, Johnny Sexton is no different. Moving to France would be an adventure, a challenge on and off the pitch, but further glory with Leinster and Ireland trumped everything; the prospect of doing it with Joe Schmidt meant he was still disposed to an improved IRFU offer.

I offered to call the Union the next morning but Johnny said he'd rather call its CEO, Philip Browne, himself. That's how he conducts business; just as no opposition is feared, no professional challenge off the pitch is left to others to deal with. The next morning he phoned Philip and, as he himself has written, he was disappointed that, even after he'd advised the Union of his decision, no effort was made to get him to change his mind.

Some might see all of this as a case of the star player wanting it both ways but what it reflected was a man with a self-belief that was matched by his coaches but not, apparently, those who controlled the finances. It represented too that pull between schoolboy Johnny who imagined winning countless more trophies with Leinster and the practical hard-edged professional who knew that, six months ahead of getting married, the Racing Metro contract was exceptional and would help him and Laura well into the future.

The IRFU got some 'stick' but I took significant abuse online though nothing compared to what I had experienced a decade earlier courtesy of fans of a well-known Glasgow football club in circumstances that were not dissimilar.

• • •

In 2004 when I negotiated for Liam Miller to leave Glasgow Celtic and sign with Manchester United, the same kind of narrative was spun by the Glasgow club. There were other similarities to the scenario of Sexton and Racing Metro. The offers Celtic had made to get Liam to sign a new contract over the previous year were poor relative to his emergence as an important member of its Champions League squad. Celtic presumed on him signing a new contract for all sorts of reasons, including how quiet he was and how settled he seemed in Glasgow. When Liam's performances in Europe started to attract scouting trips by top English clubs, Celtic woke up and started to move the needle but not nearly enough. Liam was a quiet young man but, interestingly, not to the point that he wasn't frustrated at being taken for granted.

The day before Liam and I did our recce in Manchester, I phoned the Celtic manager, Martin O'Neill, and told him exactly what we were doing. I warned him that there was every prospect the player would move. This was simply to repeat something I had told him a month previously but even then, with that threat of an asset moving for no transfer fee, the club didn't alter its approach. Like Jonathan Sexton with Leinster, Glasgow Celtic didn't have to match Manchester United to give the club real hope he would stay, but when the full and final offer arrived, it was less than one third of the basic Manchester United was offering the player.

For years afterwards I would meet people who wanted to discuss that move, many of them certain that it was one Liam had made reluctantly because he'd have known that a few more years at Celtic would have benefited him. The inference – or sometimes it was said straight out – was that we had encouraged him into it. There were three reasons he chose to go. Firstly, Manchester United, his boyhood club, was enjoying phenomenal success under the leadership of Alex Ferguson who explained to Liam that he would be important to sustaining the club's dominance. Secondly, Glasgow Celtic's complacency made Manchester United's job easier by undermining Liam's belief in how he was thought of by the club. Thirdly, there was the matter of the money.

So there were echoes of that episode with Liam Miller in 2004 but the more instructive part of this was that it showed how unstructured the business of professional rugby remains. Johnny Sexton was 28 when he moved to Racing Metro, a player at the peak of his powers, nominated for World Player of the Year in 2014, an award he would win in 2018. While Johnny may not have felt its love, the IRFU did then consider him its most valuable asset but, as a direct financial value cannot be realised from trading a player in rugby, considering players as assets is at best an uncertain science.

• • •

Johnny had signed a two-year contract, with an option for one more, but by Christmas of year two, with Racing failing to make the anticipated progress, the IRFU was circling its prey. Joe Schmidt was now in charge of Ireland. When Leinster coach he had hated the Union's control of centrally contracted players' playing time, but now he had come full circle and sought to extend and deepen that policy. It was critical for him that the best players were deployed to his agenda which was about the annual Six Nations and, most importantly, the 2019 World Cup. Johnny Sexton was the player he valued above all others to do just that.

My task was to start preparing the different options. Racing Metro owner, Jacky Lorenzetti loved Johnny as much as Joe Schmidt. I travelled to Paris to discuss a new improved contract. Johnny and Laura had settled well, they'd made new friends among the players and their partners but the lure of home, with the 2019 Rugby World Cup as a primary objective, was growing, particularly as they had started a family. Joe Schmidt had started discussions with Johnny about the playing side of him returning home. We agreed that Johnny would continue those until they got to the point where contract terms were to be discussed, at which point I would take over. In the meantime I would continue to explore the wider canvas.

It was clear he wouldn't be short of options. At that time I was also talking with Toulon about Seán O'Brien and, at the end of a meeting with its owner Mourad Boudjellal and Head Coach, Bernard Laporte, I was asked about Sexton's availability. I told them his status and Boudjellal explained that, while it was interesting to know, he and his coach had already decided that, after the World Cup, they were going to bring in New Zealand out-half, Dan Carter. When the meeting was breaking up, Bernard Laporte took me to one side and quietly asked me to keep him appraised as he would rather have Sexton.

A few weeks later, completely out of the blue, Johnny called me to say he had decided he was going to come back to Ireland and that he would be advancing the discussions with the Union himself, that he didn't want me involved. It was direct, firm and there was no attempt to dress it up as anything other than a summary execution. I was shocked. Our relationship was close and at that time I was continuing discussions with Racing, keeping in touch with a few other clubs and waiting for his deliberations with Joe Schmidt to get to a point where I would engage with the Union.

There had been not the slightest hint that anything was awry. Indeed only a week before I had been to Paris for discussions with Racing Metro which, as normal, I had reported to him in detail. I told him I had no idea that he was in any way dissatisfied. He asked me to accept that indeed that was not the case, but that it was made clear to him, if he wanted to come back, it would be better done without me.

While Johnny explained that he'd made the decision in the context of getting the best possible outcome for his family, the intensity and focus he brings to such matters meant he failed to appreciate the implications for me. Why should he? Just as with the decision to go to Paris two years earlier, he had the toughness to do whatever he thought best for him and his family. The conversation wasn't particularly lengthy. The news was too sudden and stark for that, but all the circumstances meant he'd come to understand his interests would be better served if he finalised things without my being involved. There was no escaping a level of professional embarrassment for me but I simply had to accept the outcome. I was upset but given the different elements at play, I understood the reality.

When you work in such a high-octane arena, knocks like this help to keep you grounded. Just as I constantly remind players of how dispensable they are, advisers need to remember that they are even more so. In dealing with what was in front of him, including the implications for me, Johnny was simply behaving off the field as he does on it, making the choice that gave him the safest route to the line. In contrast to others I've dealt with, while he disliked what he was doing – and I believe that he did – he felt it would be better if he fronted up on it. There would be no hiding from it. I may not have liked the outcome but I admired the directness of it. The off-field man was being consistent with the on-field player.

Months later I heard Joe Schmidt being interviewed on radio. By that stage he was so loved by the media that it was more soapbox than interview. That day, referencing the increasing role of agents, he mentioned the Sexton 'saga', slanting it as he did and lauding the management of player game time by the Union. It was amusing to hear Joe proselytising on the merits of controlling the match time of the better players, something that had driven him demented in his time as coach of Leinster.

Joe Schmidt is bright and erudite. In spite of two 'failed' Rugby World Cups, the legend that grew up around him was largely earned but for years it went unchallenged by a generally star-struck rugby media. The success he achieved with Leinster was phenomenal but much of the commentary failed to appreciate the truly transformational work of his predecessor Michael Cheika. The Leinster Joe Schmidt inherited in 2010 was dramatically different to that which the Australian had taken over in 2005. Ahead of the 2019 season, the level of public adulation reached levels that ultimately did everyone a great disservice, including him.

• • •

The Football Association of Ireland's weakness including the means by which the CEO could manage the committee structure, facilitated the emergence of an autocrat at its helm, someone who, over a period of 15 years built a personal power structure that led to a serious erosion in the effective governance of the sport. It is a real positive that the IRFU's more institutionalised approach has protected it against the risk of such a fate but the mere prevention of harm cannot be the measure of organisational success.

The IRFU's organisational structure means there's little threat of an executive being able to 'go rogue' and it deserves credit for how it has managed many aspects of this first phase of professionalism. There are limits, however, though much of those are around how the game is structured globally. It's hard to see how the sport can really flourish without more radical change initiated by World

Rugby if national unions across the sport's main territories are to be guided towards further development of the professional game. Some fundamentals about its global governance need to change if rugby is to be transported to the world of contemporary professional sport. That and the most critical consideration of all, the safety of its professional athletes.

• • •

In most markets, rugby achieved its transformation into the professional era *via* the international game, with the better players – those who represented their countries – being paid centrally by their national federations. International matches are played intermittently with one major regional competition in each hemisphere every year and, as in football, with a World Cup contested every four years. The rest of the season comprises club competitions, held on a national and a regional basis, in this respect again in Europe, similar to how football has been organised for decades.

One hundred and fifty years ago professional football was first organised as a club enterprise and the only employment contract players ever had was with their clubs; national associations only ever paid those players chosen to represent them in international competition on a fixed match-fee basis. The professional rugby model was inverted at the outset where players were paid directly by their national unions and, while that has evolved, there's now a widely diverse approach dependent on how the sport is structured in each country. This lack of organisational coherence undermines the growth potential of the sport.

In the southern hemisphere, current World Champions South Africa has eight club franchises. New Zealand operates a centralised model which works well, but Australia's approach is a chronic failure with increasingly alarming consequences for the sport. In the northern hemisphere, many of Ireland, Wales and Scotland's top players are centrally contracted by their respective unions and then allocated to the different professional clubs, most of which were formed on a provincial or regional basis.

This is different to how the sport is structured in England

and France, the other two major northern hemisphere rugby nations whose clubs contest European competition with those of the Celtic nations. Rugby union cannot grow and develop into a more successful professional sport globally without establishing a coherent approach to how it is structured with a resolution of the dynamic between the international and the club game that is applied across all its key territories.

The funding of professional sport is dependent on a number of sources but today, the appetite for media rights is central to a sustainable economic model. The popularity of a sport determines competition for those broadcast/media rights which is the biggest single source of growth for the world's main team sports. Rugby is no different and both the established 15-a-side game and the still emerging Sevens format are seeing increasing interest and economic value. World Cups and annual international tournaments generate massive revenues for the national unions but, as with football, it is the club game – the regular diet of club league and cup competitions that ultimately will create the necessary virtuous cycle of growth.

That is the reason the club game is, by definition, the preeminent form of most professional sports. World Cups apart, the form of the sport that entertains fans for upwards of between 30 or 40 weeks annually is what oils the financial wheels of all stakeholders, including the players. The IRFU is in an impossible position; it is the guardian of the sport at all levels, the promoter of the professional game and it employs, directly and indirectly, most of Ireland's professional players. That's one too many responsibilities. It has no place as a principal employer but without a global realignment where World Rugby establishes a coherent global model, rooted in the club game, the sport's real potential is hopelessly compromised.

This necessary change must be led by World Rugby and, however gradual the transformation, it must empower more private enterprise and investment so the sport can be allowed to reach its potential. The national unions, as with federations in other sports, should be responsible for the national teams as before and must retain the critical governance responsibility working under the direction of World Rugby. In Ireland it would mean decoupling professional franchises from the amateur game – Munster, for example, would be a professional club not the hybrid that combines it with its constituent clubs like Garryowen or Tralee.

One consequence of such change would be that top professional players could move across territories without any fear of their international careers being undermined. World Rugby must write into its charter that no player, eligible to represent their country, can be excluded from consideration by a member Union on the grounds of where he or she is playing their club rugby. In a new dispensation the unreasonable treatment of a player like Simon Zebo, effectively boycotted by his country for choosing to play his club rugby in France, will no longer apply as such institutional 'hang-ups' will fall away with the necessary global recalibration of the sport.

For all that some national unions, or powerful elements within them, may have frustrated the development of the club game, the more progressive elements must have known that, once the door to professionalism was kicked open, the only credible business model was one predicated on club franchises competing across national boundaries. The failure to accept all the implications such as the free movement of players, by denying or threatening their right to consideration for international duty illustrates the strain that the traditional organisational model has been taking. The most compelling adjustment – treating the players as financial assets – is likely the most contentious but the time for the establishment of a standard transfer market, with the necessary protocols, is long overdue. To enable the shift to a globally coherent club-oriented structure, players need to have a transferable value.

• • •

The Johnny Sexton / Racing Metro case helps to highlight some of these wider challenges for rugby union in this evolution. Any assessment needs to allow that, unlike football, rugby is still in its professional infancy but, 25 years on, it may be time to reset some of the essentials. The lack of consistency in its key markets makes it difficult to see how World Rugby can hope to expand the sport's reach into new territories. Without a uniform approach where its penetration is high, growing rugby's popularity elsewhere will be difficult.

In professional sport my point of emphasis is always around players. This is not just because that's where much of my experience lies, it's more that, without them, there is no potentially viable business, no industry. Football is an industry, as are countless other sports where organisational structures have evolved to make the primacy of the player central to the growth of the game. With team sports, the athlete is dependent on the employment of a club or a franchise which involves passing some of their personal asset value to the contracting party. When a footballer signs with a professional club, their playing contract may carry stipulations that grant certain of their image rights to the club, a practice that can apply also in rugby.

The great difference lies in the contracting club holding no direct value in the player as a professional athlete. So, no matter how much in demand the player may be, no matter how much he or she may have improved in the years they're contracted to the club, when they move on to a new club – from Leinster to Racing Metro, for example – the club the player leaves generally receives no revenue from the transaction.

Rewind the Sexton move to Racing Metro in a world of professional rugby where there is a formal transfer market so players' registrations can be sold. In that scenario one of the top players in the world would have moved from his home club to another major European franchise but, before any consideration of the player's personal terms, the two clubs would have had to agree a fee. Let's imagine that Jonathan Sexton was bought for €10m. This would completely change the dynamic; now there is a transaction, one which starts with the clubs but advantages all the stakeholders, now the player is really an asset.

In that scenario, Leinster would have received a considerable fee to compensate for the loss of their asset (under the current Leinster ownership structure the IRFU would have been a major financial beneficiary); Racing Metro then had ownership of an asset with a publicly acknowledged value which, provided it managed the player well, it could then trade again in the future to recoup some of its investment or potentially generate a profit. The player would, in these circumstances, be in an even better position to negotiate strong terms because there would be a correlation between the transfer fee and what he could demand.

There is another important strand to this. For generations football operated on this basis, with the club in possession of a player's registration and the buying club the only ones involved. However, about 20 years ago, FIFA turned its attention to the need to protect clubs that had played a role in the development of the player. In English football there is a quite complex but important regimen whereby clubs that brought a player through between 12 and 21 years of age, receive compensation based on a set formula.

This approach works, though sometimes it requires an FA hearing to resolve differing interpretations and, while far from perfect, it does offer some level of protection against the biggest clubs marshalling all the revenues even when another club contributed to the player's early development. In rugby it would mean that in the case of Jonathan Sexton moving to Racing Metro, some of the €10m transfer fee would be distributed to St. Mary's, arguably to both the club and the school.

In Irish rugby, most notably in Leinster, some of the so called 'rugby schools' like Blackrock College and Clongowes invest in the development of talented young men as elite schools rugby players. For a number of Irish schools, pushing every imaginable boundary to the realisation of success on the rugby field has been an integral part of the history of Irish rugby for generations.

This is not just a Leinster phenomenon; schools like Methody or Campbell College in Belfast, Christians or Pres in Cork all have a tradition of consistently producing players who go on to play for Ireland. That hasn't changed with rugby's transition to professionalism, many players who join the provincial academies at 18 come from these schools, the best of them already primed and not far from being ready for action. In professional football, the cost to the academy system of bringing a talented player to 18 years of age is considerable, a cost that is factored into the management of the asset so any introduction of commercial realities to the movement of players in rugby union should incorporate an appropriate compensation scheme for academies and, possibly, schools.

Johnny Sexton's move to Racing Metro in Paris and his return give us important insights into the management of rugby union in Ireland. When he left, it prompted some to suggest it would herald an exodus of Ireland's best players. That was never credible. As long as Irish rugby remains hamstrung by the global structural weaknesses that have a direct impact on the development of the sport in its key markets, the still somewhat conservative domestic approach of the IRFU may be for the best. Ireland's provincial club model is firmly established, proven to be successful.

Some purists decry any idea of players becoming tradable assets or 'commodities'. They are concerned that it would represent a descent into what they view as the vulgar excesses in football's movement of players for vast sums that can enrich certain club owners or that it would simply enrich player agents. There is considerable myth around how this works; there would be no advantage to player agents from this change, the player's representative earns a fee based on the value of the player's contract not the transfer fee. The material change would be that under such a regimen clubs would own players registrations that would have a tradeable commercial value, representing a step change as players would become real assets.

Ultimately, professional sport is a form of entertainment where it's inevitable that, the bigger and more attractive it becomes, the best performers must be exceptionally well paid. In European football there are too many 'professional' clubs and in most countries the domestic club model is unsustainable. Football may have a challenge with the huge salaries paid to those playing in England's FA Premier League, Germany's Bundesliga or La Liga in Spain, but it's as much too about the drain on the sport's finances from the lower leagues that draw small crowds, modest if any sponsorship and little or no media rights income.

In Irish rugby The All-Ireland League flirted with this disease early in the professional era but huge strides have been made towards a secure provincial club model which, while it needs global strategic consideration and investment, can be sustainable. In rugby union, as in other sports, the best players must be paid every cent that the game can afford. Rugby's great advantage in setting course on a global reorganisation centred on the club game is that it can clinically delineate between the professional and the amateur structures. It needs to prioritise doing so.

Professional sport has no obligation to cater for those who provide limited entertainment, those whose talents don't warrant payment. It isn't obliged to consider the welfare of those whose standard of play is coated with a veneer of professionalism when commercial or 'real' money is not attracted to it. When we consume other forms of entertainment we don't agonise over the disparity between the huge sums earned by the stars and that offered to the less gifted.

• • •

There is another, non-financial but as urgent challenge facing professional rugby union. In putting the interests of its players first it has to consider more than money, it has to prioritise the more general welfare of its employees. All employment relationships involve wider conditions especially the health and safety of the workforce. I was on the board of Mainstream Renewable Power for almost a decade and the first item on the agenda at every board meeting was the Health and Safety of the employees and our contractors. Is that the case with every professional rugby club, with each of the unions or even with World Rugby? It should be.

It's hard to see how the levels of attrition allowed in a sport where many players resemble the Terminator can continue while those responsible persist in claiming to be paying due care and attention to the athletes' wellbeing. It seems clear that the most urgent issue for professional rugby is making a series of code changes to minimise the ultimate threat to the game arising from how it is currently played and possibly introducing some protocols around the physique of many playing it.

Professional football is belatedly addressing the serious exposure of players – particularly those in certain positions – to brain damage from simply heading the football. The first concerns about this were raised decades ago but it is only in recent years that the authorities, led by FIFA, have really taken the matter seriously; fundamental changes already introduced at underage levels now seem destined to become a feature of the sport even in the professional leagues. This example, as well as the worrying developments in rugby itself, should signal a need for more urgent action in that code where the risk of upper body damage is of a wholly different scale.

That is to consider the bleakest possible outcome. Belatedly, more attention is being paid to the consequences of serious and recurring head and neck injuries but there appears a reluctance to view it as the crisis that it is. The debate seems measured when the evidence appears so undeniable that it should be fevered in search of a solution. Every business' greatest responsibility is the health and safety of its employees; that's a weighty enough burden in any sphere but when your workforce includes athletes whom you know to be, in the course of their work, placing their health at risk, you had better be sure to have more than 'return to play' protocols in place.

It's inevitable that rugby players from the professional era will be taking legal cases against their employers for not doing enough to protect them. The duty of care will, correctly, rest with the employer and it's beyond reasonable to expect that, with the level of attrition now allowed, the sport won't yield a growing number of such cases in the near future. That relates to what has already occurred and cannot be undone but it should serve to make the imperative for action now all the greater. This issue is urgent both in terms of player welfare and also as regards the potential for the sport to grow through remaining attractive to emerging talented young boys and girls.

More generally, to sustain its popularity, never mind to grow, rugby will also have to markedly increase the emphasis on the player. World Rugby needs to create an environment where the bond between the player and the fan is absolutely central to everything about the professional game. Then, if they set out to succeed by playing attractive, entertaining rugby, the fans will pay to attend, they will pay to access media rights, they will buy the merchandise endorsed by the players that promotes the sponsors. In this way rugby can grow worldwide as a form of entertainment but that's only possible if players are placed at the centre of it all.

The trade-off for the world's best rugby union professionals is that clubs must be able to 'own' their employment and, as in many other top sports, the clubs must have an opportunity to trade them in the market. Only in this way can the owners of rugby clubs be encouraged to build a standard investment approach to their business where players become among their most valuable assets. While the advancement of rugby union is complex, in part because of how it evolved, and there are many considerations, this different approach to the 'asset categorisation' of players is central to moving towards the necessary global restructuring of the game.

This doesn't mean that there will be a mass exodus of players from their domestic markets. In football where players have been tradable assets for generations, there's never been anything approaching a flight of talent from one domestic market to another: certainly not across the developed football markets. The majority of English football players play in England, Germans in Germany, Italians in Italy and most Spanish professionals play in Spain. A new approach in professional rugby could see the registration of players where transfer fees will help to oil the financial wheels but which, stewarded properly, will contribute to the growth in popularity of the sport and not the reverse.

XIII
Progression

In late November 2009, at a news conference hosted by its President, Christy Cooney, the GAA announced that it had reached an agreement with the GPA (Gaelic Players Association) on a multi-annual funding programme. The GPA, established a decade earlier to promote and protect the welfare of intercounty footballers and hurlers, would receive direct funding from the GAA to support its extensive welfare programmes. Over a number of years I had been working as a consultant to the GPA on its discussions and negotiations with the GAA.

There was some sense of a continuum from the birth of my sports business with the importance of protecting the interests of Irish footballers through the High Court action with Opel in 1990. My company, the first and, for almost two decades, the only full-service sports management business in Ireland, worked in sponsorship and major events but its most important work was always in the representation of elite athletes.

In its very earliest days, we had established that, without their explicit agreement, the FAI could not commercially exploit players it selected to represent Ireland. It was a defining moment in the treatment of international footballers. Two decades later, to be part of something just as profound within our national games, especially when the resolution had been reached by discussion and negotiation, was rewarding and humbling.

When discussions had started, the GAA team was led by its then President Nickey Brennan who was seen as forward-looking and who communicated a desire to progress things quickly in what was the final year of his presidency. It may be that this very urgency worked against progress because the first meetings weren't productive but in spite of that we weren't as optimistic when he was replaced as

President by Cork man, Christy Cooney. We were proven wrong as, from the outset, he took ownership of the process, pushed for immediate talks and urged us to accept his *bona fides* in wanting to see a positive outcome for the GPA.

The constant was the GAA's Director General, Páraic Duffy, a quietly-spoken, former school principal who had foresight and courage, an unusual mix in sports administration; when you add integrity then it puts him, in my experience, in a very small cohort indeed. Páraic Duffy accepted that the GPA wanted to bind itself with the GAA through a deal that would provide a secure funding source to provide for the welfare of its members. The funding needed to be linked to the income the inter-county competitions generated and it needed to benefit the GPA in a way that allowed it to retain its independent voice.

My clients, the GPA, had two latter-day greats of Gaelic games in charge, Cork hurler Dónal Óg Cusack as its President, and its founder and CEO, the former Dublin footballer, later manager, Dessie Farrell. It was one of the most interesting, enjoyable, if more unusual, pieces of work I did in 30 years in sports management. Dónal Óg and Dessie were bright, hard-working professional men focused on achieving something they correctly believed to be really important in protecting the welfare of amateur players whose talents and commitment generated phenomenal revenues for the governing body of their sports.

They were also good company, likeable and we enjoyed the work even when there were periods of little or no progress. The project was also deeply rewarding, not financially, but as an Irishman with an appreciation of the extraordinary contribution our national games make to who we are as a people, I was immensely proud to have been involved.

• • •

As a young boy my father cultivated my interest in all sports, so the weekends would have seen us at Bohemians or Shamrock Rovers matches in Dalymount Park or Milltown, some rugby ground in south Dublin or at Croke Park, occasionally to watch a hurling match but more regularly to see the 1960's Dublin football team that featured, the Foley brothers, Des and Lar. It was a time when more of your sporting heroes were home grown, even when it came to football. While I loved watching 'Match of the Day' in my neighbour's house, my soccer heroes included Johnny Matthews and especially Alfie Hale, both of whom played for Waterford United.

When it came to access to Croke Park I was a privileged youngster because the General Secretary of the GAA, Pádraig Ó Caoimh was a family friend, so my father would bring me and my brothers quite regularly. The GAA was part of our sporting realm although as I grew older I became conscious of my parents' disapproval of some aspects of its governance. My mother may have been of strong republican stock but they disapproved of the ban on members of the security services in Northern Ireland being allowed to play Gaelic games.

The ban was a cause of professional problems with the association when I first tried to engage professionally, after the establishment of Drury Sports Management in 1990. It seemed natural to contact the GAA which was undergoing significant change including embracing sponsorship of its main titles for the first time. There was no interest, a reticence about any form of engagement, which I was to learn later was on account of a *Morning Ireland* interview I had done with a former President on the ban. It appears I hadn't been respectful in pursuing him on the issue and the institution wasn't in a hurry to forgive!

Instead, in 1993, Bank of Ireland hired me as an adviser on its negotiations with Croke Park as it moved towards becoming the first sponsor of the Football All-Ireland Championship. At some point one of the bank's senior executives remarked that someone within the GAA had made an oblique reference to my not being beloved of the association which only served to encourage the bank to involve me more. I was curious about the source of this hostility. I had already brought Arnotts the Dublin department store to the Dublin County Board as its first ever shirt sponsor in what was then the most lucrative commercial deal in Gaelic Games. It was clear, however, that Croke Park seemed to view me with suspicion.

At that time I had an uncomfortable experience with then President of the GAA, Peter Quinn, who was a successful financial adviser. I attended a business seminar for SMEs which he addressed on the subject of entrepreneurship and business management. The speech highlighted what he saw as a failure of small business to innovate, to be flexible. When he took questions I asked how, in his position as President of the GAA, he could reconcile not opening Croke Park to other sports. I suggested its inflexibility was costing the GAA a great deal of money. While I may have been happy that it was a reasonable question, the answer suggested he didn't agree.

The response was angry. Peter Quinn chose first to point out to the room that I was a 'soccer man' with little understanding of the GAA before he went on to dismiss my analogy as having no relevance to the case he was making. It was personal with no attempt to address the question that I had raised, dismissing my intervention as mischievous and implying that I was anti-GAA.

Unusually for me, I was struck dumb but, at another table a man rose and introduced himself as Joe Connolly, captain of Galway's All-Ireland Hurling Championship winners of 1980. Joe is a legendary GAA figure whose speech in accepting the Liam MacCarthy cup is still regarded as one of the finest ever delivered in Croke Park. Quietly, but assertively, Joe said he thought my question was relevant, important and warranted a proper answer. Furthermore, he said he was perfectly happy for his young boys to have Irish soccer stars as heroes alongside Galway's hurlers and footballers. It was a powerful intervention not least because of its source.

The vignette was illustrative of how it seemed I was a lightning rod for trouble with the association. It was to become more troubled still for a period. In 2003, a year after I had assumed the position as chairman of the board of Paddy Power plc, a number of prominent hurlers took to the field with Paddy Power branded hurls in one of those clever marketing stunts then synonymous with the brand. Worse, the idea had originated from a colleague in my sports business, Eamon McLoughlin, so I found myself in the midst of a controversy with the GAA. Worse still, this episode drew the fire of the then embryonic Gaelic Players Association.

The GPA slammed it as 'opportunistic' though, as the player representative body, I thought it should have taken a different approach and pointed to the need for top inter-county names to do this kind of promotion because of the refusal of the GAA to distribute some of the wealth generated by the competitive endeavours of all inter-county players. We were involved in a few other minor skirmishes with some well-known GAA players doing their own thing, including the legendary Kilkenny hurler, Henry Shefflin, which was hardly surprising, given our expertise in representing professional athletes and the emergence of 'player power' within Gaelic games.

• • •

There was a certain irony when, a few years later, the Chief Executive of the GPA, Dessie Farrell, who'd previously been a vocal critic of mine, asked to meet. The years of shadow boxing between the GPA and the GAA appeared to be coming towards an end with those in administrative charge in Croke Park seemingly open to an accommodation with the player body. Dessie Farrell, CEO of the GPA since its foundation, had long lobbied Croke Park and government for recognition of the unique contribution inter-county players made to the finances of the game.

The GPA's autonomy was its strength but he and its board believed the point had been reached where a formal engagement with the GAA was essential. The smoke signals from Croke Park were barely visible but, in so far as they could be read, it seemed it was also accepting that a new approach was warranted. It was 2008. I was excited by the prospect of working with the GPA. Gaelic games were part of my upbringing; no one with any sensitivity to their national culture could fail to understand their unique importance. I realised that I was being invited to work on something profound in the history of our national games. I felt privileged.

There were some rumblings in GAA circles. The GPA had found its ambition to be recognised by the GAA frustrated at various points. Even a threatened strike in 2007 that was supported by an overwhelming majority of inter-county players, had failed to really advance the case. 'Official Recognition' would include a commitment to the retention of the amateur status of the players, something that neither the GPA's board nor I as its adviser regarded as in any way problematic. The protection of the amateur code wasn't only an important spiritual consideration; the games, as structured and organised, couldn't financially support any other approach. The GPA's ambition, focussed on the top level of the game, where the commitment is most demanding, was to create an environment that protected player welfare and that aligned appropriately the inter-county players' contribution with the income earned by the GAA from inter-county competitions.

The GAA is Ireland's sporting and cultural gem, an organisation with unrivalled community, local and national influence. Its games are unique and are played at the elite level, by men and women with no less dedication than by those who choose to play professional football and rugby. All Gaelic players are amateur, so the GPA had sought some form of compensation for its elite members from the huge income the GAA generated through inter-county competitions. There was no intent to break the amateur status of the sports but with the demands being made on players it was essential that some of the GAA's revenues were directed to the GPA so it could fund a range of welfare initiatives.

Some GAA people were unhappy at anything that could dilute the strictest interpretation of the amateur code. The issue had been 'live' for many years. It was contentious, often fractious, but with the passage of time, the astute commercial exploitation of the games by the GAA and the increasing demands being made on inter-county players a meaningful recognition of the player body was inevitable.

The backwoodsmen were never fully silenced but their opposition was seen for what it was, the embers of a past era which bore no relation to the modern, vibrant, commercially successful GAA that was using its resources to deepen its roots in communities across the island. That some of those resources would be channelled directly to the independent body concerned with the welfare of inter-county players was not antithetical to that mission. How could it have been? The players, whose welfare the GAA was now funding directly, would, as the heroes of the younger generations, be critical to the long-term well-being and growth of Gaelic games.

In some respects the historical importance of the agreement announced by Christy Cooney in late 2009 was reinforced by the fact that it had to be formally ratified by both the membership of the GPA and by the GAA's Annual Congress. The first agreement with inter-county players was a truly momentous point in the games' history. In getting there, the two sides had a singular focus on finding an outcome that would accommodate their respective needs. The balance was that this would see the elite players receive appropriate compensation for their commitment but reinforce the centrality of the games' amateur code, as well as reaffirming the wider ambitions of the Association.

Within the GAA community there was some pushback, most of which was just those with an agenda to undermine individuals whom they didn't like. The games were already being popularised in a way that was at the heart of the very discussions between the parties. Much of this was positive, adding contemporary glamour to hurling and football that widened its relevance to the youth and allowed it to compete with other sports that, largely through their international reach, were constantly creating imagery that appealed to the new, digital-savvy, generations.

The evolution of this had emerged from the opening up of the GAA's main properties – the Leagues and the All-Ireland Championships – to sponsorship, commercialising their broadcast, licensing the brands and permitting county boards to have shirt and subsidiary sponsors, as well as having their own merchandising agreements. It was this background to the explosion in the commercialising of inter-county competitions that fuelled the need for players at that level to be treated just as elite athletes were in other sports. The payment of players couldn't and still cannot be sustained but, had the GAA ignored the claims of other areas of player welfare, it would have been negligent.

The extraordinary growth in the importance of club hurling and football presented another challenge, this time involving all club players. Some of the same principles applied, though when established in 2016, the sole objective of the Club Players' Association (CPA) was to address the need to introduce a split season to protect the health and well-being of players in both codes. In March 2021, the CPA announced it was disbanding because that single objective had been realised.

The issue of player recognition and welfare will never end as, with the further development of its sports, the GAA will find new challenges emerging in achieving a balance between the necessary retention of its amateur code and protecting the welfare of those whose level of performance generates significant commercial revenues. For generations camogie was the only sport that women members of the GAA could play but women's football has become very popular and is attracting considerable support across the commercial matrix.

The women's All-Ireland series is an increasingly popular spectator sport where, again, the involvement of fans, sponsors and broadcasters means the GAA is generating commercial income through the talent and efforts of the players. Women's football is establishing a distinct following and as that increases so too will it need to be accommodated with a welfare model that better represents its value-add to the GAA. The GPA recognising this through securing sponsorship deals for its women members represents the start of something that will become more significant.

The first GAA/GPA deal completed in 2009 and approved by Congress in 2010 will prove to have a resonance for decades to come as other groups within the GAA community move to have their needs met in a manner more in line with the strength of their 'franchise'. That's another reason for being proud to have been involved; that first deal represents a template of sorts for others to mould into a form that meets their need to realise value and respect for their members, as the GPA managed to do for its.

• • •

There is a postscript to my work as part of the GPA's negotiating team with the GAA. It's often assumed when you're involved in professional negotiations, that it is difficult to have a positive relationship with the other party. In my experience negotiations that are grounded in market knowledge, experience and that are conducted respectfully can achieve both the optimum outcome for your client but also leave the contracting party impressed by the professionalism of your work. That should never be the ambition but the cliched aggressive, macho approach to negotiations, is rarely necessary or of value so while you often need to be tough and assertive, realising the right outcome is never simply about that alone.

My work with the GPA was about achieving the best outcome for intercounty players but while I'd been on the opposite side of the table, senior people in the GAA recognised the professionalism and realism of my approach. So, about a year later I brought a proposal to its General Secretary, Páraic Duffy, to host a Gaelic football and hurling double header at the Oval Cricket ground in south London. The largest cricket stadium in London, the Oval has hosted rugby union, football (including the first FA Cup Final in 1872), Australian Rules but with the support of Croke Park, Platinum One advanced discussions with the MCC about a festival of Gaelic Games for London. Sadly, the project didn't come to fruition but the engagement on it with the GAA was serious and meaningful. It remains a great regret but it was wonderful that the ambition of a private business was encouraged by the Association.

This was in stark contrast to the way, as the only FIFA licensed match agents in Ireland, we were actively blocked at every turn by the FAI. Over the years since I worked on that original GAA/GPA deal, I've often reflected on how Irish football would have been served so much better, if men of the calibre, commitment and integrity evident in those I worked with in Gaelic games had been involved in its governance. In common with the IRFU, the GAA has shown itself to be responsible, mature and ethical but perhaps the surprise, to me at least, is in just how adaptable and progressive it has shown itself to be.

For generations, the GAA was as closed as other aspects of Irish society but it now reflects the Ireland of today. Since the millennium, its leadership has skilfully stayed true to its unique culture but infused it with the oxygen of change so it could be remoulded to a 21st century version of its mission. The Association's deal with Sky Sports, for the first time putting some coverage of its Championships behind a TV pay wall, was especially ground-breaking but perhaps the Irish Muslim community hosting its Eid celebration on the pitch at Croke Park in July 2020 and 2021 was symbolically a more dramatic instance of just how truly inclusive the GAA has become. It's a far and welcome cry from the Ireland of my youth, when until 1965, a bishop threw the ball in to start the All-Ireland Football Final and, for years after that practice stopped, he was still introduced to the teams, with the players expected to bow and kiss his episcopal ring. Buckingham Palace had nothing on it!

There is no doubt the GAA's governance in recent decades has reflected its status as Ireland's most important, powerful and influential sports body, though some of its status is derived from its very uniqueness which means it transcends sport as no other federation could ever hope to do and merits its given epithet of 'an Irish international amateur sporting and cultural organisation'. This means that those in charge have an added responsibility as well as a greater opportunity to make a mark but they have worked assiduously to promote their sports in a way that is inclusive, true to its traditions but not constrained by them. The GAA is ahead of many international sports federations on issues like social cohesion, sustainability and player welfare. It is most certainly ahead of its peers at home.

A WIDER LENS

Peter Sutherland was appointed Ireland's Attorney General at 35 years of age and EU Commissioner at the age of 39 before he left the political arena and went on to have an exceptional career in business, leading global giants like Goldman Sachs and BP. Later he led the GATT process as Director General of the World Trade Organisation which made him a central figure in geo-politics and earned him the sobriquet 'the father of globalisation'.

Peter Sutherland was one of Ireland's great intellects of recent times and his talents were deployed with equal success in law, business and politics. The furthering of a global economy and his leadership roles in Goldman Sachs and BP – two lightning rods for those opposed to, or even just troubled by, the power of such corporate beasts – undermined for some the constancy of his interest in human rights, but he persisted.

In his sixties, his attentions turned from corporate endeavours to an increased commitment to inequality, indeed to some of the consequences of the increasingly global economy that he had helped to create. While a number of the roles that he had held meant that for some observers his reputation would always be tarnished, the global status of those positions did mean he could use his considerable influence to address what many think mattered to him most.

In 2006 he was appointed UN Special Envoy for International Migration and, body and soul, he committed himself to the cause of migrants and refugees. It was a position he relished and to which he dedicated himself until his death in 2018. I hardly knew him until we had some engagement on immigration over a number of months including one private meeting in his home in Dublin. It was a momentous experience for me, seminal even and the weekend after his death in 2018, I wrote about him in 'The Sunday Business Post' newspaper. I recalled how, in that discussion, he was deeply saddened by the global failure to deal with migration especially what he saw as the political failings of Ireland and the EU on the matter. I wrote,

"*This (migration) was, he said, the supreme challenge of our time and we were failing it. Europe was failing it. Ireland was failing it. It was a challenge of values, not just to different states or regions but to mankind. It was a challenge to the dignity and the equality of man. It was a moral issue. Peter Sutherland believed the world was short of political leadership wedded to morality.*

The EU's failings exercised him most; one of its founding features had been to curb excesses of nationalism, yet its record on refugees had been "shameful". Solidarity is at the very core of the EU but his perspective was of its value being eroded in the Balkans, gradually undermined in some of Europe's most influential states, all of which, for him, was a betrayal of the fundamentals of the European project to which he'd contributed much."

XIV
Home Thoughts From Abroad

It was 1986 and I was driving alone on a tarmac strip through Africa's giant Sahara Desert along the Sudanese Chadian border near Geneina. In remote parts of Ireland, we occasionally drive for a period without meeting other traffic but this was on a whole different level. I'd been driving for a number of hours and had seen no living thing, no vegetation, nothing that suggested life when, out of nowhere, a camel train moved across my path. It was an astonishing sight; something I'd never witnessed before and one I'm unlikely to see again.

To simply say that it 'moved' would be to bear false witness to just how wondrous it was; there seemed to be thousands of camels being herded by scores, maybe more than a hundred, colourfully-clothed Arab drivers, probably Bedouin, interspersed throughout the seemingly never-ending train. It was large-scale but it was controlled and calm, effortless almost, totally different to how cattle herdsmen work their large droves of cows. It was as though the camel train drifted in slow-motion, rhythmic but unflustered; only the occasional shout of instruction or encouragement from their masters broke the deafening desert silence as the train was guided on its sedate journey.

I was born and bred in Clonskeagh, a large south Dublin suburb today but in my youth, in the 1960s and early 1970s it was predominantly still farmland and fields dappled with small pockets of housing. The area then was dominated by a large convent with a home for the elderly and a farm directly across from the front of our house. The initial encroachment of the city was the first phase of the new Belfield campus of University College Dublin. The university that had been established in the centre of the city in the mid-1800s began to relocate to this Dublin suburb in the 1960s. It was a quiet, reserved, conservative hamlet, reflecting the Ireland of the time. The university's new campus – subsequently the epicentre of my universe during my college years – was to the vanguard of a dramatically changing Dublin in the 1970s.

Still, no matter the extent of change in Ireland through the 70s and 80s, what I witnessed on the road to Darfur was, at that point in my life, as alien a scene as any I could possibly have encountered. I was in Sudan with GOAL, the Irish relief agency, on leave of absence from my work as a broadcaster with RTÉ. For a few years I had been a young and enthusiastic, if inexperienced, member of the charity's executive committee that sought to support its founder and leader, John O'Shea, that rare phenomenon then as a layman who committed much of his energy and time to serving those most in need.

Sudan is the third largest country in Africa with a land mass of 1.8m square kilometres, much of which is part of the vast Sahara Desert that covers well over a quarter of the total landmass of Africa. The GOAL operation in Sudan was focused on the famine in Darfur, the country's western province that bordered Chad where it had a significant presence in what was then the world's largest refugee camp. Everything was of scale. Darfur, just one of Sudan's 18 regions, is the size of Spain.

Darfur's largely agricultural economy has always been dependent on the weather. Back-to-back harvest failures in 1983 and 1984 brought severe famine and the death of an estimated 250,000 people in Sudan, the majority in Darfur. As its population was about 3 million, this represented a very substantial number of lives lost, in both absolute and relative terms. GOAL's work, under the leadership of Field Director, Anne Burke, was to intervene directly in providing medical care to those survivors who were living in an enormous refugee camp close to the border with Chad.

The best way to understand any culture is by absorption so over time I came to see differences in how the Arab world seemed to function relative to ours. I was struck by the general calmness, even the acceptance that things were the way they were, however unsatisfactory that might have been on occasion. I had been to Khartoum years before as a student, but my appreciation of difference, my sense of its value as something to be celebrated, had matured. The Adhan being called by the Muezzin over the famous city where the Blue and White Nile meet seemed more striking, more soulful than the Angelus bell over the swell of the Liffey and for all its complexities, there was nothing remotely threatening about life in Khartoum.

The call to prayer is an emblem that unsettles our need to always emphasise difference. Muslims are called to pray five times daily while the Angelus bell twice rings to prompt Catholics to do the same. One is a recitation by a trained Islamic scholar, the other a bell, but both serve the same purpose of reminding believers, maybe even of tempting the non-believers to take time for reflection. The differences between the Christian and Islamic faiths are nothing when compared to what's shared – a belief that life's journey has a higher purpose. As a very small boy my first taste of formal education in Dublin was in a school run by Dominican nuns where, every day at noon, we were taught to stand and sing the Bells of the Angelus. Whenever I've been in a country where Islam is the predominant faith, the Muezzins' calls have reminded me of the connections between Christians and Muslims, not the reverse.

• • •

Thirty years after my spell with GOAL in Sudan, I spent a fortnight working in refugee camps in Greece with a friend and our 16-year-old daughters. We spent a few days on the island of Lesbos but most of our time in a camp for 8,000 refugees on the quayside of Piraeus port in Athens. It was at the height of the refugee crisis and, influenced by the urgings of the campaigner Caoimhe Butterly, we went to Greece. There was an element of a time warp for me. The only other time that I had worked with refugees was in the Sahara Desert with GOAL. I was then in my mid-20s, a cosseted Dubliner light on life-experience. In 2016, I was weighed down with it, the most recent of which had been acutely difficult. Still, my world remained of protected privilege and Ireland was a dramatically different place to the mid-1980s.

The difference was most manifest in how the two girls dealt with what was a first experience of anything approaching what they witnessed in Greece. They adapted to what they encountered in a way no Irish 16-year-olds of my generation could have done. One benefit of casting off the shackles of mono-conservatism is that Ireland's younger generations aren't bridled with layers of prejudice; most of them are adaptable and naturally open to, not at all fearful of, 'difference'.

The world of the predominantly Arab refugees was also changed from what I'd encountered in Darfur three decades earlier. Globalisation had affected them too. The number of men wearing traditional clothing was negligible and not all the Muslim women wore the hijab. Many of the refugees spoke good English and among them were large numbers of professional people who had fled lives that were not a great deal different to those we would return to in Ireland.

The experience in Greece in 2016 uncorked something buried in me; some resistance to accepted norms, especially when it came to inequity. I may have long felt it but I had, to that point, rarely actively lived it, nor given expression to my discomfort by choosing to live any differently. It had been open to me to do so but I'd chosen not to and, importantly, nor did my behaviour change fundamentally when we returned. I continued to enjoy the benefits of my well-to-do Dublin lifestyle.

Still, the experience certainly stirred something in me. I was to find that, without any grand design, I set out to invest some part of me in being a small agitator for change in how much the establishment, particularly our legislators, address the issue of migration. Even writing that is somehow uncomfortable because, for any unease I feel around much of how privileged my life is, I choose to continue to enjoy most of its benefits with hardly a thought. Why then address the inequities at all?

Within a few weeks of our return from Greece, I wrote an Opinion article for the *Irish Times* newspaper. It was informative but with an edge and made some pointed references to how inadequate Ireland's response to the migrant crisis had been. Ireland is the ultimate migrant nation but our attitude towards those most in need suggests we're not as compassionate a nation as we like to pretend. It should be troubling. Some days after that article was published, I met Peter Sutherland who had some guidance, even direction, for me.

It is to the great benefit of migrants across the world that Peter Sutherland was the first-ever UN Special Envoy for International Migration, a role to which he committed himself for the last dozen years of his life. We spent about an hour in his home discussing the scale of the migrant crisis before he asked me, now that I had written on the subject in the *Irish Times*, what more I was going to do about it. My reply was vague and he became assertive, insisting that my responsibility was to commit myself to write, to talk and to lobby and generally be an advocate for migrants. It wasn't flattery; it was blunt, matter-of-fact, partly paternalistic, but more in the line of orders from a superior officer. That afternoon, sitting in his home on what, as I discovered as I left, was his 70th birthday, I was struck by how emotional he was about global levels of inequity and deprivation. I sensed a sadness at the horror of what he saw emerging.

• • •

Within days, I approached the *Irish Times* with the idea of writing a regular column about a Syrian refugee that would, in diary form, tell his journey from the time he left Syria through to his arrival in Europe and then track his progress towards realising his dream of settling in an EU country. The series ran to 15 pieces over an 18-month period and charted the perilous journey Mustafa made from Aleppo to where we'd met in the camp in Athens and then beyond. Mustafa was one of a small group of refugees I got to know well in the short time that we were working in the camp. The first time I saw him, the Bible he was carrying caught my eye. I went over to say hello. He was friendly, spoke good, if heavily-accented English, and we sat and chatted for an hour or so. I asked him about the bible. *I like reading it,* he said, *it is just like the Koran.*

Mustafa was well-educated and his account of how he'd fled Syria was striking for its detail and lack of self-pity. What was most dramatic was his account of the boat journey from Turkey to Greece which was perilous throughout. The last time we spoke, some years ago, he was in France but we've since lost contact. Basel, an engineer from Aleppo, is now resident in France where I have visited him a couple of times. We speak quite regularly and his brother, a doctor, more recently arrived in Dublin.

There were others whose stories I could have told. Abdul was a chef from the city of Homs. The story he and his wife told us showed life's randomness. They had lived in Brussels for a decade but, when their third child was born, they had returned to Syria believing their homeland would be a safe and secure place to rear their children, something millions of emigrants feel confident to do when, after a period away, they return home.

Thousands of Irish men and women have made just that choice only to find their timing wasn't ideal, but the implications for Abdul and Marisa were a great deal more serious. Within 18 months of returning to Syria, their young children were living in a country that was at war and their very survival was at risk. Now they made the journey in reverse though this time it wasn't by commercial flights but, courtesy of ruthless smugglers, by sea. This tall, handsome, warm 50-year-old man accepted his fate without rancour expressing only mild frustration to be living with his wife and children in a couple of tiny tents on the port in Athens.

Arya was a Kurdish woman in her 50s who shared a tent with her two adult children, one of whom was a schoolteacher in Damascus before the war. The daughter had excellent English and explained that her father had feared the situation for Kurds would worsen, so he'd left a year earlier and was now in a camp in Germany waiting for them to join him. This was not uncommon; in some cases, people in the camp were the vanguard of a family effort to escape Syria, while in others they were trying to join those who'd already found some level of sanctuary.

In such a pressurised environment where people's homes were of canvas, where they queued for food in a box handed out from a truck twice a day, men and women of multiple origins talked, walked, washed, ate and most of the time, respected each other's differences. It was at times chaotic but somehow it worked and, in our time there, disagreements or incidents were rare and those that did occur were minor. It's hard to imagine a more eclectic mix of people being thrown together in a makeshift tarpaulin village where there were around 50 toilets and less than half that number of washrooms for its almost 8,000 inhabitants.

This refugee population in Piraeus included people from all walks of life from different countries and backgrounds, and yet most conducted themselves with dignity and a mutual respect that was exemplary. It was remarkable to witness the calm. I tried to imagine how 8,000 citizens of different nationalities within the EU would cope in such a situation. How would we react and interact were we thrown together to endure such awful living conditions with little prospect of a return to our previously secure lives?

When I returned to Greece just over a year later, Piraeus camp where we had worked was closed, its inhabitants dispersed to different locations around the Greek capital. The largest and where most of those I knew were held, was at the old Athenian port of Skaramanga where about 3,000 were grateful for the improved conditions, though their movement was more controlled in a camp that was enclosed with fencing, barbed wire and a strong police presence. I spoke at an international conference in Greece that year too where the predominant theme, though dressed up as migrant-focused, was more the control of borders so only those who would 'fit' would be allowed into Europe.

• • •

Freedom of movement challenges something fundamental to the relatively stable experience of western society over the past 60 years. Mass migration is undermining this and the enormity of the climate crisis makes it inevitable that migration will challenge large parts of the developed world in ways it's almost impossible to predict. One of the most concerning and immediate problems is the numbers of unaccompanied refugee children scattered across the world.

In autumn 2016, I was approached by a friend, Gary Daly, about the imminent closure in France of a refugee camp near the port of Calais. The camp, known as 'The Jungle', had been the source of political debate in Britain and France but, at short notice, President Francois Hollande announced it would be closed, and its occupants re-housed in different locations around France. Gary, a Dublin solicitor, had worked in the camp on a few occasions and knew hundreds of unaccompanied children were among its inhabitants. This was his immediate concern at the French government's planned dispersal; he believed Ireland should offer to take some of those children who would otherwise be dispersed across France.

The result was 'Not on Our Watch', a campaign targeted at getting government to offer to settle 200 of the unaccompanied minors who would otherwise be moved to centres all over France. Some weeks later after a concentrated, high-profile, fight for these children, our small team had the satisfaction of seeing the Irish government, albeit through gritted teeth, agree to intervene at EU level and offer 200 of these young people the chance to come to Ireland and make a fresh start.

It was interesting to use the political lobbying skills and experience I'd previously deployed professionally in this campaign. The government initially refused to countenance what we proposed. We were told more than once that our initiative risked making Ireland known to be accommodating of refugees, increasing the numbers coming here. Bizarrely, different people in government, warned that this would lead to a hardening of right-wing views in the community. The usual platitudes aside, there was not a scintilla of concern for the welfare of these most disadvantaged and at-risk children.

When the government continued to resist we formed a coalition of relevant NGOs, faith, and solidarity groups so that 'Not on Our Watch' could bring public pressure on the Oireachtas. Led by some able and principled parliamentarians, the Oireachtas became united in supporting the move. The strong coalition of interests we'd formed and the weight of certain voices, especially that of the remarkable Sister Stanislas Kennedy, one of Ireland's most heroic advocates for the disadvantaged in our community, shifted the political ground. Within weeks the government had to support an all-party motion it had desperately wanted to avoid. The outcome was an agreement to take an allocation of children from Calais over and above commitments already made. The government's lack of interest, limited understanding, its shallowness and lack of vision weren't unique to its ranks or indeed to Ireland.

The migrant story isn't understood; many simply pity them but not enough respect or value them as individuals of inherent value, who can and do contribute to society. Differences are accentuated, relentlessly floated on the surface of the debate, positives are kept submerged. The narrative has become deliberately laced with stories that intimidate and spread fear, all the time pressing domestic needs which, we're often told, are uniquely threatened by migrants and refugees. The idea of migrants as leeches who bleed developed economies is untrue, but in a world dominated by unresearched online opinion, it's a view that's gained ground.

The exception to this intolerance is when there's an economic need though, even then, migrants are generally seen as fit for certain types of work only. Generations of Irish emigrants to Australia, the USA and Britain, experienced this; they were welcomed because they offered necessary additional labour but normally on different terms to the native population. When contemporary Ireland experienced its 'Celtic Tiger' economic boom, it welcomed hundreds of thousands of immigrants from eastern Europe and beyond to support its construction and service industries. Many returned home following the financial crash but of those who stayed most have been integrated, have become citizens and now see Ireland as home.

The poet, Warsan Shire, expresses why people become immigrants: *no one leaves home unless home is the mouth of a shark; you only run for the border when you see the whole city running.* The migrants' motivation is 'need'. The reluctance to embrace this simple truth is in part because we fail to acknowledge that no one would uproot themselves, travel thousands of miles unsure of where they are going and how they're going to get there if their life at home was tolerable. A century ago my grandparents left Belfast for Dublin, not by choice but through circumstance. Belfast and the Glens of Antrim were 'home' but they were displaced precisely because they sensed the mouth of a great predator.

The simple truth is that the vast majority of the tens of millions of migrants on the move across the planet are doing so for that very reason; they too fear the mouth of the shark. Those who've spent their lives working with migrants know this to be the case but those, including many legislators, whom we should expect to morally-weight their decisions, are happy to allow the falsehoods prevail so they can drive some narrow political advantage.

In my experience of meeting refugees in camps overseas or migrants and asylum seekers in Ireland, those who left home out of some reckless desire for new pastures are very few in number. If increasing divisions are to be avoided, it's important to construct and promote a truthful narrative, one that builds empathy for and understanding of the plight of the migrant.

• • •

There are different levels of responsibility for the global migration crisis. Colonisers have a particular set of obligations based on their nation's wealth being built, in part, on the profits of colonisation, while the migrant's homeplace is economically compromised because its natural resources were depleted for the gain of others. While it is true that many such countries had their wealth further depleted by avaricious native leaders who followed the colonisers, there's a greater lie at the heart of how some of the world's most powerful nations profile the immigrant cause.

Many post-colonial countries in Asia, Africa and parts of Latin America have struggled to achieve political or economic stability. So, however demeaning it may have been to be colonised, in some cases it was preferable to the chaos that followed. In these cases the abuses of power are often presaged by a glorious moment of independence before the 'liberated' citizens come to realise they remain oppressed, this time at the hands of one of their own.

Colonisation isn't just about a distant past when the world order was dramatically different, nor is it only about Western powers. Russia and China are among the worst offenders in dressing up a necessary" military intervention as being about the stability of a region when it's nothing more than a lust for resources and control. In the case of the United States, once a colony, oil was long the single most essential consideration in determining US foreign policy across both Democratic and Republican administrations, but it's seldom been acknowledged as such officially.

Ireland's experience is markedly different but it's one that should also influence how we respond to migration. Ireland's history means it too has an obligation, one that carries, arguably, no less a moral imperative than that of the colonisers. Generations of our ancestors experienced the need to leave home in ways not dissimilar to what tens of millions of the world's poorest are experiencing in the 21st century. Ireland's massive global diaspora reflects how, for generations, its people left home and took often hazardous journeys in search of the fresh start that's the constant in the hearts of all migrants.

Over the history of Irish emigration, the reasons people left in large numbers have varied from oppression, to fear of starvation, to the simple hope or belief that there were greater opportunities for work and financial stability overseas. Few Irish families are without direct experience of emigration and most owe a debt to countries across the world that have welcomed their sons and daughters with little or no equivocation. Somehow this doesn't appear to translate into empathy for those who are now desperate for succour and opportunity; we seem largely indifferent to the call of migrants in our midst, our legislators especially so.

There's a cultural narrative which we contribute to and feed off which is hard to substantiate. We enjoy the legend of Ireland as an especially welcoming and caring nation. Is it true? Do we demonstrate greater levels of compassion towards the disadvantaged? The evidence suggests that, when it comes to making wider sacrifices to accommodate people who are at great risk or those who need a fresh start, we've been found wanting. Ireland's record is not one to be proud of and we have 'history' when it comes to under-performing at a time of great need. The performance of government over the last two decades, at a time of unprecedented need in Europe has been gesture-led but fundamentally, mean-spirited and inept.

• • •

Ireland today is home to Direct Provision, a system operated by the Department of Justice since 1999 when it was introduced, as a temporary measure, to provide asylum-seekers with accommodation free-of-charge and a living allowance while they awaited a hearing. The numbers of asylum seekers arriving in Ireland at the turn of the millennium were at unprecedented and unmanageable levels which prompted the establishment of this temporary measure that remains in place two decades later. The system, long since privatised and run for profit, is chaotic and the number held has increased to about 7,000, over 1,000 of whom are asylum seekers who have been granted leave to remain in Ireland.

The longevity of Direct Provision, and its failure, despite colossal public cost, to meet an acceptable standard of care of those who are among the most vulnerable of our fellow-humans, reflects an incapacity of the administration to cope. The management of migrants, of those with an obvious and legitimate right to asylum, and of the greater numbers whose cases need evaluation is challenging for most developed countries. The experience across Europe shows that managing large numbers of people seeking sanctuary is difficult but Ireland's failure to address it in over two decades is alarming.

Even allowing for its complexity, that this has prevailed for so long without any serious effort, to establish a different, more considered and humane approach, betrays both political and civic indifference. It represents an institutionalised callousness that prompted President, Michael D. Higgins, to describe it as *totally unsatisfactory in every aspect*. Ireland's shedding of a church-influenced political conservatism in recent decades hasn't altered our capacity to tidy away ugly and uncomfortable issues into a discreet corner of society's front room.

The challenge of the numbers of refugees and migrants coming to Ireland is not going to change. Ireland is a wealthy, peaceful and largely secure nation so, as the global numbers seeking refuge increase, especially with the inevitable emergence of climate migrants, it's hard to see an outcome other than ever-increasing numbers making their way to our shores. This makes the need for a fundamental re-think and overhaul of how Ireland approaches the issue more pressing.

It should concern us that it was not until the Direct Provision system, introduced as a temporary measure, moved towards its third decade that a thorough assessment of our treatment of asylum seekers was done. The reactive and tardy nature of how some of the most vulnerable people in the world have been treated in Ireland should be a matter of public shame. It is a human rights issue and we must hope that the relatively progressive recommendations offered in 2020 by the Advisory Group will be quickly implemented.

As a people, our treatment of migrants reflects poorly on our claim to be a modern progressive nation and is deeply hypocritical. There seems to be no embarrassment when we press US legislators to protect the interests of Irish immigrants there, including those who are undocumented. Indeed the use of the term 'undocumented' instead of 'illegal' contrasts with how refugees and migrants in Ireland are seen. What's certain is that, at any point over the last 20 years, if the US authorities rounded up those Irish who entered the country illegally and housed them in Direct Provision-type accommodation, there would have been outrage in Ireland, and rightly so. And while there will be hardship cases among the illegal Irish in the US, few of them could really claim to be fleeing the mouth of the shark.

A state that believes it's within its rights to manage immigrants in a way it would consider inappropriate for others to deploy with its citizens is, by definition, racist. This problem is in part rooted in deeply-held feelings which, as long as Ireland was predominantly a white, Christian, Anglo-Celtic nation, remained largely below the surface. Now, as that homogeneity is shattered, so is the facemask of tolerance. Ireland's meekness means that institutionally it has betrayed its soul; its commitment to the most disadvantaged is left to individuals with the voice and experience to influence thought. People like former Judge of the Supreme Court, Catherine McGuinness, former Presidents Mary Robinson and Mary McAleese, and the late Peter Sutherland have offered moral leadership on this issue, but institutionally, Ireland has been woefully indifferent.

Wherever people are advantaged they become suspicious of anything that could disturb things as they are. I know because I am one of them. We become defensive, reluctant to acknowledge that there may be underlying societal tensions that need to be challenged to avoid any risk that we sleep-walk into any normalisation of extremes. We need to encourage, from the youngest age, a culture of tolerance and inclusiveness, challenging in particular any last vestiges of the monochromatic Ireland of the past.

As the number of immigrants is set to increase a new approach is needed if any threat of social unrest is to be avoided. The primary motivation of a mature society should be to take a positive or affirmative outlook to immigration but nor is the defensive consideration inconsequential. The younger generations, those whose future is most imperilled by divisiveness, are more open and feel less threatened by the movement of people. It is clear that the same youthful phalanx that mobilised the world on climate change is spiritually motivated by a border-free world order.

• • •

The sleepy part of south Dublin of my privileged 1960's childhood was slowly encroached upon by the city's expansion, most notably by the re-location of University College Dublin from the city centre. UCD bought land for a new campus in the heart of our semi-rural idyll and today is almost unrecognisable from the university I attended in the late 1970s. Now it is the dominant presence in the area with a student and staff population of about 35,000, with most countries in the world among their number. Nor is the university the only transformational change. At one end of what used to be 'my road', the university campus is now neighboured by another educational establishment, 'Eurocampus', that comprises a French International School and St Killian's German School. However cosmopolitan that might appear, it's the presence of another near neighbour, whose land almost adjoins UCD, a huge Islamic Cultural Centre which opened in 1996, that most dramatically represents how Ireland has changed in less than half a century.

Clonskeagh's Roebuck Road is my personal living metaphor for the Ireland of now and then. In my youth, a large convent and farm ran almost its full length on one side, now the farm is gone and the convent has shrunk into a small enclave in a huge housing estate, within touching distance of Ireland's largest mosque. This is my home turf so, by simply mind-walking that journey from one end of that road to the other, I can capture the scale of change in Ireland over the past half century. The road hasn't changed, it still starts and finishes at the same point and it hasn't even been widened but its horizons, like Ireland's, have been transformed, dramatically so.

The impact of physical changes to a landscape is nothing compared to how what is built can influence behavioural change – either for good or ill. Societies that are homogeneous are more easily managed. They may be less interesting, they may well breed particular kinds of selfishness and fuel narrow-mindedness but, on the face of it, they are less likely to experience serious tensions or differences. When I lived in Clonskeagh everyone was white, Christian and either heterosexual or behaved as such. Today it's still predominantly Christian and Caucasian but an hour spent in the small local stores, coffee shops or walking in the neighbourhood would blow your ethnic-senses, especially if you were of a generation that remembered how it used to be and had somehow not appreciated the pace at which Dublin has become a multi-cultural environment.

In contrast, the physical landscape in the Sahara will likely have changed little since my encounter with the camel train in Darfur more than three decades ago but, if anything, the surrounding desert landscape has become even less hospitable. The Sahara, which is the size of the United States, has increased by 10% in the last 100 years. Scientists report that, in that part of Africa, climate change is resulting in even hotter summers, winters that remain as before but with rainy seasons that are shorter and less intense. So it is that the desert is eating into the agricultural land that borders it, with dire implications for those living there who can ill afford to lose more arable land.

The one change that has impacted both communities, mine and that of the Saharan herdsmen, is that they too have joined the digital age; they use mobile phones for communication, sharing information and even trading their livestock. In every other respect, however, as the material welfare of those living in south Dublin suburbs like Clonskeagh has improved, theirs has regressed. Their base was low to begin with so, as the ravages of climate in destructive mode gain pace, it's likely that survival of their way of life is already doomed. The West's relentless pursuit of economic advancement, accentuated by the actions of newer global powers, with no interest in environmental considerations is the direct cause of these native peoples' way of life being so threatened, probably destroyed. The climate crisis caused the displacement of 30 million people within their own countries in 2020, three times the number displaced by conflict or violence. Many experts expect that number to be close to 1 billion by 2050.

It seems certain that communities like that in the Sahara will be forced to leave those parts of their homeland that for centuries has provided them and their forebears with a modest existence. It is likely that any internal displacement will be followed by migration; it will no longer be a matter of choice because, even to survive, they will need to travel north. It's best they have limited expectations of us. Their fate is not their fault but, on the evidence to date, those nations whose fault it is are unlikely to support them when asked for help. Ireland, whose own sons and daughters have migrated all over the world, struggles to be any more welcoming. Its own long-standing dependency on the generosity of other nations to welcome its people during difficult times has not yet translated into an enlightened, open and caring response to the needs of today's migrants.

... Saw'

There are those who derive pleasure from taking an engine apart and re-assembling it. Quite where the enjoyment lies is beyond me but, in some respects, this book is an analogous attempt to take apart and then re-assemble my career. Since the collapse of Anglo Irish Bank, with each passing year the journalist in me, however dormant, became more curious about certain events and people, about organisational culture and leadership and how, with the benefit of hindsight I saw things as I had failed to see them in real time.

When the various experiences were dis-assembled and analysed, most of what had gone wrong was down to human failing, some my own but most where I had not been alert enough to events and behaviours. I had successes too but any clinical assessment would point to them enabling a confidence that contributed to my being passive where I should and could have been more challenging, to my being accepting where I could and should have been more doubting. Much of my success made me more comfortable about life in corporate Ireland, surer of myself and of those around me. It wasn't excessive – my own family and my closest friends wouldn't have suffered that – but it was manifest in a quiet assurance that diminished strengths which, undimmed, might have protected me, perhaps even others too.

My sense is that this assuredness is a common characteristic of business or organisational failure; too many people in or around the nerve centre whose focus is very narrow and for whom success dulls their capacity to spot trouble. News journalists are trained to sniff out a problem. It's bred into you to see behind the façade, to be doubting and unafraid to take the contrarian view. I learned that from some exceptional RTÉ colleagues who would have doubted Jesus Christ even if they'd observed him perform the miracle of the loaves and the fishes. In my first business foray, Drury Communications, we took that bloody-mindedness into our work, something that made us different and ultimately successful. Truth is integral to effective public relations; the public or the media don't have the right to know everything but your PR advisers must so they can ensure that whatever is shared with the public is correct and accurate.

• • •

Whether it was one bank, the whole banking sector or the regulatory system; the dramatic decline of a political party, the destruction of a sporting federation or the lack of a societal lens within a particular industry, crises are generally rooted in the human condition. Large organisations – corporate and other – are living entities with their own make-up and, importantly, their own distinct culture which defines how they behave and how they are seen, all of which is largely shaped by the leadership.

I held leadership positions in Irish businesses from the small ones I founded and shaped in their early years to businesses of real scale like Paddy Power plc or RTÉ. The collapse of Anglo Irish Bank and the whole banking sector was so cataclysmic that it will be of interest to historians, as much as to business analysts, well into the future. When the bank collapsed I went into a prolonged shock at its scale and at the fact that I was a board member of a business that could implode with such dire consequences for the society in which I live. In terms of leadership and responsibility there's a distinction between being either the CEO or the chair of an organisation and a more standard non-executive role but there's no escaping that board membership makes you part of the leadership cohort.

A decade on, I better understand my culpability. I realise that there was a period where I became comfortable donning the suit of big business, a time where any awkwardness I might have felt about being part of corporate Ireland fell away to be replaced by a self-assuredness that, at one level, is necessary in order to survive but, in another, weakens you. I worked incredibly hard, pushed myself to achieve and never compromised on the fundamentals but, however unconsciously, in the process I allowed myself to be corporatized.

This meant that while my personal life was unaltered, when I was in work mode I behaved differently. I embraced the corporate way of life, the high earnings and the certainty which were all very different to my years in journalism. There's an arrogance in the media world too but it's of a different nature and, however subliminally, if as a current affairs broadcaster you're some form of public monitor of how others behave, you tend to be cautious about your own affairs. In that line of work an error of judgement can have very serious consequences, more so for a leading broadcaster than for a judge of the Supreme Court it would appear, so beyond my own disposition when I was a journalist, there was a layer of caution around behaviour that went with the role.

In business, certainly in the period of exceptional economic growth in Ireland, the greatest risk was the certainty with which so many people in leadership roles went about their work. I was one of them. I assumed that Anglo was as it was seen to be and, however quietly, I adopted the corporate strut that it and all the other banks performed before shareholders and customers alike. It was my own growing sense of the corporate me that allowed me to do so and at the same time, to preside over a board that invested millions in becoming a global leader in online gambling. These businesses were growing, they were massively profitable and beloved of the institutions and private shareholders alike.

I appreciate now that such uber confidence is dangerous. Its toxicity is in how it can permeate everything, seeping into individual and collective behaviours, dulling the thirst for knowledge and compromising organisational culture. The personal analysis points to failings that, had they been more acute and my career path been different, could have led to more serious consequences. The corporate me changed as it did in some others with whom I worked but the critical difference in most cases was the degree of change and the preparedness of a few to behave in a manner outside any acceptable code of behaviour.

We are all creatures of our environment and in 20 years mine had changed from the RTÉ canteen and occasional foreign assignments flying steerage to something very different. For all that I may have shut down my journalistic instincts, the experience of working as a journalist in RTÉ stood to me. It meant I had built-in defences to any risk of behaving in a way that could appear to advantage me but, in the process, knowingly undermine the welfare of others.

The first phase of the transition from broadcaster to businessman hadn't been dramatic. The earliest years of the public relations and sports businesses would have made the security of RTÉ seem attractive but, as I moved from a purveyor of consulting services to a highly paid board director or chairman of much larger businesses, I changed professionally. Sustained success infuses the upper levels of business with a belief that sees doubt as weakness and excessive questioning as disloyal. Previously those would have been exactly the kind of criteria to make me uncomfortable but I signed up and embraced them to the full.

• • •

When Anglo Irish Bank collapsed with such threatening consequences for anyone at or near its top table, I experienced a deep trauma. It was sustained for years as I tried to understand what had happened, not to the bank, but to me. I went in on myself, spent endless hours trying to understand the events which, given my professional training meant that, almost inevitably, a personal investigative process would follow. To be of value that needs to be uncompromising but it carries risk because, the deeper the dive, the more unavoidable the murkiness of the depths. This meant, in particular, that my involvement in the gambling industry had to surface.

From early after Anglo's failure, personal analysis became my default position. Then, once the immediate economic and political dust had settled and both criminal and regulatory investigations had commenced, reflection was no longer a choice, it was an obligation. In preparing I wanted to establish a more detailed assessment of what had occurred; to offer an insider's perspective as it were. The Banking Inquiry was indifferent to this; in politics and much of the media commentary there was a near obsession with the surface wounds, whereas to better understand the events and their causes what was needed was deep tissue diagnostics.

This stimulated the second element of my personal review, carried out in the privacy of my own head and without limits of time or range. I scanned and scrutinised the deep tissue of what I'd carried over the previous decade. There was no judge, no corporate law detective, no TD, asking questions and no one, other than myself, to scrutinise my answers. It was the journalist in me that needed to probe, to pick at the scab of Anglo that had left me scarred, as a by then deeply-unattractive counsel to business, when once I had been sought after.

In this I wondered about my move into corporate life, whether with the unconscious drift from journalism to business I'd become passive, less curious or disbelieving. I liked success. I had been reared to think of it as important, not of itself but for what it represented in any field of endeavour. It was something to be strived for and once achieved, to be minded and re-invented. I wondered if the self-belief that had allowed me to build my own business had put me at risk later. Only six years after I had left RTÉ, I owned businesses that were successful: small yes, but successful, nonetheless.

I remember a sense of confidence then, believing my instincts were good but also that I could depend on those around me to ensure my naturally intuitive approach would be balanced with deep analysis. I was quite thorough and I was a good listener, careful to take counsel of experienced allies in planning the strategic direction of the businesses. I was on top of things, in conscious control of what I was doing, present in it, aware of and enjoying the success. There was a strong sense of achievement but no complacency or arrogance. I had felt ready to move on again.

When I sold Drury Communications, I had no other job that I wanted to do but I'd enough wit to know that, if its success was to be sustained, I had to get out of the way of a talented management team. Today it remains a leading consulting company 30 years after I founded it and 20 after I took my leave. Its real success, sustained over all that time, is down to Billy Murphy and others and has nothing to do with me.

Then, when I sold out of the business, ten years after I'd left RTÉ without understanding why I'd made the decision to leave journalism, I chose to leave my own company without any clear plan for where to next. I was 40. It was over the next decade that I assumed a different approach, one that saw only continued success, both for the businesses on whose boards I served and for me.

• • •

Disassembling the engine tells me that our professional journeys are likely to be better, more secure, if thought-out, a conscious process rooted in what we want and what we are proficient at. From the time I left journalism, my career path wasn't ever consciously managed and in the phase after leaving Drury Communications, that purposefulness was more especially absent.

When, a number of years later, the approaches about non-executive board positions started to emerge that seemed to represent a form of endorsement. I liked it, certainly my ego did. While I never went around town promoting myself, I did feel a sense of pride at being at the top table as it were. Even that sense can weaken your capacity to perform, make you more vulnerable to being 'managed' which is part of what happened. With Anglo Irish Bank, two of my strong attributes, both natural and trained, to be curious and to be questioning, were dulled by this subconscious feeling that I was now a 'player'.

I may never have outwardly displayed the more obvious features of success but it was quietly feeding my ego, nourishing my need for endorsement while, more seriously, blocking my nose for danger. I became an advocate for the businesses on whose boards I served which is fine externally, but it is problematic if being a 'believer' inhibits or de-sensitises your antennae for concerns or doubts about how it is conducting its affairs. To perform their duties properly, non-executive directors need to be quiet sceptics, to assume the role of questioning adherents rather than becoming disciples of the leader.

• • •

As a journalist I had once made a career of not accepting the story as presented. I was good at being doubtful, checking and probing, respectfully but thoroughly. This book arose in part from wanting to understand where that facility had gone at the height of my career in business. Anglo was the catalyst for this but what I wanted to try to see was under my own bonnet, to probe how and why it was that I had changed or allowed events to change my professional modus operandi?

I did change. I took on more than I needed to because I wanted more challenges but my behaviours reflected too how I had come to believe in my own gifts. It was more than a, necessary, strengthening of self-belief. At times it was just arrogance. In 2005, I chose to expand the sports management business, Platinum One, in a way that my non-executive chairman, Johnny Fortune thought questionable. I too easily discounted his concerns whereas only a few years previously such counsel would, almost certainly, have been accepted. Some months later when I was approached to see if I would accept an appointment to the RTÉ Authority, I asked about the role of chair. I worked hard at developing a golf resort in Budapest while with my friend, Belfast solicitor, Paul Tweed, I invested a great deal of time on making a film on football legend, George Best.

This all reveals only a level of self-confidence that was part of my graduation into fuller membership of the corporate world. Only five or six years earlier, at the point where I sold my public relations business, I would have been a great deal more cautious, more reserved. I appreciate now that my time advising business leaders through the 1990s had been an initiation of sorts which ended when I was appointed to leadership roles in larger businesses.

Graduating as I did meant mixing professionally with people, almost exclusively men, who shared that sense of self that is just part of life in the upper echelons of business. The corporate 'strut' is neither fake nor imagined, it finds its way into how you behave and in my case at least it shut down much of what had distinguished me as an adviser.

In many respects my journey – and the changes I underwent over those critical years in leadership positions – reflects just a level or degree of corporatisation. There are others where I observed people change to a much greater extent which, on account of their positions meant the impact was, in some cases, profound. Whether my more limited behavioural adjustment was to do with circumstance, training or character is impossible to know but success in any sphere carries great risk of a deepening sense of self-importance, a belief in the rightness of your position that can border infallibility. This, stripped of necessary checks and balances or absent a cohort of truly independent colleagues can poison a corporate culture. It is in these rarer circumstances that immense damage can be done, sometimes beyond the walls of the organisation involved, hurting a whole sector or even, on occasion, wider society. I never became a cheerleader but, equally, the objectivity, sometimes disdain, that had made me so good as a strategist in advising business leaders was replaced by a submission to how clever we all were.

It is undeniable that Anglo Irish Bank was the summit of this falsehood; the business where extremes of graft, intelligence, courage, humility were matched by their polar opposites without that violent swing being appreciated in real time. That was the earthquake for me and though some of the aftershocks were severe – most particularly my involvement in gambling – I came to appreciate through everything that had happened with Anglo, just how comfortable, bordering smug, I had become in the corporate world.

• • •

An excess of belief can inhibit our judgment of more fundamental issues than organisational culture, even starting with the very purpose of the business. To embrace, as some do and as I did, the idea that, once a business operates within the law a director's only job is to ensure the interests of the shareholders are protected, is not right. More should be expected of business leaders, starting with asking about the efficacy of what the business is selling and how?

I was chairman of Paddy Power when it was a world leader in the innovation that facilitated a dramatic change in how the gambling industry trades. In that role I encouraged the investment of resources and expertise in adding layer upon layer of innovation to simplify gambling, to make it more accessible to more people, more of the time. I never thought to test what I was involved in. How did I not question my role in the gambling sector? Why was it not an issue to be considered against a single focus on growth and increasing shareholder value? The corporate 'strut' is why; that assuredness that comes with success or even the perception of it can inure you to an involvement in things that personally, morally even, would, otherwise, be problematic.

In September 2016, after I appeared on a programme about gambling on BBC's *Panorama*, a young Welshman contacted me in quite a distressed state. We talked that night and for a few weeks afterwards. In his early 30s, he was addicted to gambling and was suicidal but he was confused by my messaging, by what I stood for. An unemployed professional person, he seemed out of hope that he could arrest his problem and within a few weeks we lost contact.

I wonder how, in different circumstances, if I'd ever faced an adversarial interview about my stewardship of Paddy Power during the period when online gambling was incubating, how well I would have handled it. I wonder how competently I would have dealt with my own interviewing approach if, when chairman of Paddy Power, I had been challenged on national radio about the societal damage that gambling can do. When I had quizzed Dr. Austin Darragh on morning radio I was able to address the specific death, on his watch, of one named individual.

That has to be a deeply uncomfortable experience for the interviewee, but we know that gambling is unleashing social carnage across the world, destroying lives and families through the constancy and breadth of its offer. The scale of the damage has drawn not unreasonable comparisons with the tobacco industry so while I certainly wouldn't have threatened the interviewer, in every other respect, I'm not sure that I would have fared any better than Austin Darragh did when I had interviewed him back in 1986.

• • •

Much of our professional competence in any role is centred on judgement, a capacity to make informed decisions about events, organisations and, most critically, people. Judgement requires curiosity, patience, an openness to advice, especially making space for the contrarian view. These were features of how I assisted others in business, politics, or professional sport. My capacity to think strategically, to look at challenges with a wide lens, was what clients and friends valued. It is, I think, why some long-time clients became longer-term friends.

Hindsight suggests I was less successful in applying this approach to my own career and hindsight is right. Self-belief is a double-edged sword; in order to meet fully my responsibilities, I needed to know how to temper it. That capacity was diminished in the period when my star was most in the ascendant which must, of itself, be telling.

There were important moments when I wasn't sharp enough to isolate and examine weaknesses that could have been identified. That deficit has to have resulted from success. The disassembled engine shows that I started to believe in my own status, losing some of my innate critical faculties in the process.

I could never have imagined the vicissitudes of the past four decades. Certainly when, within touching distance of my 30s, I chose to leave journalism, I would never have thought it possible to meet such an unusual cast of characters or to witness such extraordinary events.

Acknowledgements

My thanks are due to,

My friends and the publishers, PJ Cunningham and Rosemary O'Grady at Ballpoint Press for their commitment to the task and professionalism; not forgetting the patience and care of their consultant Terry MacManus. I was in the best of hands. Thanks to designer Joe Coyle for his patience and skill in dealing with this novice and to CRD for the cool sketch – love it!

• • •

To Paul Tweed for his support and guidance and to counsel, Alannah McGurk, for the attention to detail and care throughout.

• • •

There are scores of others – family members, friends, acquaintances – who read sections, different drafts, met (when you could!) and took phone calls to discuss particular issues and offer guidance. In some cases I took liberties with your time; excuse me! Without the help of this wide group the book wouldn't have been completed. As some of you cannot be identified and others don't wish to be I'm choosing not to identify anyone but you know who you are and I will always be grateful for your assistance.

Index